Queen Elizabeth II

Her Life in Our Times

SARAH BRADFORD

VIKING
an imprint of
PENGUIN BOOKS

VIKING

Published by the Penguin Group

Penguin Books Ltd, 80 Strand, London WC2R 0RL, England

Penguin Group (USA) Inc., 375 Hudson Street, New York, New York 10014, USA

Penguin Group (Canada), 90 Eglinton Avenue East, Suite 700, Toronto, Ontario, Canada M4P 2Y3
(a division of Pearson Penguin Canada Inc.)

Penguin Ireland, 25 St Stephen's Green, Dublin 2, Ireland
(a division of Penguin Books Ltd)

Penguin Group (Australia), 250 Camberwell Road, Camberwell, Victoria 3124, Australia
(a division of Pearson Australia Group Pty Ltd)

Penguin Books India Pvt Ltd, 11 Community Centre,
Panchsheel Park, New Delhi – 110 017, India

Penguin Group (NZ), 67 Apollo Drive, Rosedale, Auckland 0632, New Zealand
(a division of Pearson New Zealand Ltd)

Penguin Books (South Africa) (Pty) Ltd, 24 Sturdee Avenue,
Rosebank, Johannesburg 2196, South Africa

Penguin Books Ltd, Registered Offices: 80 Strand, London WC2R 0RL, England

www.penguin.com

First published 2012

1

Set in 12/14.75 pt Bembo Book MT Std
Typeset by Jouve (UK), Milton Keynes
Printed in Great Britain by Clays Ltd, St Ives plc

A CIP catalogue record for this book is available from the British Library

ISBN: 978-0-670-91911-6

www.greenpenguin.co.uk

MIX
Paper from
responsible sources
FSC
www.fsc.org
FSC™ C018179

Penguin Books is committed to a sustainable
future for our business, our readers and our
planet. This book is made from paper certified
by the Forest Stewardship Council.

For Will

Contents

Contents

List of Illustrations

Section 1

1. 'Us four' in the gardens of Royal Lodge, Windsor, June 1936 (Studio Lisa/Camera Press)

2. Princess Elizabeth, photographed in 1942 by Cecil Beaton, wearing the cap badge of the Grenadier Guards (Camera Press)

3. The Royal Family inspect the harvest at Sandringham, August 1943 (NI Syndication)

4. South Africa, 1947: Princesses Elizabeth and Margaret riding along the beach (Rex Features)

5. Wedding day, 20 November 1947 (ILN/Camera Press)

6. The last family holiday, Balmoral, 22 August 1951 (Fox Photos/Getty Images)

7. Tree Tops, Kenya, February 1952 (*Times*/Camera Press)

8. Grieving Queen (private album)

9. Coronation: Queen Elizabeth II enthroned with the royal regalia, 2 June 1953 (Cecil Beaton/Camera Press)

10. Annigoni's portrait of Queen Elizabeth II, 1954 (Pietro Annigoni/Camera Press)

11. *Above*, holidays at Balmoral, August 1952 (private album) *Below*, returning from Balmoral, the Queen, Princess Anne and Princess Margaret, 10 October 1954 (Topfoto)

Section 3

1. Hyde Park Corner

6 February 1952. Princess Elizabeth became Queen Elizabeth II as she perched in the branches of a tree. She was at Treetops Hotel in Kenya, peering intently at the wild animals enjoying the waterhole below, quite unaware that thousands of miles to the north, some time in the early hours of a cold dark morning, her father, King George VI, had died silently in his sleep of a thrombosis at his red brick and stone country house, Sandringham, in Norfolk. He had been found dead at 7.30 a.m. by his valet, James Macdonald, when he drew back the curtains and went to place the King's early morning tea tray by his bed.

'Hyde Park Corner last night. Go and tell the Prime Minister.' At 8.45 a.m. in London the voice of the King's Private Secretary came down the line to his Assistant Private Secretary, Edward Ford, using a prearranged code for the death of the King. 'I found old Winston in bed,' Ford recalled, 'about nine in the morning . . .[there was] a scatter of papers all over the bed, a chewed cigar and a green candle beside to relight it because it was always going out. I said, "I've got bad news, Prime Minister. The King died last night." "Bad?" said Winston. "The worsht." And there was a sort of awful flurry and flop and papers going everywhere. He was preparing a speech on foreign affairs for the House of Commons and he just threw away the papers. "How unimportant these matters seem," he said. "Our chief is dead." '[1]

The new young Queen had been in Kenya en route to an official tour of Australia and New Zealand. With typical British dottiness, the 'Hyde Park Corner' message had never been sent to her; the telegraphist, thinking the message was the address, failed to forward it. When Martin Charteris, her Private Secretary, called on her at the Sagana Hotel she knew nothing of her father's death and nor did he. She was chatting excitedly about watching rhino at the waterhole at dawn. 'She'd been at Treetops the night before actually when he [the King] died and she'd come back to Sagana Lodge [a wedding present from the Kenyan people]. I made my number at Sagana Lodge and had a bit of a gossip, she told me about the rhinoceros and all that sort of thing, [she was] looking wonderful in blue jeans. Off I went and at lunch somebody told me that the King was dead. So I got into the car and went to Sagana Lodge as quickly as I could where I found her, very composed, master of her fate.'

Churchill's Private Secretary, John 'Jock' Colville, arrived to find him sitting alone with tears in his eyes, looking straight in front of him, and reading neither his official papers nor the newspapers. 'I had not realized how much the King meant to him,' Colville recorded in his memoirs.[2] For five years, from 1940 to 1945, Winston Churchill and George VI had shared experiences and secrets during the crucial moments of the Second World War; the old Prime Minister's broadcast tribute to his friend was the most moving of many.

'When the death of the King was announced to us yesterday morning,' he said, 'there struck a deep and solemn note in our lives which, as it resounded far and wide, stilled the clatter and traffic of twentieth-century life in many lands and made countless millions of human beings pause and look around them . . .'

Public reaction to the death of the shy, stammering monarch was extraordinary, not only in Britain and Commonwealth countries around the world but also in the United States, where the King was remembered as the loyal ally of Roosevelt and Truman during and after the Second World War. The BBC's Leonard Miall, in a broadcast from New York, spoke of how the news had brought 'in this Republic, an immediate sense of personal loss'. In Washington the Secretary of State opened his weekly press conference with a formal tribute to the King, then laid aside his papers to deliver his own. The House of Representatives passed a resolution of sympathy and then adjourned for the rest of the day – 'I doubt it would do that for the head of any other State,' Miall recorded. The Senate of the State of Massachusetts, home of the Boston Irish as well as the Pilgrim Fathers, adopted a resolution which spoke of 'the beloved Monarch who was ever a symbol of strength for his stout-hearted but war-weary people – a King who was sincerely devoted to his subjects, who laboured to the point of exhaustion in showing to them, and to the world, the proper discharge of his royal duties'. More simply, President Truman wrote in his private diary: 'He was a grand man.'

Along the 110-mile railway line from Sandringham to London people gathered as the train bearing the King's coffin passed. In London the lying-in-state began on Monday, 11 February: for four days some 300,000 people filed silently past to pay their respects. Virginia Potter, an American living in England, was there on the final evening. 'It was,' she reported, 'a very awe-inspiring sight – hundreds of people slowly filing through that enormous dimly-lit hall, and *no sound* except a quiet shuffling of feet.'[3] In the street outside, thousands of people were standing completely silent in the cold night air. The BBC, then Britain's only broadcasting authority, suspended normal programmes for ten days' mourning until the funeral had taken place at Windsor on the 16th. In London during the funeral broadcast two young men in Fleet Street who refused to observe the two-minute silence and 'clumped down the street' were nearly lynched; they 'had to take refuge in a block of offices and then have police protection, the crowd was so furious. One woman hit one of them with an umbrella.' Children were given the day off to watch or listen to the funeral of a man whom they knew only as a profile on a postage stamp or as a slight high-cheekboned figure in naval uniform from newsreel photographs. Faced with the nation's utter concentration on a single event, the socialist Labour MP Richard Crossman admitted that royalty was 'the one inexhaustible subject'.

★

George VI was only fifty-six when he died; he had been continually seriously ill and under stress for the last three years of his life.
In 1948 the effects of his heavy smoking had necessitated vascular
surgery, cutting off the blood supply from the furred arteries of
his right leg from below the knee to avoid the possibility of a blood
clot reaching his heart. In the autumn of 1950 a tomography had
revealed the shadow of a tumour on his right lung; that November
the lung had been removed. Since then, as Churchill put it, 'the
King had walked with death, his life hanging by a thread from day
to day'. He had had a premonition, as a friend who accompanied
him down from Balmoral for the last time remembered. As he left
Balmoral the King quoted a line from a favourite song of the
Queen and Princess Margaret: 'Maybe you think it is the end . . .
Well it is . . .'[4]

His widow, Queen Elizabeth, always believed that the stress of
his job had killed him. As the second son of George V and Queen
Mary, he had not been in line to be King, and if his elder brother,
King Edward VIII, had not abdicated, he would not have had the
position forced upon him. If that had not happened, George VI
might not have died at such an early age and his daughter Elizabeth
would not have become Queen Elizabeth II.

2. 'Abdication Day'

10 December 1936. 145 Piccadilly, London. The two sisters, Princesses Elizabeth, aged ten, and Margaret Rose, aged six, had spent the morning hanging over the banisters on the top nursery floor of their four-storeyed London house, watching the agitated comings and goings below. Looking thin, pale and strained, their father had gone out early to witness the signing of his brother Edward's Instrument of Abdication at Fort Belvedere. The Princesses' mother, Elizabeth, Duchess of York, was ill in bed with flu or one of the psychosomatic illnesses which had seemed to afflict her at times of stress over recent years. Crowds began to gather outside the door, aware that something momentous was about to take place. Finally one of the staff told the Princesses what was happening. Their much-loved but recently rarely seen uncle, Edward, had abdicated his throne as King Edward VIII and was to leave the country that night as plain Edward, Duke of Windsor. Their father, Albert, Duke of York, was to be King in his place. 'Does that mean you will be Queen, Lilibet?' Princess Margaret asked. 'I suppose so . . .' Princess Elizabeth answered. Going upstairs to her room, she headed her diary 'Abdication Day'. At only ten years old, she knew what it meant for her future.

The Abdication was the most serious crisis for the British monarchy in living memory. On the day of the Silver Jubilee, 6 May 1935, the previous year, the two Princesses, identically dressed in pink, had ridden in an open carriage with their parents to celebrate the twenty-fifth anniversary of their grandfather King George V's accession at St Paul's Cathedral, through streets lined with cheering crowds. And they had listened to the King's broadcast from Buckingham Palace that evening, addressed to his 'very, very dear people', thanking them for their loyalty – 'and may I say? – love'. Every evening that week crowds had gathered outside Buckingham Palace – just across the park from 145 Piccadilly – to sing 'For he's a jolly good fellow' to their grandfather. Foreign envoys and press representatives, including those of the German *Deutsche Allgemeine Zeitung* in the country so soon to be at war again with Britain, commented on the warmth of the family image that King George conveyed as 'father of the nation': 'The Sovereign of Great Britain is much more than a King of England, he was the head of a world Empire and it was the personality of George V that had made it possible.' The French Ambassador in London reported that a foreign observer could not help but be 'struck by the cohesion and power which the family of the British Democracies draw from their attachment to the Crown, considered at the same time as a paternal force and the symbol of unity'.[1]

It was that 'family' image which within eighteen months was to be shattered by the determination of the King's eldest son, Edward, to marry his twice-divorced mistress from Baltimore, Wallis Simpson. Edward was the member of the Royal Family who had, both as Prince of Wales and as King, star quality. Unlike most of his family, he had an electric charm which he could switch on and off at will, and a boyish personality which came across in countless newsreels and photographs. He had been a soldier in the First World War and an active member of the Royal Family's welfare front afterwards, with a special interest in housing and unemployment. On his tours abroad in the Empire and in Britain his apparent spontaneity and unstuffy attitude had won all hearts. 'He was idolized, as no prince has ever been before or since,' a contemporary wrote. Visiting the Welsh valleys in November 1936, he had been visibly moved by the distress of the unemployed miners and their families and before he returned to London had publicly declared, 'Something must be done.' At a glamorous Belgravia dinner that night he had continued to bore the socialite guests with graphic descriptions of what he had seen. Paradoxically, however, the first thing he had done when he got back was to present Wallis Simpson with an enormous emerald ring from Cartier which would have made a more than handsome donation to any unemployment distress fund.

The Abdication crisis has to be seen against the social and political background of contemporary Britain. The era into which Princess Elizabeth had been born on 21 April 1926 was one of huge contrast between rich and poor, when the workers saw Lloyd George's promise of a land fit for heroes to live in after the First World War as having been betrayed. As newspapers cooed over the birth of the King's first grandchild, the next month brought news of the General Strike. Then came the Wall Street crash in October 1929 and the Great Depression. In October 1936, weeks before King Edward's visit to South Wales, jobless steel workers from the north-east of England converged on London in a protest known as the Jarrow March. Against this background, Edward was seen by some as 'the People's King', the one man who could help them against the politicians and the vested interests of the rich. On 10 November Mrs Simpson's name had been mentioned for the first time in the House of Commons: outside the chamber, the lobbies were filled with hunger marchers from Lancashire and South Wales protesting against the new unemployment regulations, and at the door a queue was singing 'The Red Flag'. It was less than twenty years since the Tsar of Russia had been executed and the Emperors of Austria and Germany swept away. Fear of socialism/bolshevism made the possibility of a discredited monarchy seem even more dangerous.

Yet for all his popularity Edward was in reality a spoiled rich young man whose whole life hitherto, in the intervals between being despatched to represent his father on tours of the Dominions and Empire (and during those as well), had been devoted entirely to the pursuit of women, drink and foxes. He had moments of romantic empathy with the people, but even those could partly be attributed to his dislike of his father and everything he represented – and from his own point of view, the distasteful job of 'princing' and royal 'stunts'. Far from really sympathizing with the unemployed, as soon as he inherited the family properties of Balmoral and Sandringham from his father in January 1936 he reacted by sacking gardeners and other staff, advised by Wallis, whose talent for housekeeping was legendary and who saw no point in too many gardeners when you could make use of the florist Constance Spry.

The year 1936 had been a traumatic one for Princess Elizabeth: in January her beloved grandfather, George V, had died. The two Princesses had travelled down to Norfolk for the traditional Christmas at Sandringham with their grandparents and their nurse, Alah Knight, but without their parents: the Duchess of York had been ill at Royal Lodge since mid-December, with flu which had developed into pneumonia, and the Duke stayed at home with her. A sense of gloom pervaded Sandringham, enveloped for much of the time in snow followed by fog. Their great-aunt, Princess Victoria, the King's sister, had died there earlier that month; the King himself was thin, bent and breathed with difficulty. He had never quite recovered from an abscess in his chest and, like his father and indeed his sons, smoked heavily. He was too weak to follow his passion, shooting, instead taking short walks to the stables and the gardens with his granddaughters after being visited in his room by them every morning at 9.15. Princess Elizabeth was devoted to him; he used to play with her as he never had with his own children. From Royal Lodge her mother wrote her loving but admonitory letters, hoping she was having a lovely time and being very polite to everybody. 'Mind you answer very nicely when you are asked questions, even though they may be silly ones.'[2] Her uncle the Duke of Kent and his glamorous wife Marina were there with their baby son, as was her other uncle, the bluff, gruff Henry, Duke of Gloucester, with his wife, Princess Alice, while her somewhat forbidding grandmother, Queen Mary, presided over the family teas. One notably late arrival was was 'Uncle David', the Prince of Wales, unable to tear himself away from Wallis Simpson to join his family.

The King, George V, was sleepy during the day and restless at night, when he needed help from an oxygen tank, carried up to his bedroom by a handyman. By 16 January it was obvious to his wife, Queen Mary, that he was dying; the Duke of York was sent for and two days later the children and guests left the house. On 21 January 1936 the King died, his death hastened by a merciful dose of morphine into his jugular vein administered by his doctor, Lord Dawson of Penn, with the object of timing a dignified announcement in the morning papers, *The Times* in particular. The reaction of 'David', now King Edward VIII, was described by close courtiers as 'hysterical', 'frantic and unreasonable', perhaps from guilt and regret at his emotional estrangement from his father, tinged with panic at the prospect of becoming King and, some people later surmised, because he had hoped to elope with and marry Wallis Simpson before it happened. When he recovered himself, his first two independent actions were to telephone Wallis and order that the clocks, which had been set to run half an hour fast in his grandfather's reign to give extra hours for shooting, should be put back to normal time, a change seen as deeply significant and unnerving by the old King's courtiers and servants.

From that moment the family was more divided than ever, with two powerful women dominating the scene: the Princesses' grandmother, Queen Mary, upright and dignified, whose whole life had been dedicated to the British monarchy to the suppression of her normal instincts, and their mother, a strong character who, despite her quick laugh, social ease and radiant smile, was a tough aristocrat with an abiding sense of duty and responsibility and a deep sense of religion. Both women disapproved of Wallis Simpson as a twice-divorced interloper who had split the family in two, and whose presence in the King's life threatened not just the family image but the stability of Kingdom and Empire.

Events in the family were about to reach breaking point at the beginning of the annual late summer holidays at Balmoral. On 23 September 1936 the Duke and Duchess of York were in Aberdeen to open the new Infirmary, replacing the King, who had cried off on the grounds of being still in mourning for his father. But on that same day he drove himself to Aberdeen station to meet Wallis off the London train. The local paper printed a photograph captioned 'His Majesty in Aberdeen. Surprise visit in car to meet guests' side by side with a photograph of the Yorks at the Infirmary. At Balmoral Wallis was installed in the suite of rooms used by Queen Mary during her twenty-five years as Queen; the King, perhaps understandably refusing to use his father's former bedroom, slept in her dressing-room. Three days later the Duchess of York made clear her feelings about the pretensions of Wallis. Invited to a dinner party at the castle on 26 September, she delivered a public snub to Wallis. Court etiquette decreed that royalty should be greeted only by the official host or hostess, yet as the Duchess of York entered the drawing-room, Wallis and not the King stepped forward to greet her. Either Wallis was ignorant of this convention or it was, as an observer put it, 'a deliberate and calculated display of power'. The Duchess of York walked straight past her, ignoring her attempted welcome, saying 'as if to no one in particular', 'I came to dine with the King.' The Duke of York looked 'embarrassed and very nervous'; his brother, 'looking rather startled, abruptly broke off his conversation and came forward to greet his brother and sister-in-law'. He placed the Duchess in the place of honour at his right hand; Wallis sat at the head of the table but it was the Duchess who, without a glance at her, led the women from the table at the end of dinner, leaving the men to their port.

It was a declaration of war: the Yorks did not see the King in private again at Balmoral. Edward carried out wholesale changes on the estate without consulting his brother; 'David only told me what he had done after it was over,' the Duke of York wrote sadly to his mother. 'I never saw him alone for an instant.' 'David does not seem to possess the faculty of making others feel wanted,' his wife wrote pointedly to her mother-in-law on 11 October. 'I feel that the whole difficulty is a certain person. I do not feel that I *can* make advances to her & ask her to our house, as I imagine would be liked, & this fact is bound to make relations a little difficult . . .'[3] Two days later Wallis Simpson moved into a dreary little villa in the Suffolk seaside town of Felixstowe in order to establish official residence in the county for her divorce petition, which was to be heard at Ipswich. On 27 October she received her decree nisi there; the locals were astounded by the huge contingent of international press which descended upon the town but, like everyone else in the United Kingdom, they remained in ignorance of its significance. As far as the King was concerned, the divorce meant that Wallis was now free to marry him; he presented her with an engagement ring, inscribed 'WE [private shorthand for Wallis and Edward] are ours now 27 X 36'. The stone, a magnificent emerald, had once belonged to the Great Mogul. The Yorks had travelled down from Scotland on the night train, arriving in London on 20 October still unaware of what was going on. They were warned by the King's Private Secretary that the affair might end in Edward's abdication, with the inevitable consequence that the Duke of York would have to take over. Still nothing was discussed, until on 16 November the King called on his mother at Marlborough House to give her the news that she had feared: that he intended to marry Mrs Simpson. He informed his brother the Duke of York the following day that he would marry Wallis on 27 April and be crowned on 12 May. As he put it to his brother Prince George, Duke of Kent, he would 'make her Queen, Empress of India, the whole bag of tricks'.

Pressure upon the Yorks became almost unbearable: the Duke adored his brother and at the same time was petrified at the thought that he might have to take over the throne, a position for which he felt himself mentally and physically ill equipped. The Duchess, deeply protective of her husband, was equally worried at the effect the continuing strain was having on him. Despite her proud claims that she never discussed the affair with anyone outside the Royal Family – even with her own, she herself was finding it almost impossible to bear. She and Prince Albert were staying with the Earl and Countess of Pembroke for a shooting party at Wilton the following weekend. A fellow guest recalled: 'I was staying at Wilton when [they were] there, Lady Pembroke was most tremendously keen on royalty, fawning on them the whole of the time and she noticed what frightfully poor form the Duchess of York was in and always escorted her to bed every night, and the [Duchess of York] broke down and said, "A *terrible* thing has happened, the last thing we want. We're perfectly happy as we are and suddenly have this thing put on us" – she was in a terrible state.'[4] She sent a personal appeal to the King, despite their estranged relations, asking him to 'please be kind to Bertie when you see him. I am terrified for him – so DO help him.' Edward refused to see his brother.

News of the King's romance had been kept from the British public (as it undoubtedly had from the Princesses, his nieces) by an alliance of British newspaper magnates and Establishment attitudes. Magazines and newspapers from abroad were censored, and references to the King and Wallis clipped out. Incredible as it may seem today, that summer Edward and Wallis had cruised the Adriatic aboard an Admiralty yacht, the *Nahlin*, and been photographed sunbathing, sightseeing and swimming together, accompanied by a party of English friends and courtiers. Pictures appeared in the American and European press but the blackout remained in force in Britain. No reference was made to the affair until on 2 December 1936, in an address, an obscure English bishop, Blunt of Bradford, criticized the King for neglecting his church-going duties. The Bishop had never heard of Mrs Simpson, but the press took his remarks as a coded message that the King's desire to marry her was now out in the open. 'The King's Marriage' blazed out in headlines.

For nine days controversy raged in the press and throughout the country. At first the popular press were behind the 'People's King':

why should he not be allowed to marry the woman he loved? On the other side, the old guard of Society and the Establishment, with their standard-bearer, *The Times*, were against the King marrying a divorced American because it would be bad for the monarchy and the Empire. Church-goers of all classes – including the Labour Party leader, Clement Attlee – supported the Conservative Prime Minister, Stanley Baldwin, in his efforts to persuade the King not to marry Mrs Simpson, and in his not so secret conviction that Edward should give up the woman or the throne. Over the weekend of 5–6 December the Yorks were at Royal Lodge, distraught with anxiety, and on Monday the 7th, Edward at last consented to see his brother and to tell him that he had decided to abdicate the throne. Wallis, the target of vitriolic hate mail and even threats, some allegedly concocted by the *Express*'s Lord Beaverbrook, left Fort Belvedere for France on the evening of the 3rd – her absence may have helped Edward take his decision: he could not contemplate a future without her.

On Friday, 11 December 1936 Prince Albert, Duke of York, was proclaimed King George VI of Great Britain, Ireland and Her Dominions beyond the Seas. From then on Princess Elizabeth's destiny as future Queen was set. Within the family there was no joy at their sudden promotion: the new King had sobbed on his mother's shoulder at the realization of what lay ahead of him. Queen Mary had endured the shock of losing her husband and, virtually, her son within the space of only a year. After a family dinner at Fort Belvedere that Friday evening the ex King, now Edward, Duke of Windsor, made his farewell broadcast from Windsor Castle. He declared his allegiance to the new King and his sense of duty towards his country and the Empire, continuing, in the words of his biographer Philip Ziegler, with the sentence which is the best remembered of anything he said in his whole life: 'You must believe me when I tell you that I have found it impossible to carry the heavy burden of responsibility and to discharge my duty as King as I would wish to do, without the help and support of the woman I love . . .' After a final farewell to his family, he left by car for Portsmouth to board a warship which would carry him into exile. It would be almost twenty years until Princess Elizabeth would see him again. In the meantime he would become almost a non-person and a source of bitterness and embarrassment as far as his family was concerned. Just weeks before, on 30 November 1936, at the end of the Year of Three Kings, the old glass Crystal Palace on Sydenham Hill, all that remained of Joseph Paxton's magnificent design for Prince Albert's Great Exhibition in Hyde Park, had caught fire, blazed spectacularly and burned to the ground – a requiem for the old order and an omen of the world conflagration soon to come.

3. 'Us Four'

Princess Elizabeth, unlike her father, had been brought up in a close, loving family – 'us four', as King George VI used to refer to them. The dominant figure, although she liked to pretend otherwise, was her mother, now the Queen, the former Lady Elizabeth Bowes-Lyon. She was born on 4 August 1900, the ninth child and fourth daughter of the 14th Earl of Strathmore and Kinghorne. The Bowes-Lyons were descended from King Robert the Bruce of Scotland and owned Glamis Castle, supposed scene of *Macbeth*, and the right to a private army. The heiress Mary Eleanor Bowes (whose name they incorporated with the original Scottish Lyon) brought a fortune in coal in County Durham, and two houses, Streatlam and Gibside. By the time Lady Elizabeth was born they rented a London mansion in St James's Square and also owned a house in Hertfordshire, St Paul's Walden Bury, where she spent some of the happiest days of her childhood.

Princess Elizabeth's Strathmore grandparents were strongly Christian, and unworldly despite their position and possessions. Her grandfather, Claude Bowes-Lyon, a handsome, heavily moustachioed figure, quiet and somewhat eccentric, was a popular and conscientious landlord, an expert on forestry with a passion for chopping up trees, with a high sense of duty and social responsibility. The family tradition was sporting and military: Lord Strathmore had served in the Life Guards and his recreations were the pastimes of an Edwardian aristocrat and country gentleman – shooting, fishing and cricket. His wife Cecilia, born Nina-Cecilia Cavendish-Bentinck, was the daughter of a clergyman who had been the heir to the fabulously rich 5th Duke of Portland, had he not had the misfortune to die before the Duke, thereby leaving his

children a great deal less glittering position than they might otherwise
have had. The Strathmore household – children and staff – attended
daily prayers and the children were taught to kneel and pray by
their beds every night, something which, according to her biographer, Elizabeth continued to do until the end of her life. Cecilia
Strathmore was the greatest influence on the children's lives; a talented pianist and gardener, she ran the household and the children's
lives. One of her children remembered her in a passage that could
as well have been applied to Elizabeth herself: she had 'this immense
zest for living . . . intense interest in everything going on . . . a
sense of gaiety right to the end'. There were memorable parties at
Glamis, described by guests as 'magic'. Looking back on her childhood, Elizabeth told her friend Osbert Sitwell that she had nothing
but 'wonderfully happy memories of childhood days at home . . .
fun, kindness and a marvellous sense of security'.

It was characteristic of Elizabeth to gloss over the not so happy
memories. She was just fourteen when the First World War broke
out on 1 August 1914. All her brothers except David, who was too
young, signed up and went to the front, where their experiences
were typical of the men of their generation. Fergus was killed at
the Battle of Loos in September 1915 (as was John, only son of
Rudyard Kipling, whose body was never found); Patrick, the eldest, was wounded and shell-shocked, never entirely recovering
from his experiences; a third brother, Michael, was badly wounded
and captured by the Germans. Glamis Castle was converted into a
convalescent hospital for wounded and sick soldiers after their
treatment at Dundee Infirmary, and another was set up at their
Hertfordshire home, St Paul's Walden Bury. Elizabeth's elder sister Rose trained as a nurse at the London Hospital. Even after the
war ended there was tragedy, when a young friend of Elizabeth's
was killed in August 1919 fighting for the White Russians. Elizabeth had been a child when the war started; she was eighteen when
it ended; experience of death, wounds and sickness must have
marked her, but in her letters and her attitudes she was resolutely

high-spirited and fun. The motto 'Never Complain. Never Explain' might have been invented for her.

Men found her charm, wit and sparkle irresistible; she kept them at arm's length. Of a particular friend, she wrote after his death, 'I liked him specially because he *never* tried to flirt, or make love or anything like that – which always spoils friendships.' 'People were rather inclined to propose to you in those days,' she recalled. 'You know it was rather the sort of thing, I suppose. And you said, "No thank you," or whatever it was . . . it was all very nice and lighthearted.'[1] Perhaps because of this Elizabeth had a train of admirers – aristocrats all – who seriously wanted to marry her and were heartbroken when, after three proposals, she finally accepted Prince Bertie. One of them, James Stuart, whom she is rumoured to have found the most attractive, was a well-known heartbreaker himself. He gave up hope, resigned his job as Prince Bertie's equerry and left for the wild oil business in Canada (he later married one of Elizabeth's friends, the Duke of Devonshire's daughter, Lady Rachel Cavendish). The fact seems to have been that, beneath all the gilded life, the balls, the shooting parties and the constant socializing, Elizabeth was a serious, sensitive woman. As her mother, Lady Strathmore, wrote to one of her closest, life-long friends, Arthur Penn, '. . . outside, or rather inside, that bright character is a terribly acute *sensitiveness*, which makes life much more difficult for her. However Prince Bertie simply adores her, and I think grasps her true worth.'[2]

'Prince Bertie', Albert, Duke of York, second son of King George V and Queen Mary, had qualities of goodness, niceness and vulnerability to which Elizabeth responded. People close to him described him as 'lovable', one going so far as to say that he was 'one of the very few men whom I would call lovable and the reason why he was lovable was because he was fighting every minute of the day the internal problem of his speech'.[3] Being a member of the Royal Family, however, was a black mark against him as far as Elizabeth was concerned. As her mother remarked, 'some people are attracted to royalty like sea lions are to fish', but the Strath-mores were not royalty hunters. In marrying the King's son Elizabeth would enter the royal circle, which was the very reverse of fun, particularly for the younger generation. Bertie's elder brother, the Prince of Wales, described to his friend Duff Cooper 'the gloom of Buckingham Palace, how he himself and all of them "freeze up" the moment they get inside it. How bad-tempered his father is.' He described his sister-in-law Elizabeth as 'the one bright spot there, they all love her and the King is in a good temper when she is there'.[4]

Bertie had suffered as much, if not more than his siblings, from his father's quick temper and martinet attitudes. He was born left-handed and made to write with his right, he had a tendency to knock knees and was made to wear agonizing splints to straighten his legs. He was shy and lacking in self-confidence and had long suffered in comparison with his brother David, heir to the throne, quick and charming. One of his father's courtiers described the comparison between the two as 'ugly duckling and cock pheasant'. It was hardly surprising that from the age of about seven he should have developed a stammer which could become crippling in certain situations, not helped by his father's shouting at him, 'Get it out, get it out,' as he stumbled over the beginning of a word. He had digestive problems – said to have been caused by an unkind nurse deliberately feeding him his bottle when in a rocking carriage, which culminated in a duodenal ulcer suffered as a young officer in the Navy and terminated his seagoing career. He appeared to suffer from constant stress, so much so that he was assigned a mentor, Louis Greig, to protect and guide him as a young adult. On the plus side, he was physically attractive, small and slender, a gifted athlete who played tennis almost to Wimbledon standard, and a far better natural golfer than his elder brother. He rode, hunted and danced with a natural grace. Probably because of his stressed nature, he had a volcanic temper, which showed itself in disconcerting explosions that were not directed at any particular person and which in later life only his wife and younger daughter seemed to be able to control. It was, above all, his vulnerability and essential goodness that appealed to Elizabeth; he needed her – as his future mother-in-law, Cecilia Strathmore, surmised, he was a man who would be 'made or marred by his wife'.

Furthermore, like Elizabeth, he had a fundamental sense of duty, so conspicuously lacking in Edward. Owing to his poor health Bertie had had an unhappy war. He had joined the Navy, but within a month of the outbreak of the war he had an attack of appendicitis and was transferred to hospital in Aberdeen for an operation; his undiagnosed duodenal ulcer meant that, apart from a brief exciting spell at sea during the Battle of Jutland, he spent most of his time in hospitals or hospital ships until an operation in November 1917 resolved the problem. He was miserably conscious that he had spent much of his time in hospital or convalescing in London or Sandringham with his parents and sister while his contemporaries were fighting and dying in Flanders. Men who were not in uniform were talked of as cowards and sent white feathers through the post, and Bertie had not been exempt; a letter written by the Prince of Wales to their mother after the Armistice referred to 'the very unfair questions some people asked last year as to what he [Bertie] was doing . . .' At the beginning of February 1918, in the last year of the war, he spent a short period at Cranwell in Lincolnshire, transferring to the newly constituted Royal Air Force. The years between 1913 and 1918 were probably the most unhappy and lonely of his life, but the experience he had gained of the working and organization of the Services at war was to be invaluable to him as Commander-in-Chief in the Second World War.

After the war Prince Albert was sent by his father to spend a year at Cambridge University, although quite what knowledge he was supposed to have absorbed in only one year is debatable. His father, who was becoming increasingly paranoid about the possibility of his sons 'getting mixed up in bad company', would not even allow him to live in college; he was looked after in a rented house by Louis Greig and his wife, with his brother Harry, later Duke of Gloucester, a man of limited intellect whose principal daily occupation was killing mice in the conservatory. At Cambridge, Bertie did not make friends any more than he had in the RAF. The only lasting benefit from his time there was a thorough knowledge of the British Constitution, as a result of studying Dicey's solid *Law of the Constitution* and the brilliant treatise on the subject by Walter Bagehot, which laid down the ground rules for the constitutional monarchy of Great Britain, the wider relations between Crown and people and the more trammelled relations between monarch and government. He became an expert on the subject and was on occasion to show a greater understanding of it than Winston Churchill. Like his mother, Queen Mary, he was absorbed by the history of his family and the ritual and tradition connected with it.

Moreover, as a result of his frequent periods of convalescence he had spent a good deal of time with his father and, despite his earlier relationship with him, was closer to him than any of his brothers. The King talked or wrote to him of his preoccupations, military and political. Like his brothers, Bertie found life at Buckingham Palace and Balmoral stiflingly dull; but he had absorbed the traditions of the Court and its old-fashioned, honourable and dedicated courtiers, like his father's Private Secretary, Arthur Bigge, Lord Stamfordham, who had started under Queen Victoria and had worked for Prince Albert's grandfather, Edward VII. He had seen the workings of the British monarchy close up and understood its traditions and responsibilities. After the First World War he had been active on the all-important social welfare front, designed to bring monarch and people closer together and preserve the British constitutional monarchy from the fate that had overtaken his father's cousins, the Tsar of Russia and the Kaiser in Germany. 'The Monarchy and its cost will have to be justified in the future in the eyes of a war-worn and hungry proletariat,' a royal adviser had warned the King's Private Secretary on 4 November 1918. While

David dazzled the Empire, Albert (nicknamed 'the Foreman' by his brothers) toured engineering plants, factories, mines and ship-yards. He became President of the Industrial Welfare Society, an organization dedicated to the welfare of the workers and to foster-ing relations between workers and employers, and hosted the annual Duke of York's camps, at which 200 working-class boys and 200 public schoolboys enjoyed innocent Baden-Powellesque fun. It worked at the time, as an idealistic experiment designed to prove that class war could be overcome, but, as Denis Thatcher, a veteran of the 1932 camp, wrote regretfully, 'its ideas and ethos forty years on are totally outdated . . .' The first camp was held in August 1921, the last camp at Balmoral in August 1939. It did not survive the ending of peace.

Prince Bertie may have been shy but he was single-minded in his determination to marry Elizabeth Bowes-Lyon. He first pro-posed to her in February 1921; she refused, but continued to see him and to correspond with him. He proposed again in March 1922 and was again rejected. By January 1923 even Queen Mary and her chosen intermediary, Lady Airlie, had given up their cherished idea of a marriage between Bertie and Elizabeth. Queen Mary wrote to Mabell Airlie somewhat huffily, saying that she and the King now hoped nothing would come of it 'as we both feel ruffled at E's behaviour!' Elizabeth herself was confused and ner-vous, writing to a friend, 'I don't seem able to like anybody enough to marry them . . .' On 2 January 1923 Bertie proposed to her again, but this time her response was more a delaying tactic than a definite refusal. At her request he gave her more time to think about it, until the weekend of 13–14 January when, as Lady Strath-more recorded, 'He came down to [St Paul's Walden Bury] suddenly on <u>Friday</u>, proposed continuously until Sunday night, when she said Yes at 11.30. My head is completely bewildered, as all those days E. was hesitating & miserable, but now she is abso-lutely happy – & he is <u>radiant</u> . . .' Elizabeth herself wrote: 'I <u>do</u> [underlined several times] love you Bertie, & feel certain that I shall more & more.'[5] They were married on 26 April 1923 at West-minster Abbey.

Princess Elizabeth was born by Caesarean section three years later, on Wednesday, 21 April 1926 at 2.40 a.m. at 17 Bruton Street, Mayfair, the Strathmores' new London home after they had had to give up 20 St James's Square. Her parents, it seems, had had trouble conceiving: she was born three years after their marriage and her sister four years later. 'You don't know what a tremendous joy it is to Elizabeth and me to have our little girl,' her father wrote to her grandmother, Queen Mary. 'We always wanted a child to make our happiness complete, & now that it has happened, it seems so wonderful & strange. I am so proud of Elizabeth at this moment after all she has gone through during the last few days. I do hope that you & Papa are as delighted as we are, to have a grand-daughter, or would you have sooner have had another grandson [Princess Mary's son, George, had been born on 7 February 1923]. I know Elizabeth wanted a daughter . . .'[6] No one minded the Yorks' first child being a girl, since no one seriously considered the possibility of her succeeding to the throne. Indeed, the Yorks' choice of Elizabeth for the baby's name was after her mother, without conscious reference to the great Elizabeth I, nor was the name of that other reigning Queen, her great-great-grandmother, Victoria, apparently even considered: 'I have heard from Bertie about the names,' George V told Queen Mary. 'He mentions Elizabeth, Alexandra [the child's great-grandmother, who had died at Sandringham the previous November], Mary . . . he says nothing about Victoria. I hardly think that necessary.'

Heiress to the throne or not, the Princess was a star to ordinary people from the moment she was born. She was christened on 29 May after the General Strike ended: people were fed up with dark newspaper photographs featuring men in flat caps, and the new royal baby was a welcome distraction from the dull grind of daily lives. 'Royalty makes headlines,' a disgruntled socialist, Richard Cross-man, wrote in his diary. There had been people waiting outside

17 Bruton Street since the day she was born, but never, according to her father, so many as on that day. The memory of Queen Victoria hovered over the private chapel at Buckingham Palace. The five-week-old Princess was christened in the gold lily-shaped font designed by Victoria's consort, Prince Albert, wearing the cream satin and Honiton lace dress worn by royal babies since Victoria and Albert's eldest daughter, Vicky. She cried, as babies traditionally should, and was dosed by her nurse with dill water. Tradition began early in her life – her nurse was Alah Knight, who had been the Duchess of York's nanny; that August she went with her family to Glamis and for Christmas to her royal grandparents at Sandringham. She was less than a year old when her parents left in January 1927 for Australia, where the Duke of York was to open the new Federal Parliament buildings in Canberra. At Portsmouth harbour, where they embarked on the battleship HMS *Renown*, it was evident from the enthusiastic crowd cheering them off that the Duke and Duchess of York were already popular public figures. 'If you wanted evidence that the country was not going Bolshevik, you could not have had better proof than was afforded yesterday,' an accompanying official wrote.

The tour appears to have been initiated by the Duke himself and at first had been opposed by his father, who had demonstrated his customary debilitating lack of confidence in his son's ability. The King's Private Secretary, Lord Stamfordham, had written to the Governor-General when the proposal was put to the King: '. . . the Duke of York is the only one of the Princes who could undertake this duty; and for many reasons His Majesty cannot . . . hold out much hope of such an arrangement being carried out.' To be fair, the King was probably influenced by poor Albert's miserable experience delivering the broadcast at the opening ceremony of the Empire Exhibition at Wembley in 1925, when his stammer had been painfully apparent to the listening audience worldwide, and by the outstanding success of the Prince of Wales on a previous Australian visit in 1920. Since then, however, Bertie's life had been transformed not only by the encouragement of his wife, a natural performer on public occasions, but by treatment from an outstanding Australian speech therapist, Lionel Logue, who had treated Australian soldiers traumatized in the First World War and now practised in London. Against his will (he had endured previous attempts to cure his stammer) and again encouraged by Elizabeth, who attended the sessions at Logue's Harley Street consulting rooms, he had no fewer than eighty-two appointments with Logue over the period 1926–7. Logue described him as 'the pluckiest and most determined patient I ever had'. By the time he left for Australia, he felt confident enough to write to Logue, 'how grateful I am to you for all that you have done in helping me with my speech defect. I really do think you have given me a real good start in the way of getting over it & I am sure if I carry on your exercises and instructions that I shall not go back. I am full of confidence for this trip now.'[7]

The birth of Princess Margaret Rose at Glamis in August 1930 completed the family circle. True to her later capricious form, she kept an important dignitary waiting – the Home Secretary, who by tradition had to attend the births of royal children, supposedly to prevent the substitution of another, non-royal, infant for the real one. Although there was four years' age difference between the two girls, Margaret quickly caught up and – socially – outstripped her elder sister. Partly this was due to her own quick, precocious nature, partly to the conscious efforts of their parents to treat them – even to dress them – the same. Their father never forgot the subordinate role assigned to him in comparison with his elder brother and was determined that there should not be the same imbalance in his own family. Remembering too the joylessness of his childhood, he was determined that his children should enjoy theirs. Princess Elizabeth had inherited her father's shyness but also his genuine kindness, niceness and sense of responsibility. She never seemed to mind when Margaret showed off, demanding attention. 'I've never known two sisters who were closer,' a courtier said.

Theirs was a cloistered, upper-class childhood, divided between a nursery ruled by Alah Knight and a schoolroom governed by 'Crawfie', a young Scottish girl from Aberdeen who had come to them from their aunt. Education was not considered to be at a premium, while manners were. An authorized book on Princess Elizabeth written in 1930 gives an example of the simpering cuteness expected of children's behaviour then.[8] 'On one occasion Princess Elizabeth said, "My goodness!" in the hearing of her mother and was at once told "this was not pretty and must not be repeated".' Princess Elizabeth's reaction to hearing a grown-up say 'My goodness' was described by the author as 'roguish'. The responsible Elizabeth made sure that Margaret's naughtiness and irrepressible glee were not expressed in public. At a Buckingham Palace garden party Crawfie overheard her say to her sister: 'If you do see someone with a funny hat, Margaret, you must *not* point at it and laugh. And you must *not* be in too much of a hurry to get through the crowds to the tea table. That's not polite either.'[9]

The children's parents were anxious that they should lead as normal a life as possible, difficult when they never met any 'ordinary' children. The Palace Girl Guides Company was supposed to be a substitute for going to school but, as a childhood friend of the Princesses said, 'They were all dukes' daughters and Mountbattens – it wasn't at all democratic.' The other girls were expected to curtsey to the Princesses. 'The Little Princesses', as they were always referred to in the press, became an important part of the royal brand, a family image deliberately promoted to reassure the public and erase the impression of their scapegrace uncle and his vivid private life.

For Elizabeth a key moment of childhood was her father's Coronation on 12 May 1937, an event designed to obliterate the departed King and to replace his image in the public mind with that of his dutiful brother. Indeed the date had originally been set for Edward's Coronation and it was now too late for it to be changed. Thousands of Edward mugs had to be scrapped and King

George VI and Queen Elizabeth memorabilia manufactured. The King sat in his study practising his new signature: 'Albert' became 'George' in a deliberate move to emphasize continuity with his father. Another element in that continuity would be Queen Mary, liberated by the death of her repressive husband and now a force in the family.

Privately, the King was nervous of his forthcoming ordeal, particularly the Coronation broadcast he was to make that evening from Buckingham Palace. A hugely public ceremony is a nightmare for a stammerer, and he spent nervous hours rehearsing with Lionel Logue. Rumours circulated in the City of London that the Coronation, with George VI as central figure, would not take place, even that he was subject to the 'falling down sickness', based on old memories of his youngest brother, Prince John, who had died of a final fit at Sandringham in 1917 – perhaps even on insider recollections of his great-uncle Prince Leopold, Duke of Albany, who had been similarly afflicted. *Time* magazine reported on 8 March that the King had wished a passage to be placed in the news/ gossip magazine *Cavalcade* 'denying rumours circulating on the Stock Exchange that another mild epileptic fit had been suffered by His Majesty . . .' and that 'the Gentlemen of England' (whoever they were) had 'pounced' on the printed denial and forced its excision.

The Archbishop of Canterbury, George V's great friend Cosmo Lang, whose Abdication broadcast on 13 December had caused great offence because of the language he had used against Edward, actually made matters worse for the King by referring to 'an occasional and momentary hesitation in his speech'. Lang turned down the BBC's proposal for televising the ceremony for the first time, using a camera to be 'camouflaged as stone with some Gothic ornament by the Office of Works'. His official reason was that the range of transmission was so limited, and so few people 'happened to have the necessary apparatus in their house', that it was not worthwhile doing it. His real reason, however, could be divined from a note in his hand: 'no possibility of censoring'. Clearly he was afraid that a live television broadcast might reveal incidents embarrassing to the King, who could suffer from muscular spasm in his cheeks and jaw when struggling with a word. The Coronation therefore was to be filmed, and the Archbishop and Earl Marshal would censor the film on the evening after the ceremony. Television was then in its infancy – the first television service had been opened by Leslie Mitchell in November 1936 – but although not permitted in the Abbey, 60,000 viewers were able to watch the procession.

On the day, however, the Coronation, despite the bungling of certain officials and bishops, was a triumph for the King, as was his broadcast to the Empire that evening. Princess Elizabeth kept an account of it specially for her parents, written in pencil on lined paper bound with pink silk ribbon: 'To Mummy and Papa. In Memory of Their Coronation, from Lilibet By Herself.' 'Papa [was] looking very beautiful,' she wrote; his actual crowning passed 'in a haze of wonder'. She was only surprised that 'Grannie' (Queen Mary) did not remember much of her own Coronation; 'rather odd', she commented.[10] Even odder, although she could not have known it, was that her Uncle David, now Duke of Windsor, listened to the Coronation which should have been his own while in exile at the Château de Candé in Touraine, sitting knitting a navy-blue wool sweater for Wallis, whom he was soon to marry there. You cannot help wondering – although she did not mention it – whether the eleven-year-old Princess gave a thought to her own Coronation in the future.

4. Windsor War

Windsor Castle, with its great towers and battlements dominating the Thames Valley, was to be Princess Elizabeth's home during the years of the Second World War. Even before her father's Coronation in May 1937, war clouds had been gathering over Europe and the Fascists were on the move. In March 1936 Hitler had marched into the Rhineland in defiance of the agreements which had ended the First World War; neither France nor Britain moved to stop him. The Italian dictator Mussolini took over Abyssinia (modern Ethiopia), using forbidden weapons such as poison gas and dropping inconvenient local chieftains alive out of aeroplanes. There were mutterings among the diplomats gathered at the largely ineffectual League of Nations in Geneva; the dislodged Emperor Haile Selassie, whose Coronation Princess Elizabeth's Uncle Henry had attended, fled to London but it was thought inappropriate for the King to receive him. In Spain war broke out when the Nationalist forces under General Franco attacked the Republican Government; many young Englishmen with left-wing sympathies went out to fight, including the writer George Orwell, the poet John Cornford and Winston Churchill's nephew, Giles Romilly. In March 1938 Hitler incorporated Austria into the German Reich and threatened the Czech Government on behalf of the Sudeten Germans living there. By September, it seemed that Britain was on the brink of war: trenches were dug in London parks and more than 38 million gas masks were distributed; barrage balloons flew over London. 'How horrible, fantastic, incredible it is,' bewailed the new British Prime Minister, Neville Chamberlain, 'that we should be digging trenches and trying on gas masks here because of a quarrel in a far-away country [Czechoslovakia] between people of whom we know nothing.'

Of more immediate consequence to Princess Elizabeth, however, were the death of her Strathmore grandmother in June and the beginning of the family holiday in August. It began on the Isle of Wight, where Queen Elizabeth took her daughters to visit Queen Victoria's old home at Osborne House; they then embarked on the royal yacht *Victoria & Albert* for the traditional journey to Scotland, up the east coast, stopping at Southwold in Suffolk for the Princess's father to visit his Duke of York's camp. Through the panic days of the Munich crisis the children stayed, with their ponies, nurses and governesses, at Balmoral, with a brief visit to Glasgow to see their mother launch her namesake liner, the *Queen Elizabeth*. In May 1939 the two children, with their grandmother, Queen Mary, travelled to Portsmouth to see their parents off for their State visit to Canada and the United States. At sea the next day, Queen Elizabeth wrote to her eldest daughter while the King wrote to Princess Margaret; the Queen's letter contained its usual admonition – 'be good & kind'. She wrote describing their adventures as their ship nosed through the foggy icy waters where the *Titanic* had been lost:

> Here we are creeping along at about one mile per hour, & occasionally stopping altogether, for the 3rd day running! You can imagine how horrid it is – one cannot see more than a few yards, and the sea is full of icebergs as big as Glamis, & things called growlers – which are icebergs mostly under water with only a very small amount of ice showing on the surface . . . It is *very* cold – rather like the coldest, dampest day at Sandringham – double it & add some icebergs, & then you can imagine a little of what it is like![1]

They were back in late June, after a triumphant tour when they had been ecstatically received throughout Canada and the United

States and had lunched with President Roosevelt at his home, Hyde Park. 'The British sovereigns have conquered Washington,' Arthur Krock wrote in the *New York Times*. Queen Elizabeth described it as 'the tour that made us'. And it had: in Canada, the United States and Britain the couple had established themselves as the royal representatives of their country and Empire, banishing the spectre of Wallis and Edward, which perhaps had loomed larger in their imagination than it had in reality.

Princesses Elizabeth and Margaret joined their parents on the liner off the Isle of Wight, and crossed the Solent accompanied by a patriotic flotilla of steamers, yachts and small boats. The train track back to London was lined with waving spectators; when they arrived, they were met by the Prime Minister and more crowds greeted them along the route to Buckingham Palace. In Parliament Square the members of both Houses of Parliament welcomed them home, shouting and cheering. As Harold Nicolson recorded: 'We lost all dignity and yelled and yelled. The King wore a happy schoolboy grin. The Queen was superb. She really does manage to convey to each individual in the crowd that he or she has had a personal greeting . . .' Carried quite away, he added: 'she is in truth one of the most amazing Queens since Cleopatra'.[2] In a speech at the Guildhall the next day, the King spoke movingly of 'our great Commonwealth of Nations' and of the Crown as 'a force for promoting peace and goodwill among mankind'. The sense that peace and goodwill were at serious risk from Hitler's manoeuvres and that the Royal Family represented a focus for patriotism, for good against evil, was at the heart of the huge emotional response they evoked on their return from across the Atlantic.

For Princess Elizabeth, however, what Hitler did was of far less importance than an encounter with the man who was to occupy her thoughts and her heart for the rest of her life. She was thirteen in July 1939 when with her parents and sister on board the *Victoria & Albert* she visited the Royal Naval College at Dartmouth, where her father had once been a cadet. Prince Philip of Greece was eighteen and, as a direct descendant of Queen Victoria, a royal connection. She had apparently already met him at family gatherings but, on this occasion, she fell in love with him, as her father's official biographer was authorized to confirm. He was extremely handsome, with fine features and blond Viking looks. He was also, in the view of Crawfie, who accompanied the party, an outrageous show-off who found a willing audience in his two royal cousins as he jumped over nets on the tennis courts and ragged 'plump little Margaret. I thought he showed off a good deal but the little girls were much impressed. Lilibet said, "How good he is, Crawfie. How high he can jump." '[5] When the *Victoria & Albert* left harbour, Prince Philip was conspicuous in the last of the little boats accompanying them, rowing furiously in the yacht's wake. Within months he would be a serving officer in the King's Navy, fighting for his adopted country against the Fascist dictators, and Princess Elizabeth would be the Princess in the Tower, immured for safety behind the walls of Windsor Castle.

She was at Balmoral as usual when Hitler invaded Poland at dawn on 1 September 1939. Britain and France had guaranteed that they would fight to maintain Polish independence, and now delivered an ultimatum threatening war unless hostilities ceased: at 11 a.m. on 3 September the time limit expired, and fifteen minutes later the Prime Minister, Neville Chamberlain, declared the country at war. The King and Queen were already back in London; that evening the King delivered a moving speech:

> In this grave hour, perhaps the most fateful in our history . . . for the second time in the lives of most of us we are at war. Over and over again we have tried to find a peaceful way out of the differences between ourselves and those who are now our enemies . . . [but] . . . We have been forced into a conflict. For we are called, with our allies, to meet the challenge of a principle which, if it were to prevail, would be fatal to any civilized order in the world . . . that might is right . . .

The children listened from Birkhall, where they had been moved for safety in case the Germans chose to bomb Balmoral. They continued on their usual outdoor holiday, the only impact of the war on their isolated life being the arrival in the locality of evacuee children from Glasgow and their mothers, who were housed at Craigowan Lodge on the royal estate. 'We have got hundreds all around about from Glasgow,' Princess Elizabeth told Crawfie. Their arrival was part of the early war plans for civilians; a million people were moved out of the cities to escape the expected bombing. It was a huge culture shock on both sides: the country people were dismayed by the language and habits of the city children and their mothers, the children and their mothers unnerved by the boredom and to them unnatural quiet of their rural surroundings. Queen Elizabeth recalled that they 'couldn't bear the noise of the trees'. A rather more stately refugee, Queen Mary, was sent to spend the war years with her niece, the Duchess of Beaufort, at Badminton, where she was equally surprised by rustic quiet and tedium. At Birkhall the two Princesses continued their lessons with Crawfie and their French teacher, Madame Montaudon-Smith ('Monty'), and Princess Elizabeth wrote historical essays set her by Henry Marten, the Vice-Provost of Eton. They joined a local sewing circle and knitted socks and scarves for the soldiers. They listened to their mother's Armistice Day broadcast to the women of the Empire: 'When I told our little daughters that I was going to broadcast they said, "Oh Mummy please give our love to all the children." '[4] War touched them for the first time when on 13/14 October 1939 a German submarine penetrated the defences of the northern naval base at Scapa Flow and sank the battleship *Royal Oak*. Eight hundred men drowned. 'We were continually studying *Jane's Fighting Ships*,' Crawfie wrote, 'and the little girls took a personal interest in every one of them. Lilibet jumped from her chair, her eyes blazing with anger. "Crawfie, it can't be! All those nice sailors." ' She was still thinking of them at Christmas when she wrote to Crawfie from Appleton House at Sandringham (the big house was closed for the duration). 'Perhaps we were too happy. I kept thinking of those sailors and what Christmas must have been like in their homes.'[5]

Dressed in naval uniform, the King delivered a dramatic Christmas broadcast warning of dark times to come, but it was the period of the 'Phoney War', when apart from accidents caused by the darkness, when street lights and car headlights were banned, and windows heavily curtained or painted over, nothing happened. Fuel and food rationing were to follow. Poland suffered terribly, but in England no bombs fell. For six months it seemed that the war was unreal, until in April 1940 the Germans attacked neutral Norway and a British expedition sent to help the Norwegians ended in disaster. On 9 May 1940 Chamberlain, who had foolishly declared that Hitler had 'missed the bus', was defeated in the House of Commons with members taunting him, 'Missed the bus, missed the bus.' He was as popular with the Royal Family as his successor Winston Churchill was distrusted by them for his manoeuvrings in support of Edward VIII. 'I *cried*, Mummy,' Princess Elizabeth wrote after hearing his resignation speech. He was replaced as Prime Minister by Winston Churchill at the head of a National Government, with Clement Attlee, the leader of the Labour Party, as his deputy, a coalition which was to last until the end of the war. Within just over a month, the Germans had swept through Holland, Belgium, Luxembourg and northern France, driving the British Expeditionary Force into the sea. The famous flotilla of 'little boats' helped to rescue more than 300,000 British and French soldiers from the beaches of Dunkirk, but they did not include Princess Elizabeth's first cousin on her mother's side, John Elphinstone, who was captured and spent the rest of the war in German prisoner-of-war camps, ending up in Colditz. The Dunkirk operation ended on 3 June, and the following day Churchill issued his famous promise that Britain would fight on – 'we shall fight them on the beaches . . . we will never surrender'. But on 14 June the Germans marched unopposed into Paris, the sixth European capital to fall under their control within nine months, and France, led by the former hero of the Battle of Verdun, General Pétain, asked for an armistice. Britain now stood alone against the Fascist powers (Mussolini declared war on Britain on 10 June), supported only by its Empire and Dominions; the United States, although friendly, was determined to remain neutral.

Royal refugees from Europe began to arrive at Buckingham Palace: King Haakon of Norway had come over in April, and on 13 May Queen Wilhelmina of the Netherlands was brought to England on a British warship, having narrowly escaped a German parachute force sent to capture her. Many observers thought that Germany – allied with Russia, Spain and Italy, and in control of most of Europe – would win. There was a panic voluntary exodus of upper-class children and an involuntary one of their working-class counterparts to Canada and the United States. The Queen, a vociferous patriot – 'we must keep the old flag flying', as she told her friends, was determined that neither she nor her children would leave, despite warnings that the Germans would capture them. She had, however, instructed Crawfie to move the Princesses from the Royal Lodge to the safety of Windsor Castle, where they were to remain for five years, through the Battle of Britain in August 1940 when the young pilots of the RAF battled in dogfights with the Luftwaffe in the clear summer skies over the Channel and the British coast. Then came the Blitz, when London was bombed every night from 7 September to 2 November. On the night of 7–8 September more than 200 German bombers attacked London: by dawn more than 400 Londoners, most of them East Enders, had died, and 1,357 had been seriously injured. A bomb dropped on the 9th destroyed the King's new swimming pool; more seriously, on 13 September a direct and deliberate day-time attack was made on the Palace. 'The aircraft was seen coming down the Mall . . . having dived through the clouds & dropped 2 bombs on the forecourt, 2 in the quadrangle, 1 in the Chapel & the other in the garden. There is no doubt it was a direct attack on the

Palace.'[6] Queen Elizabeth with her keen touch for propaganda
famously declared, 'Now I feel I can look the East End in the face';
the King was privately convinced the Germans intended to substitute him with his brother, the Duke of Windsor. The King in
uniform and the Queen in hers – feathered hat, crêpe coat and
dress, strings of pearls – visited the bombed areas, while Princess
Elizabeth did her bit for the family war effort.

Aged fourteen and a half, she made her first broadcast from
Windsor on 13 October, addressed to 'the children of the Empire'.
Ostensibly directed at British children evacuated to the United
States, it was actually intended to influence American opinion in
favour of Britain. 'As Her Royal Highness's first broadcast, delivered at an historic moment,' the Director-General of the BBC
advised, 'it would reach the minds of the millions who heard it
with a singular poignancy.' Reading in a clear, high-pitched voice,
she linked her own recent life and that of her sister to the lives of
displaced British children overseas: 'My sister, Margaret Rose, and
I feel so much for you, as we know from experience what it means
to be away from those we love most of all . . . My sister is by my
side, and we are both going to say goodnight to you. Come on,
Margaret.' 'Good night,' her ten-year-old sister chirped. 'Good
night and good luck to you all,' Princess Elizabeth ended. Despite
what Churchill's Private Secretary, Jock Colville (later to work for
the Princess as her Private Secretary), described as its sloppy sentiment, the broadcast was a huge success, making the front pages in
all the New York newspapers.

The impact of the bombs dropping on London could be felt
shaking the chalk hill on which the castle stood; in October there
were two attacks on the town of Windsor and on the moonlit night
following Princess Elizabeth's broadcast wave after wave of enemy
bombers passed over the castle heading north, to devastate the
Midlands industrial city of Coventry. Her father saw the terrible
effects for himself when he visited by train the next day: all but
7,000 of its 12,000 houses destroyed, 35,000 of its 47,000 citizens

homeless, the historic centre of the city with its towering four-teenth-century cathedral destroyed. The Germans had invented a new verb, '*coventrieren*' – to obliterate.

The years at Windsor were the formative period of Princess Elizabeth's life, a time when she absorbed the symbolism and traditions of the British monarchy as she could have done nowhere else. Founded as a wooden castle on a hill by William the Conqueror in the eleventh century, Windsor has been the home of nine monarchs and is the oldest royal residence in Britain to have remained in continuous use. Samuel Pepys, friend of Princess Elizabeth's Stuart ancestor King Charles II, called it the most romantic castle in the world, and for more than 900 years it has been a potent symbol of the British monarchy. Charles II celebrated the splendour of his restoration in 1660 by turning the royal apartments into the grandest baroque State apartments in England, the rooms filled with recovered works of art collected by Charles I and sold by Cromwell, including the great Van Dyck portraits of the King and his family. George III, the first of the Hanoverians to live again at Windsor, employed James Wyatt in 1796 to re-gothicize the castle. Blind and afflicted with porphyria, the poor King spent his declining years of madness here until his death in 1820. The nephew of a courtier remembered being taken, while a boy at Eton, by his aunt to listen at the King's door: 'If he were having a disturbed day he would be pacing up and down, and sometimes roaring; at other times the stillness would be broken by snatches of Handel as he groped in his darkness upon the keys of the harpsichord.'[7]

But for Princess Elizabeth, the presiding genius of the castle was her great-great-grandmother, Queen Victoria, whose principal home it was – 'the Widow of Windsor', as she was known after the death there on 14 December 1861 of her adored husband, Prince Albert. Elizabeth was fascinated by stories of Victoria told to her by Victoria's granddaughter, Princess Marie Louise. Reminiscing one Christmas at Windsor about conversations with the old Queen, Princess Marie Louise stopped and said to Elizabeth that it must be boring for her to hear old people talking about things that happened long ago. 'But Cousin Louie,' Elizabeth said, 'it's *history* and therefore so thrilling.' Her father and others were even beginning to compare her with Victoria. It was Victoria and Albert who had established the image of the Royal Family, with the emphasis on 'family', recorded in a series of portraits by their favourite painter, Winterhalter. And it was this Victorian ideal of the monarchy that King George VI and Queen Elizabeth were determined to re-establish. Pictures were issued of the identically dressed Princesses wielding rakes while haymaking on the Home Farm in Windsor Park, and of their father prodding an enormous pig in the farm sties, setting an example for an embattled nation that would have to grow its own food. At Windsor, as at Buckingham Palace, black lines were painted round the baths, allowing only five inches of water to be drawn; the great paintings and works of art were taken down to be stored in the cellars; the huge chandeliers in the Waterloo Room were lowered to within three inches of the floor so that they would not be shattered if they dropped. Windows were blacked out so that the huge castle loomed dark against the sky and the inhabitants groped their way around just as His Majesty's subjects did in the streets of their cities.

Windsor Castle is more than a royal residence, it is a community in a very real sense. Beside the massive towers and glittering State apartments a conglomeration of houses of different periods occupy courtyards and corners, clinging to the ancient walls like swallows' nests. The historian of Windsor, Mark Girouard, has described their inhabitants as 'a race apart' – the people who live and work in the castle: members of the Household, acting or retired; the archivists of the Royal Archives; their fellow scholars in the Royal Library; the Governor, the Dean and fellow Canons, the vergers, choristers and whole administrative world of St George's Chapel; the Military Knights, retired military men, emerging from their houses on Sundays or special occasions in their handsome uniforms; and a network of porters, maintenance men and policemen, helpful and jolly in a distinctive Windsor way. In wartime it was a cosy community, the members sending each other soup, eggs and other treats to beat the rationing. It was and is like a hive, its workers clustering round the Royal Family at the centre. One of the great royal events of the year is the Garter ceremony, the annual celebration of the 'Most Noble Order of the Garter', the senior British Order of Chivalry founded by King Edward III in 1348, membership of which is conferred by the Sovereign. In June, on the Monday of Ascot week, the Sovereign and the Knights of the Garter, wearing blue velvet mantles with the badge of the Order and black velvet hats topped with white feathers, process from St George's Hall to St George's Chapel for the Garter Service.

This was Princess Elizabeth's world, then as it is now. During the war years the King and Queen drove up to London for the day, coming down to Windsor to sleep and spend the weekends. The two Princesses lived in the Augusta Tower, the floor they occupied being still known as 'the nursery floor' although in 1940 Elizabeth was fourteen and Margaret ten, and Alah Knight was very much in charge. Nursemaid Bobo Macdonald slept on the floor above. Meals were served in the nursery, brought up from the Great Kitchen, at least five minutes' walk away, by the 'nursery footman', Cyril Dickman. Crawfie was still their principal companion, and they had other governesses, Mrs Montaudon-Smith, 'Monty', and Antoinette de Bellaigue, 'Toni', a Belgian aristocrat who had escaped just before the German invasion, who not only taught them French but gave them an idea of European culture and civilization. The eccentric Vice-Provost of Eton, Sir Henry Marten, came up to give the heir to the throne lessons in history and, above all, on Bagehot and the British Constitution, mastered by all recent monarchs since Queen Victoria, even such anti-intellectuals as George V and George VI (although not, apparently, Edward VIII). Apart from lessons, there were rides in the park and walks with the dogs, the three corgis and Ching, the Tibetan spaniel. The girls kept rabbits and worked on their allotment gardens in the Dig for Victory campaign; the beds on the East Terrace were planted with vegetables and the King kept huge pigs in the Home Farm in the park. At weekends they lunched with their parents, and with courtiers and young officers from the Castle Company of Grenadier Guards, officially stationed at Windsor to protect the Royal Family.

The chief wartime entertainment for the Windsor Castle community was the annual pantomime, in which the Princesses took leading roles. There were entertainments in St George's Hall – a Nativity play on 21 December 1940, in which, according to a spectator, 'Princess Margaret acted the part of a little child who saw the star of the Nativity in a dream: & when she sang a little hymn, kneeling and unaccompanied, the Queen had to resort to her handkerchief, the Dean said that he was not ashamed to admit that he wept copiously . . . it was extraordinarily moving. The dresses were beautiful, Princess Elizabeth looked marvellous as one of the 3 Orient Kings in red & gold brocade.' On 13 July 1940 there was a concert/variety show given by 'the children of Windsor Great Park', in which the Princesses took part in a duet and other sketches. 'The King told the Dean that he was glad to think that if he was dethroned his daughters would be able to earn their living.' On 12 December 1941 they organized a pantomime, *Sleeping Beauty*, written and produced by Hubert Tannar. 'The Princesses took part in all the principal dances, & their dancing is worth all the money, they are so graceful. Princess Elizabeth as the Prince Salvador was delightful, and in the 2nd act, dressed in white satin with a white wig was quite lovely. Princess Margaret as the principal fairy had a rather bigger part & acts so well,'[8] an observer wrote.

Princess Margaret was always destined to be a star – extrovert, capricious, attention-seeking, imaginative and naughty. 'The King spoiled Princess Margaret dreadfully,' the daughter of one of his courtiers said. 'She was his pet . . .' Crawfie worried about the effect of the contrast in temperament between the two sisters, asking friends, 'Could you this year only ask Princess Elizabeth to your party? We really are trying to separate them a bit because

Princess Margaret does draw all the attention and Princess Elizabeth lets her do that.' Princess Elizabeth herself admitted as much, saying, 'Oh, it's so much easier when Margaret's there – everybody laughs at what Margaret says . . .' In contrast, Princess Elizabeth was deeply shy, a trait inherited from her father, and from her grandmother, Queen Mary. It was a predominant characteristic which all her contemporaries mention; as a young officer friend put it: 'She didn't find social life at all easy . . . I don't think she particularly enjoyed being a young girl . . . dances, all that sort of stuff. She quite enjoyed it once she could get going, but it didn't come absolutely naturally. She needed confidence.' In that way, he said, she was a typical member of the old Royal Family, so different from her mother and sister with their sparkling vivacity.[9] In character Princess Elizabeth resembled her father, shy, dutiful and extremely kind; fortunately for her, however, she did not share his nervous tension or his fits of explosive temper. She had a calmness and reserve which in many ways was like that of her grandmother, Queen Mary, whose slightly canine looks and quiet dignity she had inherited. She had inherited useful qualities from her mother, an inner toughness that was to stand her in good stead when she became Queen. In her views she followed her father: '[the King] tried very hard to be impartial. What I think is true of hereditary royalty is that their political opinions are relatively idiosyncratic and that they don't fall neatly into party categories and it's quite interesting to compare that position with . . . the Queen Mother's, who's a natural old-fashioned Tory. It's quite a different attitude. They've always thought of themselves as above politics and I think they don't like politicians as a breed. They find them uneasy and they don't like ideas . . .'[10]

June 1940 had been a time of particular stress for the King: Owen Morshead, the Royal Librarian, who was also head of the castle's Home Guard, told Queen Mary that the King 'seemed rather oppressed and tired – sick of reading & reading the endless stream of Cabinet papers and war reports sent daily to him . . . It is a misfortune for him in these days that he has to know so much of what is going on . . . Happily,' he added, 'the Queen is a perpetual tonic, with her sunny and buoyant nature.'[11] Even the children behind the thick walls of Windsor could not escape the stress of war, as their mother wrote to Queen Mary: 'I am afraid that Windsor is not really a good place for them, the noise of guns is heavy and then of course there have been so many bombs dropped all round, & some so close.'[12] One of the worst Blitz episodes of the war came on the night of 29 December 1940 in London, when the Guildhall, eight Wren churches, five railway stations and sixteen Underground stations were damaged or destroyed, and there were 700 fires. For her fifteenth birthday in April 1941 Winston Churchill sent Princess Elizabeth a bunch of roses, with a cheerful message that things would get better. Unfortunately they did not: on 10 May 1941, 400 bombers attacked London, over 1,000 people were killed and 1,800 injured, 2,000 fires were started and 11,000 houses were destroyed. Both Houses of Parliament were hit and Westminster Abbey was damaged. In Queen Elizabeth's words, '. . . poor London, an even more violent & cruel raid Saturday night. Our beautiful shrines and monuments – It seems such *sacrilege* that they should be destroyed by such wicked lying people as the Germans.'[13]

In 1941 two events turned the eventual outcome of the war: in June Hitler attacked Russia, ostensibly an ally since August 1939 but actually a long-term target of his hatred of bolshevism, and in December Japan bombed Pearl Harbor in Hawaii, bringing the United States into the war. Nonetheless Britain suffered a dismal litany of imperial defeats in 1941 and 1942, the surrender of Tobruk in North Africa, the evacuation of the British Expeditionary Force from Crete, and heavy losses of merchant shipping to German submarines in the Battle of the Atlantic. The sinking of the battleships *Prince of Wales* and *Repulse* by the Japanese off Malaya in December 1941 was followed by the humiliating surrender of Singapore in

February 1942, when a superior force of 85,000 British and Australian solders surrendered to Japan. When the Archbishop of Canterbury suggested a National Prayer Day, Churchill is said to have quipped, 'If we can't fight we might as well bloody pray.' The tide only began to turn in the West with Montgomery's victory over Rommel at El Alamein in November 1942, followed by the Allied landings in North Africa, and on 3 September 1943, four years to the day after the declaration of war, British troops landed on the Italian mainland.

On 6 June 1944 – D-Day – the final stage began with the Normandy landings, but it was only the beginning of the end. By the end of the month 8,000 Allied soldiers had been killed (the Queen's friend, artist Rex Whistler, and Kathleen Kennedy's young husband, Hartington, among them) and almost a year of bitter fighting lay ahead. In retaliation Hitler launched his worst weapon, the first flying bomb, the VI, nicknamed the doodlebug, on London. At Windsor there were almost daily air-raid alerts: on 7 July a bomb had the temerity to be shot down near the great statue of George III, known as the Copper Horse, dominating the skyline of the Great Park, and there were so many alerts that the residents' diarist, Charles Fulford, lost count. On 8 August he counted 137 planes flying over the castle; later Allied bombers were continuous overhead from 10 p.m. until midnight, returning from 4 a.m. onwards.

Earlier that summer, shortly after D-Day on 15 June, a bomb fell on the Guards' Chapel within yards of Buckingham Palace during Sunday service, killing more than 100 people including friends of the King and Queen. Another doodlebug hit the Palace wall bordering on Constitution Hill. In the first month alone the doodlebugs destroyed 10,000 houses and damaged almost 200,000 more. The situation was considered dangerous enough for the King, Queen and Prime Minister to hold their Tuesday meetings in the Palace underground shelter. During that doodlebug month of June both Princess Elizabeth's parents made wills – 'in case I get done in by the Germans!' as Queen Elizabeth put it in a letter to her daughter, adding, 'Let's hope this won't be needed, but I *know* that you will always do the right thing, & remember to keep your temper & your word & be loving – sweet.'[14]

In October 1944 the Germans produced an even worse bomb to attack London with, the V2, but the end was now in sight. At Windsor Castle people were beginning to take down their blackouts – 'After tea we removed the black paper from the bathroom window,' Charles Fulford recorded on 11 September 1944, 'an epoch-making event!' The King and Queen worried about their children, longing to get them away from Windsor; as Queen Elizabeth told Queen Mary, 'because life is rather un-normal, & though they are so good and composed, there is always the listening [for air-raid alerts and bombs] & occasionally a leap behind the door, and it does become a strain'.[15] They gave a small dance for them in May, with Ambrose, the same bandleader they themselves had used to dance to before the war, and – despite constant alerts and explosions that day – another party to celebrate Queen Elizabeth's birthday on 4 August. They even felt free enough to go to Balmoral that autumn, and gave a Christmas pantomime in the Waterloo Chamber at Windsor which the King thought was better than ever. It was *Old Mother Red Riding Boots* and Princess Margaret as usual shone, performing a solo dance 'in Victorian costume with frilly pantaloons'.[16]

As heir to the throne, Princess Elizabeth was trained by her father as if she had been a man. The royal link with the armed forces was emphasized: on her sixteenth birthday, 21 April 1942, she was made honorary Colonel of the Grenadier Guards and given a Grenadier brooch to celebrate her appointment. The ceremonial involved a parade at which she reviewed the regiment marching past, standing on a dais with her father, mother and sister – again, even on this occasion, the Princesses were identically dressed in pale blue, although Princess Elizabeth now wore stockings while

Princess Margaret still had long white socks. As usual the shy Princess Elizabeth hung back – a castle witness noted that 'the King prodded the Princess in the back to make her take the front place to receive the salute'. The war had touched the family in August 1942 when her uncle, Prince George, Duke of Kent, had been killed in a flying accident in Scotland, not far from Balmoral where they were on holiday, leaving a wife and three young children. The Duke was on active service en route to Iceland when the bomber in which he was a passenger smashed into a hillside in low mist, known locally as 'haar'.

Part of Princess Elizabeth's training was to meet important visitors. Eleanor Roosevelt, invited by the Queen to observe the part played by British women in the war effort, came to stay at Buckingham Palace in October 1942, met her at tea and was impressed, despite her shyness. Mrs Roosevelt noted that she was 'quite serious and asked me a number of questions about life in the United States and they were serious questions'. However, Princess Elizabeth's own life experience was limited: on her eighteenth birthday, 21 April 1944, the King made her a Counsellor of State. Brought up as she had been in an innocent world surrounded with love and kindness, she was horrified when faced with the more distressing facts of real life. When the King was away visiting the Eighth Army in Italy, her duty as Counsellor in his absence included signing the reprieve of a murderer. 'What makes people do such terrible things?' she asked. 'One ought to know. There should be some way to help them. I have so much to learn about people!'

She longed to join the war effort but her father would not allow it; the conscription of women had been announced at the end of 1941, and by January 1942 the registration of women at the Labour Exchange was under way. She formally registered under the wartime youth service scheme at the local Labour Exchange on 25 April 1942 and was given a registration card, E.D.431. By 1943, a total of 90 per cent of single and 80 per cent of married women were in work, most in industry and the armed forces. But it was not until the spring of 1945, a short time before her nineteenth birthday, that she was at last allowed 'out' to join the Auxiliary Territorial Service, always known as the ATS, as No. 230873 Second Subaltern Elizabeth Alexandra Mary Windsor, and was enrolled on an NCO's cadre course. She had already been given instruction in driving and in maintaining the various vehicles she would have to drive on the course, and on the morning of 23 March 1945 she put on her hideous khaki uniform – cloth-belted tunic and skirt, khaki stockings and heavy flat regulation shoes, and presented herself to her father for inspection. Princess Margaret was jealous – 'madly cross'; as Princess Elizabeth used to complain to Crawfie, 'Margaret always wants what I've got.'

But if it seemed like freedom to Princess Elizabeth, it was closely guarded. While she was driven back every evening to spend the night at Windsor, the other women slept in dormitory huts. At lectures she was surrounded by officers, with the lower ranks sitting behind. At the intervals between lectures she was 'whisked away' by the officers and lunched in the officers' mess. Later she managed to extricate herself from her praetorian guard and join the other women for a break: 'These cups of tea are getting a nice chatty institution,' Corporal Eileen Heron wrote. 'She talks much more now she is used to us, and is not a bit shy.' The course ended on 16 April 1945, just before her birthday; she told her new friends how sorry she was that it was over. 'She says she will feel quite lost next week,' Eileen Heron recorded, 'especially as she does not know yet what is going to happen to her as a result of the course. She would *love* to join HQ Crawley Rise as a junior officer.'[17] But being an expert driver and being familiar with the workings of the combustion engine were not to be essential parts of Princess Elizabeth's future, and this pioneering expedition into unfamiliar territory outside the castle walls lasted only a few months, as the King, of course, had known it would. As head of the armed forces and Churchill's confidant at their weekly lunches, he knew perfectly well that when his daughter had started in the ATS the end of the war could not be far off.

President Roosevelt died on 27 April 1945, the day Italian partisans captured Mussolini and his mistress Claretta Petacci, executing them next day. Hitler committed suicide in his Berlin bunker on 30 April. 'Events are moving very fast now,' the King wrote in his diary. Germany signed a document of Unconditional Surrender in the early hours of 7 May, and on 8 May, VE-Day, the end of the European war and Allied victory was announced. Churchill and the King met at Buckingham Palace for their usual Tuesday lunch: 'We congratulated each other on the end of the European War,' the King wrote. 'The day we have been longing for has arrived at last & we can look back with thankfulness to God that our tribulation is over. No more fear of being bombed at home & no more living in air-raid shelters. But there is still Japan to be defeated & the restoration of our country to be dealt with, which will give us many headaches & hard work in the coming years.'[18]

Princess Elizabeth, dressed in her ATS uniform, stood with her parents, Churchill and Princess Margaret on the balcony of Buckingham Palace, and later slipped away with young Guards officer friends to join the crowds cheering, singing and dancing. 'Everyone was very jolly,' the Princess's friend Lord Porchester recalled, 'linking arms in the streets and singing "Run, Rabbit, Run", "Hang out the Washing on the Siegfried Line", "Roll out the Barrel", that sort of thing all night.' They came back to stand outside the Palace incognito, chanting: 'We want the King, we want the King.'[19]

Princess Elizabeth's only real taste of life outside Windsor Castle had come towards the end of the war when she had joined the ATS, but even then she did not share the experiences of her contemporaries. She slept at the castle and was chauffeured to training every weekday. She learned to drive and learned the workings of the combustion engine and became a fast and skilful driver on the private roads at Balmoral, but the scope of her life was extremely limited. She met and talked to international figures like Eleanor Roosevelt and General Eisenhower, but she remained in a royal cocoon, shy, reserved and cautious with outsiders, devoted to her close family, an apparently ordinary figure in an extraordinary situation. Women of her age had jobs, worked on the land and in factories and as code-breakers, served in the armed forces (although not in the front line), went on espionage missions to occupied Europe. Princess Elizabeth's life experience barely extended beyond the castle circle. It was, perhaps, a good preparation for a dutiful and circumscribed life.

5. Enter the Prince

The year 1945 began a new era – Churchill lost the General Election in July, rejected in a landslide by the people he had led since 1940 in favour of the Labour leader, Clement Attlee, who had promised and would give them a new world of greater social justice. The eclipse of Churchill as a public figure focused attention even more on the King and his family, as the monarchy was seen as a guarantee of stability in a time of change.

On the evening of VE-Day, 8 May, the BBC broadcast a 'Tribute to the King' preceded by live contributions from people from different walks of life. This was followed by George VI's address to his people, delivered live at 9 p.m. It was the longest live broadcast he had ever made; he was exhausted, stumbling more than usual over his words, but apart from the occasional hesitation it was ecstatically received. 'We all roared ourselves hoarse,' Noël Coward, who was among the crowd, recorded. 'I suppose this is the greatest day in our history.' One of Mass Observation's investigators went into a Chelsea pub and recorded people's reactions:

> . . . the King's speech is turned on. Several women at the back of the lounge stand up, assuming reverent attitudes. There is a sense that people have been waiting all this time for something symbolic and now they have got it: the room is as hushed as a church. A local Marxist puts his feet on the table and groans. At the phrase 'endured to your utmost' there are deep cries of 'Hear Hear!' Whenever the King pauses the Marxist reacts with loud Ts Ts and becomes the centre of looks of intense malevolence from all corners of the room . . . When the King says 'of just (long pause) – of just triumph' several women's foreheads pucker and they wear a lacerated

look. At 'strength and shield' [the] Marxist unaccountably removes
feet from table. When God Save the King is sung, the whole room
rises to its feet and sings, with the exception of the Marxist and his
twin brother, who remain sullenly seated [but] the wife of one [of
them] gets up. Because, she explains, 'she felt like being in har-
mony with everyone else'.[1]

At midnight on 14 August 1945, Japan surrendered. VJ-Day on
the 15th was celebrated in much the same fashion – although generally less enthusiastically – as VE-Day three months before. For
some people the invention and devastating use of the atom bomb at
Hiroshima and Nagasaki threatened a different and more dangerous
world, as, for others, did the advent of a socialist government in the
July election. Less than a fortnight after VJ-Day Britain was faced
with unpleasant economic reality when the US cancelled Lend–
Lease, the financial support that had got the country through the
war, precipitating austerity Britain. The acute observer Mollie
Panter-Downes predicted the dreary period to come:

> The factories which people hoped would soon be changing over to
> the production of goods for the shabby, short-of-everything home
> consumers are instead to produce goods for export. The Govern-
> ment will have to face up to the job of convincing the country that
> controls and hardships are as necessary a part of a bankrupt peace
> as they were of a desperate war. People are suddenly realizing that
> in the enormous economic blitz that has just begun, their problems
> may be as serious as the blitz they so recently scraped through.[2]

Another diarist wrote ruefully at the end of the year 1945:
'Housing, food, clothing, fuel, beer, tobacco – all the ordinary
comforts of life that we'd taken for granted before the war and naturally expected to become plentiful again when it ended, became
instead, more and more scarce and difficult to come by.'[3]

An observer in the crowd on a visit by the King and Queen to Birmingham commented on the undoubted fact that Queen Elizabeth

'looked a little too matronly for her age. Considering the rationing of the people she certainly looked well fed.' Yet *Time* magazine
reported in the spring of 1946 that Princess Elizabeth's twentieth
birthday at Windsor had been 'medium-austere' – a family lunch
featuring a pink cake with 'the thinnest icing'. Dressed in a 'pow-
der-blue ensemble', she appeared at a window to 'blow kisses' to a
huge garden party of 40,000 people. She carried on her public role
with a radio broadcast on the Empire, somewhat fancifully comparing it to a garden: '. . . it has grown like a garden but one that
makes use of nature for its beauty, of the sort that used to be
known abroad as an English garden'. The King announced that
there would be no more courts, which had historically featured
men in knee breeches, women in tiaras, ostrich feathers and evening dresses with trains – they would be substituted with garden
parties. 'It's the clothing shortage,' *Time* commented. Some royal
customs carried on as usual. At Balmoral that autumn Princess
Elizabeth bagged a twelve-point stag, and General Eisenhower
with his wife Mamie and son John spent the night there, arriving
for hot scones and tea, followed by grouse for dinner and High-
land dancing. As a sign of the times, royal servants at Buckingham
Palace and Windsor were unionized, 256 out of 260 joining the
Civil Servants Union (though four traditionalist stalwarts refused
to join).

    'Class resentment and class feeling are very strong,' Harold
Nicolson noted as the war ended. But while there was feeling
against the rich – aristocrats, industrialists and bankers – the Royal
Family were exempt and seen as a family representative of the
nation, despite the royal way of life being essentially aristocratic
rather than popular. Stalking, racehorses, hunting, and balls and
dances at Buckingham Palace were hardly the thing East Enders
did for relaxation, yet the Royal Family were seen as democratic
and essentially on the side of the people. The King was a keen
spectator of the national sport, football, and in February 1944 had
taken his daughters to watch the England *v.* Scotland match, tradi-

tionally an occasion for the expression of ancient hatreds and rivalries. Princess Elizabeth was torn. Asked if she had enjoyed the day, she said, 'Oh very much! It was most exciting. But the difficulty was knowing who to back, England or Scotland. I found it rather difficult to follow because I don't know much about the game, but I hope to go to another & then I shall perhaps know more about it . . . but it was exciting watching the crowd, I enjoyed it immensely.'[4]

Princess Elizabeth was seen as the future. She had become legally able to rule as Queen on her eighteenth birthday, the age Queen Victoria had just reached when she succeeded to the throne in June 1837. In recognition of Elizabeth's coming of age she had been assigned a lady-in-waiting of her own, and a suite of rooms to use as an office at Buckingham Palace. More practically, she was now entitled to forty-four clothing ration coupons a year.

Rumours began as to who her future husband might be: three aristocrats were mentioned – Charles Fitzroy, Earl of Euston, son of the Duke of Grafton; Johnny Dalkeith, son of the Duke of Buccleuch, who was also seen as a possibility for Princess Margaret; and Charles Manners, the Duke of Rutland. All had super-aristocratic backgrounds as rich landowners and all were officers in her beloved Grenadier Guards. All of them had stately homes (Buccleuch had no fewer than five). She herself enjoyed dancing with them – they were jokingly known as her 'flirts' – but as far as marriage was concerned, she had quite a different man in mind, the man she had been in love with since July 1939 and whose photograph, dashingly bearded and in naval uniform, she kept on her desk.

Prince Philip of Greece had had what was known as a 'good' war in the Royal Navy, which he had joined in January 1940 after Dartmouth Naval College. As a Greek prince he had been kept out of the main theatre of war, in order to preserve the image of his country's neutrality, until Germany invaded Greece in the autumn of 1940. He had joined the battleship HMS *Valiant* in the eastern Mediterranean and had taken part in the Battle of Cape Matapan against the Italian fleet in March 1941, had been mentioned in despatches and awarded the Greek Cross of Valour. Seven weeks later he endured the constant threat of German bombing in the Battle of Crete, when three British cruisers and six destroyers, including his uncle Mountbatten's HMS *Kelly*, were sunk. In January 1942 he had become one of the youngest first lieutenants in the Navy on board the destroyer HMS *Wallace*, accompanying the Allied landings on Sicily in July 1943. In July 1944, as second-in-command of the destroyer HMS *Whelp*, he had sailed to the Far East to join the war against Japan and he had been in Tokyo Bay for the final surrender of the Japanese on 2 September 1945.

Philip had been at Windsor for Christmas 1943, when he was in the audience for the Christmas pantomime, *Aladdin*, with Princess Elizabeth in the title role, wearing the classic 'principal boy' costume of jacket, revealing stockinged legs, and with Princess Margaret as her beloved Roxana. According to the diarist C. L. Fulford, there was an unscripted episode when 'One tiny boy came on clad only in an inadequate leopard skin, which slipped off as the curtain fell & he appeared with an entirely undraped posterior presented to the King who was nearly reduced to hysterics.' Philip's cousin, the fatherless Princess Alexandra, had a small part and having done her bit came and sat at her mother's feet, Fulford recorded. Prince Philip stayed at Windsor over Christmas, when, Princess Elizabeth wrote to Crawfie, 'we had a very gay time with a film, dinner parties, and dancing to the gramophone'.

Prince Philip's Greek royal relations and his uncle Mountbatten had apparently had the Princess in their sights as a future bride for him as early as 1941. Chips Channon, who knew the Greek royal family through his friendship with the Duke of Kent and Princess Marina, Philip's cousin, was on a visit to Athens in January that year when he met Prince Philip 'looking extraordinarily handsome' at a cocktail party. 'He is to be our Prince Consort,' Channon wrote, 'and that is why he is serving in our navy.' In March 1944 the prospect of Princess Elizabeth's imminent eighteenth birthday had prompted his cousin, King George of Greece, to raise the possibility of an engagement between them with the Princess's father and he had not been encouraged. 'We both think she is too young for that now,' the King wrote to Queen Mary, 'as she has never met any young men of her own age. I like Philip. He is intelligent, has a good sense of humour & thinks about things in the right way . . . We are going to tell George that P. had better not think any more about it for the present.'[5]

For the King, no doubt, Philip's 'naval' sense of humour was a serious recommendation; by 'thinking about things the right way' he meant that, more importantly, Philip was royal himself and understood the Windsor context. He was connected to the King and Princess Elizabeth through both his father and his mother. His father, Prince Andrew of Greece, was the King's second cousin, the nephew of his grandmother, Queen Alexandra. His mother, Princess Alice of Battenberg, was the sister of Philip's uncle, Lord Louis Mountbatten (the Battenbergs had anglicized their name to Mountbatten in 1917 on George V's orders, when he had adopted the family name of Windsor). She was a great-granddaughter of Queen Victoria and had been born in Windsor Castle.

Unlike his future bride, however, Prince Philip had had a difficult and – in royal terms – impoverished childhood, belonging to a pool of European royalty exiled and disinherited by the fortunes of war and revolution. He was born on a kitchen table in the family villa on Corfu on 10 June 1921, and eighteen months later his family were rescued by a British warship after his father had been sentenced to perpetual banishment. He was the only son and youngest child of the family, separated by eleven years from his nearest sibling. In exile they lived in a house at St-Cloud near Paris, virtually on the charity of a rich aunt-in-law. When Philip was nine his family disintegrated: his father to live a nomadic life moving between Paris, Germany and the south of France; his mother, suffering from mental problems, spent some eight years in clinics. She then went to live in Athens, where she spent the war years rescuing Jews from the Nazis and founding a charitable order of nuns. His elder sisters by then had all married German princes (one, Cecile, died in an air crash in 1937 with her husband, George Donatus of Hesse). Philip lived with his Mountbatten relations in England, where he was sent to school at Gordonstoun; the out-break of war separated him from his sisters in Germany. By the time he returned from the Navy, he was virtually an orphan: his father had died in Monte Carlo in 1944, bequeathing Philip only a pair of monogrammed hairbrushes, cufflinks and some old suits, and his mother still lived in Athens. He lived with his grandmother in her flat at Kensington Palace or with the Mountbattens, Louis and Edwina, at their smart house in Wilton Place, dependent on his Navy pay and subventions from Mountbatten's rich wife.

He was blond and extremely handsome, even glamorous; self-reliant and self-assertive, cocky to the verge of being arrogant. Women swooned over him; he was flirtatious but emotionally cool: 'Basically the Mountbattens were Germanic,' Mountbatten's great friend in later life, Barbara Cartland, said. Prince Philip of Schleswig-Holstein-Sonderburg-Glucksburg was not, as the sati-rists later dubbed him, 'Phil the Greek', but 'Phil the German'. The British upper classes, who would rather their future Queen married a Duke's son than a penniless German princeling, were against the marriage. The antis included almost all the King's circle, his courtiers and some of his close friends, and it was rumoured also to include Queen Elizabeth and her brother, David Bowes-Lyon. For them it was not only that he had no money and had been to the wrong school, but that the Second World War and indeed the First were too close for a 'Hun' to be acceptable as royal consort. Many of them disliked the Mountbattens as being too 'pushy' and 'left-wing', denouncing them as 'champagne socialists'. He was not a part of the magic circle of Old Etonians; the breezy democratic style he had learned in the Navy was not appreciated by courtiers, one of whom described him as 'rough and uneducated'.

The reaction of the wider British public was quite different – to them and indeed the rest of the world, this was the Great Romance. The love of the handsome sailor prince (the fact that he was penniless was an advantage rather than a hindrance) and the popular Princess, whose life had been a part of contemporary myth for as long as even the youngest could remember, was the headline story. Like all fairy stories there were obstacles before the handsome Prince could obtain the Sleeping Beauty – in this case her parents' conviction that she was too young and had not seen enough of the world to know her mind. Princess Elizabeth's love for Prince Philip had never wavered, and never would; his for her seems to have grown as he got to know her better. The pressure from Mountbatten and the Greek royal relations had acted on him as a brake rather than a spur. 'I am not being rude, but it is apparent that you like the idea of being the General Manager of this little show,' Philip warned his uncle Mountbatten in January 1947, 'and I am afraid that she might not take to the idea quite as docilely as I do. It is true that I know what is good for me, but don't forget that she has not had you as Uncle *loco parentis*, counsellor and friend as long as I have.'[6]

They had come to an 'understanding' at Balmoral in the late summer of 1946, the year he returned to England, and rumours about a possible marriage surfaced in the British press some two months later. One source was the left-wing Labour MP Tom Driberg, who described Prince Philip as being 'intelligent and broad-minded, fair and good-looking', for which he was derided as a 'monarchist' who had sold out and 'joined in building up the royal wedding ballyhoo'.

The King had made the couple promise that nothing would be said until the family returned from their visit to southern Africa in February 1947. He was, above all, anxious that 'us four' should be together for one last time. The visit would be the first he and

Queen Elizabeth had made to Africa since their honeymoon safari in 1923; for the Princesses it would be the first time they had ever been out of the country. There was no doubt that the King and Queen needed a holiday from the strain of war, but the principal reason for the visit was realpolitik. Both Labour and Conservatives, and indeed the great majority of the British population, liked to believe that despite the economic crisis and the looming independence of India, Britain was still a Great Power, a belief that underlay what may now seem to be inexplicable attitudes.

The eleventh year of the King-Emperor's reign, 1947 was the moment of truth for post-war Britain. The previous year, 1946, had been a year of full employment and a confident flood of welfare legislation, but in 1947 things began to go seriously wrong. The worst winter of the century ushered in an unprecedented fuel crisis. On 28 January Big Ben struck once and then fell silent, and the next day the Thames froze at Windsor. Coal pits were blocked by snow, ports by ice. By the end of the first week in February electricity cuts of five hours a day were imposed; unemployment rose to 2.5 million and production fell. The weather improved in mid-March but by then the damage had been done; the fuel crisis was succeeded by a financial one. The dollar credits on which the British Government had been surviving were almost exhausted; on 5 June the Chancellor, Hugh Dalton, was to tell the Cabinet that if the present rate of drawing on them were to continue, they would have run out by the end of the year. On 20 August he was forced to announce the suspension of the convertibility of the pound, a serious blow to Britain's international credibility, bringing home the unpleasant fact that Britain was no longer a world power and could not afford her Empire. War had hastened the progress of imperial disintegration that had already been evident before 1939; post-war ideology, coupled with a growing realization that Britain no longer possessed the resources in money and men, accelerated the process.

That year the King-Emperor stood in Windsor Great Park

looking sorrowfully at a plantation of trees, each representing a colony of his Empire. 'This is Singapore,' he said, pointing to one. 'There is Malaya . . . Hong Kong is over there. They have all been lost to the Empire Plantation. Burma too over there. The time may soon come when we shall have to cut out the Indian tree . . .' The Victory Parade on 8 June 1946 had in truth been the swansong of his Empire.

With British losses of their Asian and Indian territories glaringly obvious, people in power had increasingly turned towards their African territories as the hope for the future. The American commentator Walter Lippmann wrote: 'The Royal Family did not go to South Africa in order to escape the cold weather in England but to mark and to promote change in empire and the revolution in imperial strategy. In South Africa, which is a rich and undeveloped land, Britain may find the means of becoming, despite the liquidation of the Indian and Near Eastern empires, an independent Great Power in the world.'

One of the reasons for the trip was to prop up Britain's friend, the war hero General Jan Smuts, who was facing the threat of defeat by the anti-British apartheid Nationalist Party in the forthcoming election. In the light of the crisis enveloping Britain, the King wanted to remain with his people, but Attlee refused to let him postpone or cancel the trip for fear of magnifying the situation. And so the family set sail on HMS *Vanguard* on 1 February 1947, leaving a shivering nation behind.

It was Princess Elizabeth's first experience of the Commonwealth, or of anywhere outside Britain, and was to have a profound, lifelong effect on her. Arriving in South Africa on 17 February, the tour was a two-month marathon, including thirty-five nights on a special train, the 'White Train', travelling though the Orange Free State, Basutoland, Natal and the Transvaal, Northern Rhodesia and Bechuanaland. South Africa was a deeply divided country – British and Afrikaners spoke different languages and had historic rivalries – but although it was divided on racial grounds the apartheid system in legal terms did not yet exist. While the British community, black, coloured (Asian) and white, welcomed the visit, the Nationalist (Boer) politicians and press did not. At the presentation of addresses of welcome by the members of the Senate and House of Assembly in Cape Town on 17 February, only eleven out of forty-six Nationalist Assembly members put in an appearance and not one single Senator. The Nationalist press, described by the British High Commissioner, Sir Evelyn Baring, as 'unrelenting in its hatred of the British connexion', either ignored the visit or wrote abusive articles. There were endless receptions, even a 'Coloured Ball', two indabas in Southern Rhodesia where the King opened the Rhodesian Parliament, inspected Cecil Rhodes's hilltop tomb (where the Queen as usual tottered on high heels until forced by Princess Margaret to put on more sensible ones), and gazed on the magnificent Victoria Falls in what was then Northern Rhodesia. The King, however, sick of being expected to perform like a travelling salesman, became tired and nervy, losing seventeen pounds. He told journalists travelling with him on the White Train that he should be at home and not lolling about in the summer sun; but both Princesses enjoyed the new experience hugely.

The focus of the tour turned out to be very much on Princess Elizabeth. Her twenty-first birthday on 21 April was declared a public holiday throughout the Union of South Africa. She reviewed a large contingent of soldiers, sailors, women's services, cadets and veterans, gave a speech to a 'youth rally of all races', and at a ball in her honour in Cape Town General Smuts presented her with a twenty-one-stone gemstone necklace. But for Elizabeth the key to her future was marked by a broadcast she gave to the Empire and Commonwealth. In her high girlish voice, speaking with confidence and sincerity to her own generation, 'all the young men and women who were born about the same time as myself and have grown up like me in the terrible and glorious years of the Second World War', she made what she called 'a solemn act of dedication':

I declare before you all that my whole life, whether it be long or short, shall be devoted to your service and the service of our great Imperial family to which we all belong, but I shall not have the strength to carry out this resolution alone unless you join with me, as I now invite you to do. I know that your support will be unfailingly given. God help me to make good my vow and God bless all of you who are willing to share it.

The speech may have been written by a middle-aged courtier (her father's Private Secretary, Alan Lascelles) with the worldwide image of the British monarchy at home and abroad in mind, but it struck home with incredible conviction, bringing tears to listeners' eyes. Above all, it expressed what Elizabeth felt herself and would feel all her life, a sense of duty and dedication to the ties that bound Britain and the entity developing out of Empire into the Commonwealth. Forty-eight years later, when she would visit an independent South Africa to be greeted as an old friend by President Nelson Mandela, the people held up signs saying simply 'Welcome back.'

The significance of the tour and of Princess Elizabeth's twenty-first birthday was lost on no one. Every British newspaper carried a photograph and a profile of her; *Time* magazine put her on its March cover, a fresh-faced young woman silhouetted against a multi-faceted diamond with the regulation royal double string of pearls round her neck, captioned pertinently 'For an aging Empire, A Girl Guide?' The image projected was one of absolute normality. The British monarchy had absolved itself of the stain of the Abdication by projecting itself as being decent and normal, the image of what a family should be, representing the people but yet with the touch of glamour given by royalty. The public worldwide had followed Princess Elizabeth since she was a child – for her third birthday *Time* had featured her on its cover, suitably chubby but prematurely serious and with her first (single) string of pearls. (The caption was ' "P'incess Lilybet". She has set the babe fashion for yellow.') Through press photographs they had seen her grow up and liked what they saw. The fact that she was rich beyond most people's dreams — her income had been increased to £15,000 a year — lived in palaces and holidayed on enormous country estates seemed irrelevant. Through careful management — much of it due to her mother's control — she had projected an image which was not very far from the truth. The British Prime Minister, Clement Attlee, leader of the Labour Party, declared that her simple dignity and wise understanding had endeared her to all classes.

On 10 July 1947 Buckingham Palace at last announced Princess Elizabeth's engagement to 'Lieutenant Philip Mountbatten, R.N.', the wedding to take place in November. (Later, shortly before his marriage, the King created him Duke of Edinburgh and made him a Knight of the Garter.) At the garden party given to celebrate, Prince Philip wore his old naval uniform. The couple were — in their undemonstrative way — radiant, but the economic situation was dire, and about to get worse. 'Work or want' was the slogan. In the House of Commons the Deputy Prime Minister, Herbert Morrison, grimly told members that no matter how hard Britons worked they would still want. In a year Britain had spent 60 per cent of the US Dollar Loan ($2.2 billion out of $3.75 billion); worse, most of the money had gone on buying American consumer goods: tobacco (32 per cent), food (24 per cent), oil (12 per cent), raw materials (11 per cent), films (5 per cent), ships (3 per cent), while a 3 per cent increase in US commodity prices had made things even worse. There could be no more belt-tightening as far as food was concerned. The British diet, one observer said, 'had remained on the thin line that divides discomfort from malnutrition'. On 20 August the Chancellor, Hugh Dalton, suspended the convertibility of the pound. In the circumstances, the allowances made for the Princess and her husband by the Labour Government were extremely generous: an annuity of £50,000 for the Princess upon her marriage (later whittled down to £40,000 by the House of Commons), 90 per cent of which was tax free, and £10,000 for her husband. In return the

King handed over to the Treasury £100,000 savings made on the Civil List during the war years' economies, just as his father, George V, had done in the First World War.

And, as in 1918, the Second World War cast its shadow. Among the royal relations (recently described as 'the flotsam of two world wars and many revolutions'), Prince Philip's own family – apart from his mother – were conspicuous by their absence. Philip's three surviving sisters had not been invited to the wedding. Anti-German feeling in Britain in the immediate post-war period ran too high for the King to risk the embarrassment of underlining how many of his and the bridegroom's relations were Germans, indeed Nazis. The Eton-educated Duke of Saxe Coburg and Gotha, a grandson of Queen Victoria, had been a *Gauleiter* and had his estates confiscated after the war. Prince Philipp of Hesse, another descendant of Queen Victoria, had been arrested by the Americans for Nazi activities. A more noticeable absentee was the Duke of Windsor, who was not invited to his niece's wedding, the first great royal occasion since his brother's Coronation, a sign that family attitudes had not softened since the Abdication and the quarrels in its aftermath.

Nobody seems to have cared. Amid the bleak reality the royal wedding provided an opportunity for pure escapism. It was, as Winston Churchill put it, 'a flash of colour on the hard road we have to travel'. It became the occasion for a national jamboree: thousands queued to see the wedding presents on display at St James's Palace, which included nylons and food parcels from well-wishers in America (one lady in Brooklyn sent a turkey to Princess Elizabeth 'because she lives in England and has nothing to eat'), a wreath of diamond roses from the Nizam of Hyderabad, a gold tiara from the Emperor of Ethiopia, and a woven 'fringed lacework cloth made out of yarn spun by the donor on his own spinning wheel', given by Gandhi. This object was misidentified by the bride's grandmother, Queen Mary, as one of the Mahatma's famous loincloths. 'Such an indelicate object . . . what a horrible thing,' she exclaimed as Prince Philip attempted to silence her comments by loud praise of Gandhi. More appropriately, perhaps, Lord and Lady Melchett gave a sixteenth-century psalter in which Elizabeth I had written her name and a poem. The wedding dress designed by the Princess's mother's couturier, Norman Hartnell, was made of ivory silk from Chinese silkworms, embroidered with York roses entwined with ears of corn, star flowers and orange blossom encrusted with pearls and crystals. Like the wedding presents, it was put on display and the queues waiting to see it stretched down the length of the Mall.

The wedding was a huge event, described as 'a movie premiere, an election, a World Service and Guy Fawkes Night all rolled into one'. 'There was a tremendous crowd reaction,' one of the Princess's friends recalled as the couple returned together from the Abbey. 'Suddenly to see the state coach was marvellous, with Princess Elizabeth with her wonderful complexion and Prince Philip so devastatingly handsome – they were a dream couple.'[7] The press coverage was extraordinary, greater, one historian claimed, even than for the Coronation: the BBC broadcast was worldwide. The service was filmed and shown on television that evening, and copies were flown to the US. It was even shown in Allied-occupied Berlin, still scarred by the devastation left by the end of the war just over two years earlier.

In line with previous publicity, the 'ordinary family' aspect was officially underlined. The Archbishop of York in the Wedding Address claimed that the service was 'in all essentials exactly the same as it would have been for any cottager who might be married this afternoon in some small country church in a remote village in the Dales', despite the fact that the congregation of 2,000 included 'one of the largest gatherings of royalty, regnant and exiled, of the century'. In the face of the Cold War between Communism and the Western democracies, it was also a celebration of the continuity of the monarchy as a symbol of constitutional freedom.

6.   Young Couple

While the young couple were still on honeymoon, the King wrote his daughter one of his most touching letters:

> . . . I was so proud & thrilled at having you so close to me on our long walk to Westminster Abbey, but when I handed your hand to the Archbishop, I felt that I had lost something very precious. You were so calm & composed during the Service & said your words with such conviction, that I knew everything was all right . . . Our family, us four, the 'Royal Family' must remain together . . . I have watched you grow up all these years with pride under the direction of Mummy, who as you know is the most marvellous person in the world in my eyes, & I can, I know, always count on you, & now Philip, to help us in our work . . . I can see that you are sublimely happy with Philip which is right but don't forget us is the wish of your ever loving and devoted Papa.[1]

Recently published letters have revealed that the Royal Family was as it had been pictured, a truly loving and close relationship. 'I think I've got the best mother and father in the world,' Princess Elizabeth wrote to the Queen while on honeymoon at Broadlands, the Mountbattens' country house, 'and I only hope that I can bring up my children in the happy atmosphere of love and fairness which Margaret and I have grown up in.' She added, 'Philip is an angel – he is so kind and thoughtful, and living with him and having him around all the time is just perfect.'[2] 'Lilibet is the only "thing" in this world which is absolutely real to me,' Prince Philip wrote to his new mother-in-law, 'and my ambition is to weld the two of us into a new combined existence that will not only be able to withstand the shocks directed at us but will also have a positive existence for the good.'

It is unclear what 'shocks' Prince Philip anticipated, but among them were undoubtedly run-ins with his father-in-law's courtiers, who treated the prickly young man with a certain amount of disrespect. 'They were bloody to him,' said a relative. The situation was made worse by having to live with his in-laws at Buckingham Palace, where he was assigned a room in his wife's suite. The country house planned for them to use had burned down the previous summer, and Clarence House, which was destined to be their home in London, was dilapidated and uninhabitable. However, his position vis-à-vis his wife's courtiers was improved when it became known that the Princess was pregnant. Even 'Tommy' Lascelles, previously a stern critic, was converted: 'Such a nice young man,' he gushed to Harold Nicolson, 'such a sense of duty – not a fool in any way – so much in love poor boy – and after all put the heir to the throne in the family way all according to plan.'

Prince Charles Philip Arthur George was born at Buckingham Palace at 9.14 p.m. on 14 November 1948, while his father distracted himself on the Palace squash court and outside crowds chanted, 'Good old Philip.' Charles was the first royal baby to break with the tradition that the Home Secretary attended the birth in order to verify that there had been no hanky-panky with bedpans and substitute babies. Queen Elizabeth, always conservative and a traditionalist, had been against this new departure, but when Lascelles pointed out that under the Constitution as laid down in the Statute of Westminster of 1931 there could be – including the representatives of the Dominions – some seven people in the waiting-room, she acquiesced. The Prince was christened on 15 December in the White and Gold Music Room at Buckingham Palace, the King being among his godparents.

The goodwill generated for Britain by the royal wedding was continued with the opening of the 1948 Summer Olympics by the King at Wembley Stadium on 29 July. After a twelve-year hiatus because of the Second World War, this was the first Olympiad since the notorious 1936 Games in Berlin, which had provided an international showcase for Hitler and the Nazis. A record fifty-nine nations were represented, but because of their role as aggressors in the late war, Germany and Japan were not invited; the USSR was invited but chose not to attend. Britain had considered passing the opportunity to hold the Games to the US, owing to the dire economic climate, but the King stepped in to insist that this was a chance to restore British confidence and prestige after the war. At the time of the Games, food, petrol and building rationing was still in place in Britain and the 1948 Olympics became known as the 'Austerity Games'. There was no specially constructed Olympic Village for the athletes: male competitors were housed in R A F camps near London, women in London colleges. As a concession they were given the same rations as dockers and miners – 5,467 calories a day, more than twice the amount allowed to the rest of the population. Nonetheless, when the King declared the Games open, the sun shone brightly, 2,500 pigeons were released into the blue sky and the Royal Horse Artillery fired a twenty-one-gun salute as the last runner in the torch relay ran a lap of the track (created with cinders from the domestic coal fires of Leicester) to light the Olympic flame. (The original torch was later discovered converted into a table lamp.)

That summer, on 22 June, a former German troopship and Nazi cruise liner, rechristened the *Empire Windrush,* arrived at Tilbury docks from Kingston, Jamaica. Aboard were 492 black males and one stowaway woman, looking forward to a new life in the 'mother country', Britain. Also aboard was the calypso singer known as Lord Kitchener, who in anticipation had already composed a song, 'London is the Place for Me'. His recollections of his feelings at the time are touching in the extreme in view of the prejudice many of the Jamaican immigrants were to encounter there. 'The feeling I had to know that I'm going to touch the soil of the mother country, that was the feeling I had . . . That's why I compose the song.' Sadly, the reception these men were going to get in the mother country was a less happy experience. Even before the *Windrush* had docked, eleven Labour MPs had sent Attlee an anxious letter, quoted by David Kynaston in his *Austerity Britain*:

> This country may become an open reception centre for immigrants not selected in respect to health, education, training, character, customs and above all, whether assimilation is possible or not.
>
> The British people fortunately enjoy a profound unity without uniformity in their way of life, and are blest by the absence of a colour racial problem. An influx of coloured people domiciled here is likely to impair the harmony, strength and cohesion of our public and social life and to cause discord and unhappiness among all concerned.[3]

The issue was to rumble on under the surface during the future Queen's reign, occasionally flaring into race riots in areas like Notting Hill, Brixton and Toxteth.

In the public eye the King, much loved and respected though he was, was fading into the background and the Princess, a world celebrity since her wedding, had come to the fore, seen as the future. Already her Private Secretary, the experienced Jock Colville, a diplomat on secondment from the Foreign Office who had been Private Secretary to both Chamberlain and Churchill, had been preparing her for her role. She was included in the circulation of Foreign Office telegrams, and attended a debate in the House of Commons and a dinner party given by the Prime Minister to introduce her to members of his Labour Government. In May 1948 she and Prince Philip had made their first, triumphal visit to Paris. Thanks to Antoinette de Bellaigue's teaching she spoke excellent French, and the youth and beauty of the couple had impressed the French capital. Colville, often acerbic in his comments on his contemporaries, dipped his pen in sugar when describing the Princess's effect on the public in Britain, as in Paris: '. . . a visit by a young princess with beautiful blue eyes and a superb natural complexion brought gleams of radiant sunshine into the dingiest of cities . . .'[4]

The state of the King's health had been concealed from Princess Elizabeth until after the birth of her son. At Balmoral that August the King had been complaining of cramp in his legs; on returning to London he was diagnosed just two days before Prince Charles's birth as having a condition known as Buerger's disease, early arteriosclerosis with a danger of gangrene and even the possibility of amputation of his right leg. He was confined to bed and the family Christmas at Sandringham was cancelled, although he did manage to go there for New Year, much enfeebled. Rest was not enough. On 3 March 1949 his surgeon, Professor James Learmonth, told him that if he wanted to live a normal life, he would have to have a right lumbar sympathectomy operation. This involved cutting a nerve at the base of the spine which functions as a thermostat regulating the flow of blood to the arteries in the leg. The operation, carried out on 12 March 1949 in a specially set up operating theatre at Buckingham Palace, was a success; but from now on prognostications for the King's life could not be good. As Winston Churchill was later to put it, 'the King walked with death'. He had less than three years left to live.

Unaware, as her mother also appeared to be, of her father's dangerous state of health, Princess Elizabeth was experiencing the happiest stage of her life, living in her own home with the husband she adored and a new baby. In June 1949 they moved into Clarence House, down the Mall from Buckingham Palace, which had been redecorated and equipped to their own taste; Prince Philip, being very interested in practical design and gadgets, made expeditions to the Ideal Home Exhibition, coming back triumphantly with the latest modern pieces of kitchen equipment, many of them, according to his valet John Dean, designed specifically as aids for servantless couples.

Martin Charteris arrived to replace Jock Colville as the Princess's Private Secretary. Recently a serving officer, he was aristocratic but easygoing, intelligent and thoughtful, and quite unlike the more stuffy, strait-laced courtiers who had worked for the Royal

Family since time immemorial. Like the other men in Princess Elizabeth's Household, he was more than a little in love with her, falling for her at his first interview with her in November 1949: 'There was this really pretty woman,' he later recalled, 'bright blue eyes, blue dress, brooch with huge sapphires. She was so young, beautiful, dutiful, the most impressive of women.'[5] She was also, he said, extremely businesslike. Prince Philip's own Private Secretary was as unlike the standard courtier model as he could find, his close friend and boon companion from the Navy war years, Commander Michael 'Mike' Parker. The Comptroller of the Edinburghs' Household was General Sir Frederick Browning, survivor of the Arnhem disaster, married to the writer Daphne du Maurier. Always known as 'Boy', he was exceptionally handsome, a disciplinarian but greatly loved by the Household and domestic staff, which included of course 'Bobo' Macdonald as the Princess's dresser, a power in the land and inseparable from Princess Elizabeth, whom she had referred to as 'my Little Lady' since her days as nursemaid. The present nursemaid to Prince Charles was Mabel Anderson, later a key figure in his life, as Bobo had been in his mother's, and still holidaying with the Royal Family in 2010.

One other key figure from the Princess's past sensationally re-emerged: Crawfie. The much-loved Scottish governess retired from royal service in 1949, having married, two months before Princess Elizabeth's wedding, a dubious character with a shadowy war record named Major George Buthlay. She was by now a thirty-eight-year-old spinster who had lived an admirable life of total dedication to her charges: he was divorced, a philanderer who had managed to wangle a job at the Royal Bank of Scotland through the Keeper of the Privy Purse. Crawfie was given a grace and favour house, Nottingham Cottage, at Kensington Palace, a pension and an honour, the CVO. Meanwhile Bruce and Beatrice Gould, editors of the *Ladies' Home Journal*, had been angling for a story on Princess Elizabeth, to be written by Dermot Morrah, a favoured royal correspondent. No doubt encouraged by her husband, who sniffed a potential fortune, Crawfie wanted to write the story herself and approached Queen Elizabeth, only to receive a discouraging response. In April 1949 the Queen wrote to her: 'I do feel most definitely that you should not write and sign articles about the children, as people in positions of confidence with us must be utterly oyster, and if you, the moment you finished teaching Margaret, started writing about her and Lilibet, well, we should never feel confidence in anyone again.'[6] Egged on by her husband, who apparently worked up feelings of resentment against her treatment by the Royal Family, Crawfie delivered herself into the hands of the Goulds and signed a contract with them.

The result was to be *The Little Princesses*, the first insider's account of the Royal Family, utterly sympathetic and uncritically treacly in sentiment, which nevertheless earned Marion Crawford their undying resentment. 'Doing a Crawfie' became the royal term for spilling the beans. Crawfie received 80,000 dollars; in November 1950 she bought a house in Aberdeen and moved there with Buthlay, by now aware that in Court circles she was to be 'shunned by colleagues from top to bottom'. She went on to write more articles and books on royal subjects (or, more accurately, they were written for her by journalists at *Woman's Own*), until on 16 June 1955 *Woman's Own* published her gushing account of Trooping the Colour and Royal Ascot, events which were both cancelled due to a rail strike in the six weeks between press date and publication. In the words of Queen Elizabeth's biographer, Hugo Vickers, Crawfie became a figure of public mockery and was never heard of again.

It was a tragic story: Crawfie lived on in Aberdeen, a lonely life after the death of her husband in 1977, apparently making at least one suicide attempt in her old age. She died in 1988, in an Aberdeen nursing home, at the age of seventy-eight. As a last gesture of love and loyalty she left a collection of royal letters and cards from her past to the Royal Archives. Although the Royal Family, taking the lead from Queen Elizabeth, never forgave Crawfie's 'betrayal', its real significance was yet to come. As the Queen's biographer,

Ben Pimlott, was to write more than half a century later, '*The Little Princesses* marked a watershed. For the former governess had stumbled on a discovery that was to blight the Royal Family for the rest of the century: the market in intimate details of royal lives was a rising one ... What ... would henceforth grow, with increasing rapidity, was the voracity of the public appetite, and the profits-led crumbling of inhibitions about feeding it.'[7]

In October 1949 Prince Philip, to his great delight, had been given an active command as first lieutenant and second-in-command of HMS *Chequers*, based in Malta, where 'Uncle Dickie' Mountbatten, having descended from the lofty heights of Viceroy of India after Independence the previous year, was now Vice-Admiral of the Mediterranean Fleet. Prince Philip stayed with his uncle at Villa Gardamangia; their relationship had always been a slightly edgy one, with the fiercely independent Philip on the lookout for attempts by Mountbatten to patronize or boss him. Relations between Mountbatten and Princess Elizabeth were far warmer; when she came out to join her husband, her uncle-in-law was delighted and immediately fell in love with her. She had flown out on 20 November, leaving Prince Charles to spend Christmas with his grandparents at Sandringham, returning to England on 28 December, then out to Malta again in March. Philip's naval career had been progressing, and that July he was given command of his own ship, HMS *Magpie*. 'Philip will be remaining in the Mediterranean for some time as he has just got command of a ship which has been his goal ever since he returned to naval duties and he ... is very thrilled about it,' Princess Elizabeth told a friend. She flew back to London to await the birth of Princess Anne; Prince Philip followed later and was in London in time for Princess Anne's arrival at Clarence House on 15 August 1950.

At her christening two months later, among her godparents Prince Philip's relations outnumbered the Princess's by three to one, an indication of his status as head of the family. He returned to his ship at the beginning of November, and a month later Princess Elizabeth followed him, leaving her two children behind with her parents at Sandringham for Christmas. Towards the end of February – according to *Time* magazine – 'scolded by British newspapers for two and a half months' absence from her children', Princess Elizabeth flew back from Malta. Her brief time in Malta was perhaps the happiest of her entire life, enjoying herself without responsibility at beach parties and even going to the hairdresser like the other naval wives. Perhaps not quite like other naval wives: there is a poignant picture of her looking out at the inhabited caves behind Gardamangia and wondering about those people's lives. It had been a recurrent theme ever since she had watched ordinary people from the windows of Buckingham Palace after she first moved there.

But while Princess Elizabeth was still enjoying her young married life, the world was changing around her. The Labour Government, which had come into power with promises of a 'New Jerusalem' of social welfare and equality, had achieved much in education and housing. Its programme for the creation of a modern welfare state culminated in 1948 with the launching of the National Health Service by the Minister of Health, the dynamic, physically impressive Welshman Aneurin 'Nye' Bevan. Health provision was to be free and universal and involved the nationalization of all hospitals, whether local or voluntary. Traditionally the Royal Family had been greatly involved in the patronage of the hospitals, many of which had 'Royal' in their title. 'The Royal Family could only watch with dismay as loyal institutions came first under government scrutiny and then control,' the historian Frank Prochaska wrote.[8] Queen Elizabeth in particular, with the training of her family background, was a fervent advocate of the voluntary hospital tradition, and probably influenced her daughter, Princess Elizabeth, to say, when as President of the Queen Elizabeth Hospital for Children she attended the annual Court of Governors in May 1948, 'I feel a very special sense of regret because of the long connection

my family has had with this hospital.' However, not even Bevan,
the scourge of social distinction, who had famously described the
Tory Party as 'lower than vermin', could bring himself to 'black-
ball the Royal Family from the NHS', as Prochaska put it; Royal
Family visits and support of hospitals continued into the new era.

It was a tribute to the secure position which the monarchy had
re-established as a symbol of security, democracy and freedom,
which in that year of 1948 seemed threatened by the advance of
Communism and Stalinist socialism in Europe and the Far East. A
Communist coup in Czechoslovakia was followed by the Soviet
blockade of Berlin and the airlift of supplies into the beleaguered
city from the Allied sectors in what was then West Germany. Symbolically, the BBC dismissed the actor who played 'Jock' in the
immensely popular radio serial *Dick Barton Special Agent* for being
a Communist. NATO was founded in 1949 as Communism seemed
ever more threatening: on 25 June 1950 the tanks of Communist
North Korea crossed the 38th Parallel invading South Korea. Britain joined the US in supporting a UN-backed force and sending in
troops to fight in Korea; the North Koreans were pushed back
across the 38th Parallel almost to the Yalu River.

The People's Republic of China joined the war on the side of
the North, materially supported by the Soviet Union. Fears that
the Americans were contemplating the use of the atomic bomb
sent Attlee on a flying visit to President Truman in December. In
the end nuclear weapons were not unleashed, but it was a savage
war. From 22–25 April 1951 a fierce battle was fought on the Imjin
River. An entire Chinese army, the 5th, fell upon three British
infantry battalions of the 29th Brigade; outnumbered by ten to
one, they fought on for three days. Denied orders to withdraw,
they held on while Allied forces regrouped; then, surrounded,
they ran a gauntlet of fire to break out. All but one battalion, 'the
Glorious Glosters', as they became known because of their heroism:
cut off, they fought on until their ammunition was exhausted.
Only then did they try to escape, but just forty men succeeded.

Seen as a tragedy at the time, the Imjin River is now considered one of the epic defensive stands of modern warfare. Fighting continued until an armistice was declared in 1953. (To celebrate the Queen's Coronation in June that year, the British enjoyed teasing the enemy by firing red, white and blue smoke at them.)

On a more light-hearted note, on Christmas Day 1950 it was revealed that four young Scots, members of the recently formed Covenant movement demanding a national parliament for Scotland, had stolen the 'Stone of Scone' from the Coronation Chair in Westminster Abbey. The King was outraged; the news was kept from him before his Christmas broadcast, and when he was told, his reaction, despite his detestation of broadcasting, was to go back on air demanding it be brought back. The general reaction was much the same: 'As if there was not enough trouble in the world. They should go and fight in Korea . . .' a contemporary diarist commented.

Meanwhile the Government continued to promote its vision of a country with a new-look post-war future symbolized by the Festival of Britain, which was opened by the King on 3 May 1951. It was the brainchild of Gerald Barry and the Labour deputy leader Herbert Morrison, who described it as 'a tonic for the nation'. The Festival was sited on the south bank of the River Thames, replacing warehouses and working-class housing with International Modernist buildings, a riverside walkway and new public spaces. There was a Dome of Discovery – at the time the largest dome in the world – the Royal Festival Hall, which still exists, and, most memorably, the 'Skylon', a stunning cigar-shaped aluminium-clad steel tower, balanced on cables slung between three steel beams, which was the symbol of the exhibition. In an unworthily vindictive gesture, Winston Churchill, who saw it as a symbol of the Labour Government, had it cut into pieces and toppled into the Thames in 1952. Not everyone appreciated the Festival: the young aesthete Roy Strong, who saw it as a schoolboy, among them. Later he saw the point of it: 'It is clear to me now,' he wrote in

2011, 'that, like the much-reviled Millennium Dome in 2000, the Festival of Britain was in many ways an attempt to reconfigure a new national identity based in an imagined present.'⁹ History repeats itself – Herbert Morrison's grandson, Peter Mandelson, was among the foremost promoters of the Millennium Dome.

The King had looked a shadow of his former self when opening the Festival. He had managed to attend the FA Cup Final at Wembley on 28 April (known as the 'Matthews Final'; however, despite Stanley Matthews's individual brilliance for Blackpool, Newcastle won 2–0). He was tired and depressed. The Korean war had weighed heavily on his mind: 'The incessant worries & crises through which we have to live have got me down properly,' he wrote to a friend. In June he was too ill to attend a dinner at Buckingham Palace for King Haakon of Norway and to take part in the annual Trooping the Colour. Princess Elizabeth took his place instead, in uniform, riding sidesaddle, trim and comfortable in her position – 'a woman alone' – at an all-male event, as *The Times* put it. There could have been no clearer emphasis on her position as successor to the throne.

Four separate doctors' reports from June to the end of July stated that there was inflammation of the lung but no one mentioned the word 'cancer'. Courtiers described the King's 'awful cough', and he himself, believing he had nothing worse than a touch of pneumonia – 'pneumonitis', went to Balmoral as usual, only to be summoned back to London for a day from 7–8 September for a tomograph. The royal doctors had moved at a stately pace, almost two months having passed since the first round of tests dated 10 July 1951. The result of the tomograph was as bad as it could be, showing a tumour on the King's left lung. They recommended a bronchoscopy as soon as possible. The King was back at Balmoral but returned for the procedure, which showed that the tumour was malignant. Lord Moran, Churchill's doctor, reading the runes through the cautious bulletin issued by the doctors, told Churchill he was sure it meant cancer. Again the King was not told, only that an operation had to be carried out at 10.30 a.m. on Sunday 23 September. The King's left lung was removed. No news was given to the public, of whom an estimated 5,000 waited outside the Palace, surging forward when the bulletin was pinned to the railings: it took police three-quarters of an hour to form them into an orderly queue. Two at a time they filed past, from 5 p.m. until almost midnight. The bulletin was bland but expert prognosis was doom-laden. The editor of the *Spectator* telephoned Harold Nicolson to ask him to write the King's obituary. Moran's opinion was that 'even if the King recovers he can scarcely live for more than a year'.

Ever practical, on the day after the operation Princess Elizabeth wrote to her young couturier, Hardy Amies, asking him 'in the strictest confidence' to prepare sketches for her in the likelihood that she would have to take the King's place on the tour of Australia and New Zealand scheduled for the following spring, which 'I have strong reason to believe he will be unable to undertake.'[10] On 7 October she left with Prince Philip for a long-planned visit to Canada and the United States, the fact that they travelled by plane indicative of anxiety about the King's health; it was the first time a member of the Royal Family had flown the Atlantic. As a precaution, her Private Secretary, Martin Charteris, travelled with the documents necessary for her accession should her father die.

Perhaps unsurprisingly in the circumstances, the Princess was not at her best. It had not been her year in the media. In March she had featured on columnist Igor Cassini's annual list of the ten worst-dressed women in the world (with Rita Hayworth, Eva Perón and Margaret Truman), her outfits condemned as 'shapeless, matronly clothes that make her look years older'. In Rome for her twenty-fourth birthday that April, the smart Italian society women had sneered at her unfashionable looks and flirted with her husband. (She had had, however, a private audience with the Pope.) In contrast, Princess Margaret, since her eighteenth birthday in August 1948, had become the new media star, photographed wearing the 'New Look', cheered at the Cup Final and swooned over by teenagers on her provincial visits. In Canada crowds wildly applauded Prince Philip but criticized the Princess for her unsmiling look. 'Instead of the poised and charming beauty most Canadians had expected, she was nervous and inarticulate,' *Time* magazine reported. Apart from worrying about her father, she had not yet discovered the skill with crowds that came so easily to her mother and her husband. Queen Elizabeth's smile had become her trademark (she was nicknamed 'Grinners' by some of her more irreverent friends), while handsome Prince Philip always found it easy to adopt a relaxed democratic attitude in public. As the tour wore on, however, the Princess too relaxed and the crowds became more and more enthusiastic. At a small settlement in the Rockies they were greeted by the town band and the entire population singing 'The Loveliest Night of the Year'. By the end, everyone was pleased. According to *Time*: 'Elizabeth was the first happy news in years from troubled Britain . . .' In the Canadian prairies, she soothed many a farmer's gripe about Britain's reduced food-buying. She was convincing proof of what the London *Times* called 'the benign influence of the British monarchy'. It was a successful reminder to everyone of the royal connection: since the Statute of Westminster in 1931 the King of Great Britain was separately also King of Canada.

Yet, ahead of her Washington visit, the US press had its reservations. 'Judged by Canada's impression, Elizabeth is unlikely to match the tremendous personal success scored by her mother on her 1939 visit,' *Time* wrote on 5 November 1951. 'In contrast to the radiant Queen, who often broke royal routine to comfort a weeping child or to chat spiritedly with onlookers, Elizabeth's manner has been more consciously regal. In the ceremonies, Canadians found her a charming and perfectly trained heiress presumptive. But on the human side Elizabeth is still a shy girl of 25, self-conscious and tense on her first major public appearance abroad without the overshadowing presence of her parents.' In contrast, it said, 'Philip's warm interest in the people and sights made him a solid hit with the crowds along the Canadian tour route.' One US correspondent who had travelled with them on the royal train said: 'Philip could run for Congress on the Republican ticket in Texas and win.'

Yet from the moment the couple arrived from Canada in Washington for a three-day visit, the Princess, to everyone's surprise, eclipsed her husband. 'From the moment she stepped down the ramp from a Royal Canadian Air Force DC-4M at Washington's National Airport,' *Time* reported, 'it became apparent that newspaper pictures had never done justice to Elizabeth's delicate colouring or warm smile. She was both tinier and prettier than most who saw her had guessed . . . Within the hour she had smiled repeatedly for cameramen . . .' She rode up Constitution Avenue with President Truman through waving crowds estimated at half a million, many of them with Union Jacks. At a dinner in her honour that night Truman set the seal on the visit with his gallantry: smiling, he told her, 'When I was a little boy, I read about a fairy princess. And there she is.' He went further in a speech in the White House Rose Garden: 'We have had many distinguished visitors here in this city,' he said, 'but never before have we had such a wonderful couple, that so completely captured the hearts of all of us.' 'Truman was like an uncle and loved her,' Martin Charteris recalled. 'We've just had a visit from a lovely young lady and her personable husband,' the President wrote to the King. 'They went to the hearts of all the citizens of the United States . . . As one father to another we can be very proud of our daughters.'

When the President had introduced Princess Elizabeth to his deaf, bedridden mother-in-law, the confused old lady told her, 'I'm glad your father has been re-elected.' The cause of her confusion was the recent General Election on 25 October, in which Attlee's Government had been defeated and the Conservatives elected with a small working majority. The King had invited his old friend and hero Winston Churchill to form the next Government. He had liked Attlee and worked well with him, but both he and the Queen worshipped Churchill. Churchill, however, was no longer the man he had been during their wartime partnership. He was seventy-six, rather deaf, and in 1949 had suffered the first of his strokes. His spirit remained indomitable and he still had the magical power to turn a phrase, but there was, as his doctor, Lord Moran, said, a difference: then that indomitable spirit had been battling a deadly threat to the world's freedom, now it was 'struggling only with the humiliations of old age and with economic problems quite beyond his ken'.

Princess Elizabeth and Prince Philip arrived back in England having once again missed Prince Charles's birthday – his third. The King had been well enough to attend his birthday party – a charming photograph shows them sitting side by side on a sofa at Buckingham Palace. This occasion was to be Prince Charles's first – and only – recollection of his grandfather. There was the usual family Christmas at Sandringham; the King was too weak to make the traditional broadcast and for the first time it was pre-recorded. Princess Elizabeth was preparing to leave for yet another tour – to Australia and New Zealand, which the King and Queen had had to postpone in 1948. There was a family theatre party on 30 January to see *South Pacific*; the next day the King took the unusual step of going to Heathrow airport to see his daughter off. Had he a premonition he might not see her again? Bobo, who as usual accompanied the Princess, recalled that his last words to her had been, 'Look after the Princess for me, Bobo,' and that she had never before seen him so upset at parting from her. He stood hatless in the cold wind, his face gaunt, straining for a last sight of his daughter. It was to be the last time Princess Elizabeth saw her father.

7.   Coronation

From the moment the Queen, a small neat figure in black dress and hat, stepped out of the door of the aeroplane at Heathrow airport on 7 February 1952, she became the focus of a growing worldwide media interest culminating in the explosion of patriotism and splendour of her Coronation sixteen months later.

At the foot of the steps waited her first Prime Minister, Winston Churchill, soon to become as besotted with her as just over a century before Queen Victoria's first Prime Minister, Lord Melbourne, had been with the young Victoria. Behind him were ranged up a funeral row of ancient royal Rolls-Royces. 'I see they've brought the hearses,' the Queen had joked grimly as she had spotted them through the aircraft window. The sight of them emphasized the final end of her freedom as the royal life closed in on her for ever. At Clarence House, her grandmother, Queen Mary, ever a stickler for royal protocol, curtseyed to kiss her hand, to her granddaughter's great embarrassment. Round the corner at St James's Palace the next day the Garter King of Arms, dressed in a medieval-looking tabard which her ancestor Queen Elizabeth I would have recognized, sonorously pronounced her accession as 'Queen Elizabeth the Second, by the grace of God, Queen of this Realm and of all Her other Realms and Territories, Head of the Commonwealth, Defender of the Faith'. On 11 February, accompanied by her mother and grandmother, she waited at the station for the body of her father to be brought up from Sandringham for his funeral at Windsor. Heavily veiled to protect the privacy of their grief from the public, the 'Three Queens', as the photograph was inevitably captioned, looked, an observer said, 'like Muslim women'.

In private their grief was real and severe. While the young Queen had her husband and children to sustain her and her new duties to fill her time, the world seemed to have come to an end for Queen Elizabeth, now known to her public as the Queen Mother, and Princess Margaret. 'He was the very heart and centre of our family,' Princess Margaret wrote to a friend. Queen Mary would survive the blow by barely a year. For Prince Philip the life change was almost as difficult: in future not only would he have to walk two steps behind his wife, but as if to emphasize the difference, the chair which he occupied at the State Opening of Parliament would be two inches lower than the Queen's.

Worse still, within days of the King's funeral a behind-the-scenes row broke out over the Royal Family name. Queen Victoria's family had taken the name of her husband, Prince Albert of Saxe-Coburg-Gotha, which had remained the family name until George V had changed it to Windsor in 1917 under the stress of anti-German feeling during the First World War. Queen Mary had heard that at Broadlands Lord Mountbatten had boasted that since the accession of his niece-in-law, 'the house of Mountbatten reigned'; Prince Philip naturally but apparently belligerently and tactlessly argued that, as in the case of Victoria and Albert, his children should bear their father's name. Churchill, the Cabinet, and the older generation of royals represented by Queen Mary and Queen Elizabeth the Queen Mother, and the royal Household, all came down against Mountbatten pretensions. The Queen, constitutionally obliged to take the advice of her Government, issued a proclamation to the effect that it was her pleasure that she and her descendants should continue to bear the name of Windsor. It was a blow that Prince Philip's male pride found hard to accept. 'I am the only man in the country not allowed to give his name to his children,' he raged. Later, when the Queen came fully to realize how much it meant to him, a compromise was reached, but at the time, realistically, with the recent death of her popular father and the coming prospect of her own Coronation, she had little alternative but to fall in with the majority opinion.

It was Churchill, with his rolling sense of history, who inspired the notion of a New Elizabethan Age in a broadcast on the evening of the new Queen's return from Kenya. The idea of a British renaissance had been in the air since the Festival of Britain the previous year, and Churchill now gave it fresh impetus: 'Famous have been the reigns of our Queens,' he declaimed, harking back to Elizabeth I and Victoria. 'Some of the greatest periods in our history have unfolded under their sceptre.' He spoke of the monarchy as 'the magic link which unites our loosely-bound but strongly interwoven Commonwealth'. The 'magic' of the monarchy was demonstrated by two royal events, the lying-in-state and funeral of George VI and the Queen's Coronation, both of which drew large crowds to London.

'Under the reign of George VI,' *Time* magazine wrote, 'Britons learned to queue . . . for food, for fun, for clothing, for travel, for life's necessities and life's rewards. Last week they queued for George himself.' Londoners called it 'the Great Queue': more than 300,000 people lined up to pass the King's coffin lying in state in Westminster Hall. Among those who attended the funeral were General Eisenhower, then chief of NATO, who was there unofficially as a friend of the Royal Family, and the Duke of Windsor, who was described as noticeably 'jaunty' as he followed his brother's coffin. He was not to be invited to his niece's Coronation the following year, principally because the Queen did not want him there, as the Archbishop of Canterbury recorded after a meeting with her on 6 November 1952. Siding with her mother and grandmother's view of her uncle as a reprehensible embarrassment to the family, 'The Queen would be less willing than anyone to have him there.' Fortunately Churchill took the same view and saved the Queen from embarrassment by telling the Duke bluntly when consulted by him later that month that it would be 'quite inappropriate for a King who had abdicated to be present at the Coronation of one of his successors'.

Queen Mary, who had been such an influential figure in the

family, would also not be present to see her beloved granddaughter crowned. She died on 24 March 1953, aged eighty-five; typically she had let it be known at Buckingham Palace that, should she no longer be there for the Coronation, it must on no account be postponed because of mourning. Equally typically, the last letter she wrote was to a friend thanking him for sending her a catalogue of the Goya exhibition in Basle. She had been a rock for her family during the Abdication and during Princess Elizabeth's childhood. Erect and dignified, always seen in her old-fashioned long frocks, toque hats and strings of pearls, most of the people lining the streets as her coffin passed could not remember a time when she had not been an essential part of the royal scene.

The second, more glittering royal occasion was the Queen's Coronation on 2 June 1953. Discussions about the date had been going on since before the King's funeral; a day in 1952 was ruled out because the Abbey was still under restoration and, equally importantly, the serious economic situation would have made expensive celebrations unthinkable or, as Churchill put it to Robert Menzies, the Prime Minister of Australia, it was 'vital that not a single working day should be lost in this year of crisis'. 'Can't have Coronations with the bailiffs in the house,' he told 'Tommy' Lascelles. Typically, since the Queen, the Prime Minister and the Earl Marshal, the Duke of Norfolk, were keen racing fans, the choice of the date seems to have been, at least partly, to avoid a clash with Derby Day, a sacred day in the British horse-racing calendar. The composition of the Coronation Commission, appointed by the Queen, reflected the importance that she and the Government placed on the Commonwealth. She had been the first British sovereign to be specifically entitled 'Head of the Commonwealth' at her accession, and the Royal Titles Act of 1953 stipulated that she was separately Queen of each of the Commonwealth territories which were not republics; representatives of all the Commonwealth governments were to be present at Commission meetings. Perhaps to compensate Prince Philip for the hurt caused by the family name-change row,

1. 'Us four' in the gardens of Royal Lodge, Windsor, June 1936: the Duke and Duchess of York with Princesses Elizabeth and Margaret and their dogs at Y Bwthyn Bach (The Little House), given by the Welsh people

2. Princess Elizabeth, photographed in 1942 by Cecil Beaton, wearing the cap badge of the Grenadier Guards. She was made Colonel on her sixteenth birthday

3. The Royal Family inspect the harvest at Sandringham, August 1943

4. South Africa, 1947: Princesses Elizabeth and Margaret riding along the beach with Group Captain Peter Townsend in the background between them

5. Wedding day, 20 November 1947. Princess Elizabeth and Prince Philip, Duke of Edinburgh, returning to Buckingham Palace from Westminster Abbey

6. The last family holiday, Balmoral, 22 August 1951. *From left*, Prince Charles, his grandmother Queen Elizabeth, Princess Margaret, Prince Philip, King George VI, Princess Elizabeth with Princess Anne in the pram

8. Grieving Queen, 8 February 1952

7. Tree Tops, Kenya, February 1952. Princess Elizabeth was staying here at the time of her father's death

9. Coronation: Queen Elizabeth II enthroned with the royal regalia against the background of Westminster Abbey, 2 June 1953

10. Portrait of Queen Elizabeth by Pietro Annigoni, 1954

11. Balmoral, August 1952. *Top left*, Princess Margaret enjoys a cigarette with her mother; *inset*, Prince Charles and his beloved grandmother; *top right*, The Queen outside the castle; *right*, Prince Philip at a picnic. *Below*, returning from Balmoral, the Queen, Princess Anne and Princess Margaret, 10 October 1954

12. Peter Townsend confronts the paparazzi, October 1955

13. In love again: a happy Princess Margaret with her husband Antony Armstrong-Jones (1st Earl of Snowdon) at a Hollywood banquet on their American tour, summer 1965

14. The Queen square dancing, Ottawa, Canada, 1951

15. The picture that shocked the Afrikaaners: the Queen dancing with President Nkrumah of Ghana, Prince Philip in the background, 19 November 1961

16. The Queen and Prince Philip meet competitors at a sheep-shearing contest at Lower Hutt, New Zealand, February 1963

17. The Queen visits the Snowy Mountains hydroelectric scheme, Island Bend, Australia, 1963

18. Gordon Richards is congratulated by the Queen and Prince Philip after winning the Derby on Pinza, 6 June 1953

19. England celebrates: the Queen, watched by a smiling Prince Philip, congratulates captain Bobby Moore on England's World Cup victory over Germany, Wembley Stadium, 30 July 1966

20. The Queen and her old friend Lord Porchester at the Derby, June 1978

21. Winston Churchill greets Princess Elizabeth at a Guildhall dinner. Prime Minister Clement Attlee and Mrs Attlee are in the background, 23 March 1950

22. The Queen, shortly before the birth of Prince Andrew, visits Oxford accompanied by Chancellor Harold Macmillan, January 1960

23. The Queen and Harold Wilson at Downing Street for dinner on his retirement as Prime Minister, 24 March 1976

24. The Queen and Prime Minister Margaret Thatcher at the Commonwealth Conference, Lusaka, 1 August 1979

the Queen chose Prince Philip the modernizer as Chairman, with the deeply traditionalist Norfolk as Vice-Chairman.

Ironically for an event which was to cause a media revolution with the monarchy as television, the Commission's decision was to exclude the cameras from the heart of the ceremony – the anointing. It was the Queen herself who felt that she did not want such an intrusion and it was only when the decision caused uproar – 'Let the People see the Queen,' the *Daily Express* demanded – that she changed her mind, telling the Prime Minister in an audience that 'all her subjects should have the opportunity' of seeing her crowned as their Queen. Privately she remained wary of this new medium; perhaps with memories of her father's agonized experiences, she later vetoed televising her Christmas broadcast in favour of a still photograph of herself at the microphone instead.

The combination of ancient ceremonial with the youth and beauty of the Queen and her Prince made the Coronation of Queen Elizabeth II a visual spectacle that still has the power to move people who see it. It was the culmination of months of increasing anticipation and growing national pride in the British monarchy as the symbol of British identity. It was, as Princess Margaret recalled, 'a Phoenix-time' expressing optimism and stability – a young Queen, a re-invigorated people. No less than 56 per cent of the adult population tuned in to the televised service, and despite the grey drizzly weather hundreds of thousands crowded the streets along the procession route and the public parks, singing, dancing and doing comic turns. Elsewhere there were street parties. Pop songs were composed: 'In a Golden Coach' ran, 'In a golden coach there's a heart of gold/ That belongs to you and me . . .' A young Trinidadian, billed as Young Tiger, performed a calypso, 'I Was There' (at the Coronation), also focused on the Queen. 'Her Majesty looked really divine/ In her crimson robe furred with ermine/ The Duke of Edinburgh, dignified and neat/ Sat beside her as Admiral of the Fleet . . .'[1] The hushed, reverential tone of BBC commentator Richard Dimbleby, 'an increasingly integral part of the British

Constitution', as one historian put it, set the scene. It was a turning point both for the monarchy and for the media. 'From now on,' wrote the Queen's biographer Ben Pimlott, 'the expectation that royal events would be televised became automatic . . . television became the means by which the public would perceive the Royal Family and with ever more fascinated intimacy relate to it.'

Eight years after the war food rationing was still in force: rationing of tea had ended in October 1952 and of sweets in February 1953, but sugar, butter, cooking fats, cheese, meat and eggs were all still rationed. Restrictions were lifted for the Coronation, and while the working classes in towns and villages celebrated with parties and with extra rations of sugar allowed and eggs de-rationed, the upper classes so heavily represented at Court attended the Household Brigade's Coronation Ball at floodlit Hampton Court Palace. The men wore tailcoats and decorations, the women ballgowns and tiaras. 'We danced in the Great Hall and supped in the orangery,' Jock Colville wrote. 'A world that vanished in 1939 lived again for the night.' But for all the official emphasis on the Commonwealth future replacing the imperial past, many people could not grasp the concept. The Queen might insist that symbols of Commonwealth countries were embroidered on her Coronation dress, but the *Evening Standard* editorial titled 'Onward to Glory' celebrated the recent ascent of Everest (announced on Coronation Day) by the New Zealander Edmund Hillary and the Nepalese Sherpa Tensing as both a symbol of the new age and an achievement of Empire. 'Long live the Queen! Long also may there live the Imperial unity which can make her reign one of peace and wondrous glory.'

The beautiful young Queen travelled to her Coronation at the Abbey in the huge eighteenth-century Gold State Coach, with her handsome husband, wearing the uniform of Admiral of the Fleet – cocked hat, gold bullion epaulettes and Garter star – by her side. In her ermine and velvet cloak and wearing Queen Victoria's diadem in her hair, her carriage drawn by four pairs of Windsor Greys in scarlet and gold harness, attended by postillions, grooms and Yeo-men Warders (Beefeaters) in scarlet and gold uniforms, she could have been the young Victoria.

The maintenance of that world symbol that the British mon-archy represented would require its sacrifice. Even as she went through the extraordinary day the Queen was already aware of trouble looming for the family: her sister was in love with her father's handsome war-hero equerry, ex-fighter-pilot Group Cap-tain Peter Townsend. Within hours of the day ending, the world was too. Unwarily, even perhaps characteristically defiantly, Prin-cess Margaret, standing in the Abbey porch waiting for her carriage, had tenderly flicked a patch of fluff from Townsend's uniform, an intimate gesture which had alerted the world's press to a potentially explosive situation.

For the Palace entourage the Townsend affair raised uncomfort-able comparisons with the Abdication scandal: since November 1952 the Group Captain, father of two young sons, had been divorced from his wife Rosemary on the grounds of her adultery. Innocent party though he may have been, his status as a divorced man was incompatible in Establishment eyes with the Queen's position as Supreme Governor of the Church of England. The Queen, characteristically, when she and Prince Philip were told by Princess Margaret and Townsend of their love for each other, had been sympathetic but had taken no positive action. Equally charac-teristically, the Queen Mother's reaction had been appalled dismay despite the fact that the relationship had been carried on under her nose. After the King's death she had appointed Townsend, her late husband's favourite equerry, Master of her Household, not notic-ing or choosing not to notice the situation developing between her beautiful, capricious younger daughter and the handsome, charming Group Captain, who was sixteen years older. And so the Royal Family had carried on through the Coronation with this time-bomb ticking beneath their feet. The romance threatened the image of family happiness and respectability that had been so carefully cultivated over the years since the Abdication in 1936. The Queen's life, as *Time* put it in their cover story for 5 January 1953 naming her Woman of the Year, 'had provided a quiet well-behaved fairy tale in which the world could believe'. Foreseeing trouble when the story broke in the international press – it was published in New York the next day (although not yet, as in 1936, in the relatively obedient British media) – the Queen's Private Secretary, 'Tommy' Lascelles, drove down to inform the Prime Minister, Winston Churchill, what was going on and seek his advice.

In a re-run of his reaction to the Wallis Simpson/Edward VIII love story, Churchill (he was now seventy-seven and within days of a severe stroke on 23 June) was romantic and sympathetic: 'What a delightful match! A lovely young lady married to a gallant young airman, safe from the perils and horrors of war!' His wife Clementine's reaction was significant: 'Winston, if you are going to begin the Abdication all over again, I'm going to leave! I shall take a flat and go and live in Brighton.' Despite Winston's more humane instincts, the Clemmie/Lascelles official line prevailed: if Princess Margaret wished to marry Townsend she should give up her rights to the royal succession and possibly her Civil List income as well. Churchill was also firmly of the opinion that Townsend should disappear from the scene for at least a year and should not be allowed to accompany the Queen Mother and the Princess on their forthcoming tour of Rhodesia.

The day after the Chartwell meeting, on 14 June, the *People* broke the story, smoking out the Palace in an article entitled 'They Must Deny It Now'. It was 'quite unthinkable', the article ran, tongue-in-cheek, 'that a Royal Princess, third in line of succession to the throne, should even contemplate marriage with a man who has been through the divorce courts'. This public exposure forced a choice: Princess Margaret could either renounce Townsend now and for ever – or she could, she hoped, under the Royal Marriage Act, be free to marry on her twenty-fifth birthday in August 1955. Agonized, the couple decided not to give each other up but to wait and hope for two years. In the meantime, the official sentence for Townsend was exile as air attaché to the British Embassy in Brussels. Princess Margaret left for Rhodesia with the Queen Mother on 30 June, still expecting to see him again to say goodbye on her return on 17 July. Churchill's orders, however, were that Townsend should leave Britain within seven days of his posting: halfway through her tour Princess Margaret received the devastating news that Townsend was to leave two days before her return. 'She collapsed as she does when things go terribly wrong. She was so upset she wouldn't be able to see him when she got back,' a member of her party said. 'Officially it was put out that she was ill but she just collapsed from emotional shock . . .'

The Queen, as always, went along with the official line, acquiescing in what was the deception of her sister, but making a farewell gesture of friendship towards Townsend by inviting him to be her official equerry on her post-Coronation visit to Belfast. 'I thought it was a most generous and admirable act on her part,' Townsend later recalled. 'She shook hands with me on the tarmac. It was the last time I saw her until many years later.' Duty called the Queen; Princess Margaret might be 'utterly lost and lonely' but it was not the end of the story, and meanwhile the royal bandwagon had to move on.

The next stop was to be the Commonwealth. For six months, from 14 November 1953 to May 1954, the Queen and Prince Philip were out of the country on her post-Coronation Commonwealth Tour. They visited Bermuda, Jamaica, Fiji, Tonga, the Cocos Islands, Aden, Uganda, Malta and Gibraltar, spending three months in Australia and New Zealand and ten days in Ceylon. 'Such a marathon of travel, speeches, national anthems, handshakes, troop inspections, Parliament openings, performances, banquets, bouquets and gifts, had never before been undertaken by a British Head of State – or perhaps by anybody.'[2] Some 6,000 people were at London airport to witness their departure. 'It was immensely moving,' Noël Coward recorded after watching the television coverage. 'The Queen looked so young and vulnerable and valiant, and Prince Philip so handsome and cheerful. A truly romantic couple, star quality *in excelsis*. True glamour without the Windsors' vulgarity.'[3]

As Ben Pimlott pointed out, it was the last occasion for an extended royal tour of a still-surviving Empire and of Dominions that fervently believed in their Britishness. After the glamour of the Coronation, Queen-mania had reached new heights. The crowds were huge: in New Zealand, after a disappointingly wet start, the UK High Commissioner's report estimated that two out of three New Zealanders saw the Queen, many of whom had travelled considerable distances to do so. In Bluff, whose normal population was less than 3,000 people, 200,000 were estimated to have crowded in to see her.

> Few, I think, could have predicted the adulation which Her Majesty and His Royal Highness – who also in his own right, made a great and lasting impression – inspired wherever they went, or indeed the emotions which Her Majesty's presence aroused . . . no longer is she a remote personage to her New Zealand peoples: she is now to them, the Queen of New Zealand, and moreover, the relationship between the Crown and the various members of the Commonwealth has been brought home to them in a manner in which no amount of writing and talking could ever have accomplished.[4]

The Queen's Christmas broadcast (live from New Zealand, a considerable technical achievement for the BBC) emphasized and updated the concept of the Commonwealth: 'The Commonwealth bears no resemblance to the Empires of the past. It is an entirely new conception,' the Queen said. 'To that new conception of an equal partnership of nations and races,' she added, in a direct echo of her South African speech of six years earlier, ' I shall give myself, heart and soul, every day of my life.' She opened the New Zealand Parliament, the first time a sovereign had done so since its establishment a century before, bringing home to the people, as the British representative reported, 'the importance of the constitutional changes, formalized in the Royal Titles Act, 1953, by which HM has become Queen of New Zealand'.

The adulation and enthusiasm with which the Queen had been greeted in New Zealand was more than equalled by the reception she received in Australia. Since her Coronation the twenty-six-year-old Queen and her husband had become worldwide celebrities. Millions had seen the Coronation on film, a magical, mysterious and glittering ceremony which had elevated the central figure to the level of myth. Now people saw the reality, a lovely, shy, dignified, very young woman with a radiant complexion and a rare but glorious smile. *Time* magazine – and sections of the British press – contrasted the tumultuous welcome she received in Sydney with the 'dignified, orderly' reaction of the New Zealand public. 'A million goggling Aussies whooped it up on the shore as the royal liner *Gothic* steamed into Sydney harbour,' *Time* reported. 'There were 1,000 private yachts, several Australian warships, scores of sightseeing steamers, and a school of hot-rod teenagers, who seemed more eager to swamp the police boats than to welcome their Queen. Cannon roared; sirens blew; wave after wave of fighter aircraft swooped over the royal yacht [*sic*]. Her Majesty, helped by Philip, stepped ashore at Farm Cove, where the first English settlers (290 freemen and 717 convicts) landed in 1788.' Two days later, during a twenty-three-mile State procession, some of the crowd of 1,200,000 burst through police barriers, halting the royal car on eight separate occasions. 'Men and women clutched Philip's arm, tried to shake his hand, patted the royal shoulders and tossed confetti and flags into the car.' Later even Prince Philip was flustered by a crowd of teenagers wolf-whistling and screaming: 'Isn't he nice? . . . He's beautiful.' At the Lord Mayor's Ball that evening many of the 2,000 guests, instead of dancing, stood round the dais staring at the Queen.

The huge success of the 1953–4 Commonwealth Tour inevitably

invoked the law of diminishing returns: no royal tour could ever reach those heights again. The spread of television would mean that it was not necessary to line the streets in order to see the Queen. Moreover, there were already signs of trouble in the former colonies: making a detour from the Red Sea on her way home, the Queen visited Uganda. Papers reveal that the scope of her visit was limited by fear of terrorist incursion from neighbouring Kenya Colony, where the bloody Mau Mau uprising had begun. Between October 1952 and the end of 1954, thirty white European farmers and 1,800 loyalist Africans were murdered, a State of Emergency was declared and the Mau Mau leader and future President of an independent Kenya, Jomo Kenyatta (who had been educated at a Scottish missionary school and spent many years in England), was sentenced to life imprisonment. The winds of change were already blowing through Africa.

At Gibraltar the Queen and Prince boarded the new royal yacht *Britannia* to be met by Prince Charles and Princess Anne, whom they had not seen for five months, before returning home for a triumphant, choreographed welcome. Warships of the Royal Navy and the greatest flotilla of private craft seen since Dunkirk escorted *Britannia* up the Thames. Lights blazed from the cranes of London Docks, ships blew their hooters and a forty-one-gun salute thundered. Crowds rivalling those that thronged London for the Queen's Coronation lined the royal route from Westminster Pier to Buckingham Palace. During the 174 days she had been away from Britain she had travelled more than 40,000 miles by land, sea and air. Her tour made the Coronation theme of the Commonwealth take on reality.

In the aftermath of the Coronation, Britain was an optimistic country, proud of itself and of its recent achievements, first the conquest of Everest and then a world record for the one-mile race when a young medical student, Roger Bannister, ran the distance in under four minutes. 'So Britain has been the first to conquer Everest and to achieve the four-minute mile,' a newspaper crowed.

'Both feats may be equalled, but they will never be erased, for first is always the first. Britain has pioneered the way. So let us have no more talk of an effete and worn-out nation.' It was, an historian has written, 'the apogee of the determinedly hopeful, optimistic "New Elizabethan" moment'. There seemed much to cheer about – full employment without inflation and the end of rationing, with a ceremonial tearing-up of ration books in Trafalgar Square. A year later, New Year 1955, the *News Chronicle* was predicting 'ANOTHER BOOM YEAR', with Britons getting ready for a spending spree. Mollie Panter-Downes reported that Britain was turning into a land of 'new television masts sprouting from roofs, new cars in garages, and markets bulging with every conceivable necessity and luxury'. At the other end of the scale, however, punitive taxation resulted in the destruction of an old feature of English life: in 1955, according to the historian J. Mordaunt Crook, 'country houses were coming down at the rate of one every two and a half days'. England was beaten at football by Hungary in the World Cup, which was won by Germany; in April there was a third crash of a Comet, the hope of the British aircraft industry which would be totally outclassed by the Americans. The West German economic miracle had begun and, however rosy it might appear on the surface, Britain might have won the war but it was about to lose the peace.

8.   A New and Dangerous World

While in Australia Prince Philip had been handed a mulga wood box containing chunks of Australian uranium ore. It was not merely a tribute to his reputation for forward thinking and interest in science, more importantly it was also a symbol of a new nuclear era and of Commonwealth involvement in the global Cold War between the Western powers and the Communist world.

In November 1953 the British had tested an A-bomb in the Australian desert. On 7 January 1954, US President Eisenhower had delivered his State of the Union message, in which he stated that his aim during his second year in office would be 'to reduce the Communist menace without war'. 'We shall not be the aggressor,' he declared, 'but we and our Allies have and will maintain a massive capacity to strike back.' Weeks later, at Bikini Atoll in the Pacific Ocean, the US tested the first hydrogen bomb; it was more than 500 times more powerful than the atomic bomb dropped on Hiroshima nine years earlier. A Japanese fishing boat, the *Fukuryu Maru*, was cruising for tuna off Bikini when a vast explosion occurred and the crew was covered with radioactive ash; the wireless operator died from radiation sickness in September. Later, radioactive rain fell on Japan: its source, however, was not the US hydrogen bomb but a series of H-bomb tests initiated by the Soviet Union in the Urals. Eight years earlier the Labour Foreign Secretary, Ernest Bevin, had come out for a British atom bomb: 'We've got to have this thing over here whatever it costs,' he told Prime Minister Attlee. 'We've got to have the bloody Union Jack on top of it.' Now, in the spring and late summer of 1954, Churchill had to contemplate upping the ante in Britain's nuclear weaponry from the atomic bomb to the hydrogen bomb. Faced with an apocalyptic warning from the military chiefs of staff ('There is no theoretical limit to the destructive power which can be achieved with the latest techniques'), he responded along much the same lines as Bevin had: 'We must do it. It's the price we pay to sit at the top table.' On 16 July 1954 Churchill warned the Queen that 'the Cabinet are considering whether it would be right and advantageous for this country to produce the hydrogen bomb . . . There is very little doubt in my mind what the decision will be.' It was taken on 26 July 1954 and announced in 1955. The Queen was therefore aware of the realities of 'The Bomb', which haunted the minds and imaginations of her subjects of all ages through the 50s and early 60s. And not just the British: in the wake of Bikini Atoll and the experience of the *Fukuryu Maru*, the 1954 Japanese film *Godzilla*, featuring a monster created by a nuclear explosion which climbs out of Tokyo Bay to destroy the city, became a much-repeated image through into the twenty-first century.

Meanwhile the Princess Margaret/Peter Townsend affair, which had been brushed under the carpet the previous summer, continued to pose a threat to the Royal Family's image and stability. The one-year ban on Townsend's presence in the United Kingdom had been extended to two, but neither the Princess nor Townsend had given up hope: the key date for decision was to be Princess Margaret's twenty-fifth birthday on 21 August 1955, when she would be free to marry without the Queen's consent (wishfully overlooking the fact that that of the Cabinet and Commonwealth would be necessary). In February 1955 the Princess made a tour of the West Indies – Trinidad, Barbados and the Leeward Islands – making up for the people's disappointment at not seeing the Queen on her Commonwealth tour. She was enthusiastically received, as the Governor-General of Trinidad informed the Colonial Secretary: 'The behaviour of the people throughout has been magnificent and their remarks as the Princess passed by gladdened me, and I am sure the Princess also. Remarks like "she nice" and "she like a fairy" were met everywhere, and I do not believe that ever in the past has such enthusiasm been shown for any person or persons . . .'[1]

The Princess returned from her tour happy and eager; the day after her return Townsend revived all the speculation about them by giving an interview to the *Daily Sketch* in Brussels, where he was stationed. When asked whether he would marry Princess Margaret he replied, 'Wait and see.' There was an absolute furore and he claimed to have been misquoted, while the newspaper's proprietor was adamant that the initiative had come from the Group Captain. It is difficult to believe that this was not the opening shot in the final campaign for their marriage. The two of them corresponded passionately and frequently and it would seem unlikely that the move had not been co-ordinated between them. For the moment, however, nothing happened; there was the usual royal reluctance to discuss anything awkward. As 'Tommy' Lascelles had commented on a previous occasion, it was always much easier to act 'before the waters have started to rise than to bury your head in the sand, and trust that the flood won't incommode you, which is the usual technique of the Royal Family'.

According to Princess Margaret's friends, the success of her West Indian tour was not even acknowledged. In early August at Sandringham, where she was staying with friends and with the Queen Mother as hostess, there was great tension. Cecil Beaton had taken a series of birthday photographs of the Princess and much time was spent choosing one to be sent to 'Peter'. Princess Margaret, no doubt in an agony of apprehension and resentment, was 'very moody and difficult', refusing to go to bed at night and doing the opposite of what her mother said. 'We felt sorry for Queen Elizabeth, she knew what was the matter and she didn't know how to cope with the situation and she was much too reserved to talk to anyone about it.'[2] Princess Margaret knew that the time for decision, her twenty-fifth birthday, was imminent: 'She rationalized her behaviour and said it would do no harm if she did marry him.' When friends warned her that marrying Townsend, a divorced man, could harm the Queen's position, even daring to mention the Windsors, she riposted that that was nonsense. Any comparison with the Windsors made her furious. 'She has always regarded them as beyond the pale.'

Meanwhile Winston Churchill, the first member of Government to be officially informed of the Townsend/Margaret saga, had finally resigned on 5 April 1955, to the relief, it must be said, of his colleagues and even, perhaps, of the Queen, who had steadfastly and typically resisted pressure to urge his resignation. He was now eighty years old but had recovered remarkably from his stroke and was still full of fire and fun, rising to the occasion when needed. On his eightieth birthday, on 30 November, his response to an unprecedented tribute address from both Houses of Parliament had been a classic, the enthusiastic reaction to it confirming him in his reluctance to leave the scene. He dithered almost to the end, writing to the Queen with a decision and then asking her if she minded if he changed the date before finally informing her on 31 March of his decision to resign five days later. He was replaced by Anthony Eden, long seen as his successor, to whom Churchill had been wont to refer as 'my Princess Elizabeth'. Handsome and highly strung, Eden's self-confidence in the top job had been seriously undermined by his long apprenticeship, as was all too soon to become apparent. And in one direction, at least, his position was severely hampered. He was the first Prime Minister to have been divorced (he had remarried, in April 1952, Churchill's niece, Clarissa) and was, therefore, hardly in a position to take the lead in the decision as to whether the Princess should marry Townsend.

To British public opinion, however, whatever Eden thought was not of primary importance. The private life of the Royal Family was no longer private: the Abdication had lifted the corner of the curtain. Swiftly dealt with as it had been by those in power, the curtain had fallen again. But with the huge public, indeed worldwide interest aroused by the Coronation, when the people had been invited to join the party, 'their story' was becoming 'our story'. Some 300 members of the press were encamped round Balmoral on Sunday, 21 August, Princess Margaret's twenty-fifth birthday, hoping for a decision. 'COME ON MARGARET,' the *Daily Mirror*'s headline had shouted two days before, 'please make up your mind!' But nothing happened, either in public or in private. Then in September Peter Townsend arrived in London en route for the Farnborough Air Show: making no attempt to keep a low profile, he was seen around the city in a chauffeur-driven red Daimler, pursued by a posse of newsmen who staked out houses of friends of the Princess from which he put through private calls to Balmoral. On one memorable occasion, when one of the go-betweens used to put in the calls to Balmoral was late, he rang the castle himself. 'You should have seen the look on their faces when the page came in and said Group Captain Townsend was on the telephone for Princess Margaret,' one of those present recalled. Still nothing happened and at Balmoral nothing was discussed, setting a pattern for royal behaviour at later crises in their family life (Fergie's toe-sucking and, more seriously, Diana's death). On the day Princess Margaret was due to leave, the Queen saw to it that she avoided the private discussion that her sister wanted, taking the dogs for a walk and returning only in time to say goodbye. Rightly, the Queen was refusing to put pressure on Princess Margaret. The Princess was too intelligent not to know for herself what was at stake. At Balmoral she had sat down and written, 'Reasons why I shouldn't marry Peter: because it does harm to the Queen' and 'Reasons why I should marry Peter: because I couldn't live without him.'

Princess Margaret arrived back in London by the overnight train from Scotland on 12 October. Townsend had flown in the same day and they met that evening for tea at Clarence House. Public interest was at fever pitch; the Palace press officer, Commander Colville (known to the press as the 'Abominable No-man'), issued a statement pleading in vain for the public to leave the Princess alone and declaring to widespread astonishment and disbelief that 'no announcement concerning Princess Margaret's future was at present contemplated'. On the surface and in the press it seemed a re-run of 1936, but there was one vital difference that everyone seems to have overlooked. Edward VIII had been King; his niece was neither Queen nor, since the birth of Prince Charles and Princess Anne, heir to the throne. The fuss, emotion and hysteria which raged in October 1955 was symbolic of divisions in the country between progressives and Establishmentarians, religious and non-religious, at a time when belief in the monarchy had itself become almost a kind of religion. Sir William Haley's leader in *The Times*, still just as much a voice of the Establishment as it had been in 1936, thundered:

> Now in the twentieth-century conception of the monarchy the Queen has come to be the symbol of every side of life in this society, its universal representative in whom people see their better selves ideally reflected; and since part of their ideal is family life, the Queen's family has its own part in the reflection. If the marriage which is now being discussed comes to pass, it is inevitable that this reflection becomes distorted . . .[3]

This was the moral straitjacket into which the Royal Family was to be confined, trapped by an image of its own creation.

By the time Haley delivered his broadside (on 26 October, Budget Day, which passed almost unnoticed), the couple had already come to a decision. Princess Margaret spent 23 October at Windsor. Childhood memories of her father, reinforced by the recent dedication of a memorial statue to him, must have weighed heavily on her, and she must have known that he, as King and Supreme Governor of the Church of England, would not have approved. Even in terms of upper-class and royal traditions, he would not have welcomed the marriage of his twenty-five-year-old daughter to a divorced RAF officer, sixteen years older than she was, with no money and two sons to be educated. On 24 October she and

Townsend mutually agreed that they could not go ahead with the marriage. Contrary to what has been claimed, the Government did not threaten the Princess with loss of her title and income if she married Townsend, only that she should renounce her right to the succession of herself and any children she might have, hardly a deadly deprivation in the circumstances. Religion and royal duty undoubtedly influenced the Princess – 'Princess Margaret was very religious,' a friend claimed. Under the rules of the Church of England a divorced person with a spouse living could not contract a church marriage; Princess Margaret felt strongly that she could not go through with a civil marriage both from her own point of view and out of consideration for the Queen's position as Supreme Governor of the Church and Defender of the Faith. Status was probably a factor: in a structure still so rigid as the Court and Society with a capital 'S' as it was in the 50s, the Townsend marriage would have been regarded as a huge step down for the Queen's sister. Asked whether Princess Margaret had been sacrificed on the altar of the monarchy, a courtier responded briskly, 'She sacrificed herself.'

The decision, publicly announced on 31 October, was greeted at first with stunned semi-silence; then the anti-Establishmentarians began a ripple of protest that was to become a wave during the 1960s. Keith Waterhouse in the *Mirror* stood up for Townsend, 'a man of intelligence and personal courage', against what he called 'the stiff-collar classes . . . already crowing in their clubs that Peter Townsend has been shown the door. These are the people who would have bowed the lowest if he had married Princess Margaret . . .' Not mincing his words, he went on in bold type: 'THESE ARE THE PEOPLE who from now on will watch Princess Margaret like hawks crossed with vultures.' In the *Express*, a letter signed by Kenneth Tynan, Lindsay Anderson and others claimed that the decision had revived old class distinctions in public life: 'it has shown us "the Establishment" in full cry, that pious group of potentates who so loudly applauded the Princess's decision', who had, they said, 'exposed the true nature of our national hypocrisy'. Among the people at large the reaction was not so clear-cut. While a Gallup poll on Archbishop Fisher's ruling that the Church of England should not remarry a divorced person while the other party was still alive showed 59 per cent against the Archbishop and only 28 per cent pro, a Mass Observation panel of opinion set in non-religious terms seemed to indicate that Middle England tended to think Princess Margaret had done the right thing: 'the man's a Cad' was one woman's response.[4]

A few months later, in April 1956, the Queen was deployed as a lure to defuse the Cold War between Britain and Russia when Nikita Khrushchev, General Secretary of the Communist Party, and the Soviet Prime Minister, Marshal Nikolai Bulganin, arrived on a State visit. Earlier that year Khrushchev had denounced the dead leader Stalin, in a closed party conference in the course of which he had announced his intention of pursuing a policy of 'peaceful co-existence' with the West. This visit was to be his reward. 'Bulge' and 'Crush', as the two leaders were nicknamed by the disrespectful British press, arrived in London on 18 April to a very mixed reception on their first drive through the capital. Some 60 per cent of the crowd remained silent, about 20 per cent cheered and 15 per cent actively booed, something which the *Spectator* correspondent had never heard a British crowd do before. The two had earlier attended the Grand National race meeting at Aintree (as guests of the Central Electricity Authority), when the Queen Mother's horse, Devon Loch, ridden by Dick Francis, had been spooked only forty yards from the finish when leading by five lengths, falling on his stomach, struggling to his feet, only for his hind legs to give way again. The explanations were various – a reaction to the noise of the crowd, trying to jump an imaginary fence, even a Soviet conspiracy. The Queen Mother remained calm in this disaster, patting the trainer on the shoulder and comforting the tearful jockey and stable lads. 'I hope the Russians saw it,' the Duke of Devonshire commented. 'It was the most perfect display of dignity I ever witnessed.'[5]

Eden arranged that the Queen and Prince Philip should invite the pair to tea. 'I don't know what the hell we shall give them,' the Prince had grumbled beforehand to the Labour politician Richard Crossman. 'I think it's bloody silly. But they think we should give them too much importance if we had them to lunch.' 'Eden told us that we would find the Queen to be a simple but very bright and very pleasant woman,' Khrushchev recorded. He described her as 'the sort of young woman you'd be likely to meet walking along Gorky Street on a balmy summer afternoon'. The students of the Oxford Union had been less respectful, treating the Russian pair like a comedy turn, holding up pro-Stalin posters and singing 'Poor old Joe'. 'Bulge' and 'Crush', unaware the mickey was being taken, appeared on television at the event waving and smiling. But later Harold Nicolson vouchsafed that 'the Russians are furious at the undergraduates ragging them at Oxford'. Khrushchev made a contemptuous speech at a formal House of Commons dinner given for the delegation by the Labour Party, in which he boasted that it was Russia alone who had defeated Hitler; George Brown exclaimed, 'May God forgive you!' Khrushchev broke off and asked the interpreter what he had said. It was translated. Khrushchev then banged the table and said, 'What I say is true!' . . . George Brown retorted, 'We lost almost half a million men while you were Hitler's allies.' 'There was a painful silence (*silence pénible*),' Nicolson wrote. 'At the Speaker's luncheon yesterday George Brown went up with outstretched hand to apologize, but Khrushchev put his hand behind his back and said sharply, "Niet!" My [Labour] friend told me that in a long experience of unsuccessful banquets, that will live in his memory as the most acid failure that he has ever witnessed.'[6]

A few months later, in November 1956, the Russians showed that they had not been tamed by the Queen's invitation when they took advantage of the world's attention being turned on the disastrous

Suez affair to attack Hungary, moving with great brutality to crush the nascent democratic government in Budapest. On the morning of 1 November, 75,000 Soviet troops and 2,500 tanks crossed the Hungarian–Soviet border, moving on the capital. By 7 November they had succeeded in re-installing their puppet Prime Minister: reportedly 25,000 Hungarians, mostly civilians, and 7,000 Russians, mainly soldiers, were killed. As many as 200,000 Hungarians, almost 2 per cent of the entire population, fled their country as refugees.

With the Suez campaign in 1956, Britain faced an experience far more destructive to its own, and the world's, image of itself as a Great Power. On 26 July the new President of Egypt, Colonel Nasser, nationalized the Anglo-French Suez Canal Company, which had been responsible for the administration of the water-way since its construction. Eden's immediate reaction was secretly to plan a full-scale invasion to capture the Canal, while a subsequent international conference, boycotted by Egypt, supported a plan put forward by John Foster Dulles, American Secretary of State, for an international Suez Canal Board, associated with the United Nations, to manage the Canal and ensure that it was kept open to the ships of all nations (the Egyptians had refused to allow Israeli ships, or ships bound for Israeli ports, to use it). Early in September Nasser turned down the Dulles plan, and later that month the British and French took the question to the United Nations Security Council in New York. Meanwhile the French and Israelis met secretly in Paris to co-ordinate military action against Egypt, and when the Security Council failed to support the Anglo-French position, Anthony Eden and his Foreign Secretary, Selwyn Lloyd, travelled to Paris to discuss military action against Egypt with the French. In a further meeting on 21 and 22 October in a villa at Sèvres, just outside Paris, which resulted in the secret Sèvres Protocol, the Israelis and the French were joined by Selwyn Lloyd. The discussion focused on how the three countries could co-ordinate their planned action in such a way that it would not seem to be collusion. The Israelis would cross into the Egyptian Sinai and advance towards the Suez Canal. This would give Britain and France the opportunity to intervene militarily, in order to 'protect' the Canal.[7]

On 29 October the Israelis duly attacked, and on the 30th Britain and France issued their ultimatum and Eden made a statement in the House of Commons revealing his plans. At a meeting of the United Nations Security Council in New York, Britain and France enraged the United States and the Soviet Union by vetoing a US resolution calling on the Israelis to withdraw; on 31 October they bombed Egyptian airfields, destroying the Egyptian air force. In the House of Commons the fact that Britain had bombed a country with which it was not actually at war raised the political temperature to heights equalling those of May 1940. On 4 November 10,000 demonstrators protested against the action against Egypt; early the following day, Monday, 5 November, British paratroops landed at Port Said, at the northern entrance to the Suez Canal, at the same time as French forces landed at Port Fuad, on the opposite side of the Canal. A run on the pound developed and Britain's gold reserves fell by 15 per cent that month. When appealed to for help, the United States told the British bluntly that none would be forthcoming without a ceasefire. Eisenhower, re-elected President on 6 November, was afraid that the Soviet Union might step forward as Egypt's protector, bringing Soviet influence to the shores of the Red Sea, and was determined to halt what he saw as the Anglo-French aggression against Egypt. 'Ike scuppered us,' Eden later was wont to claim. That day, 6 November, at the United Nations, Canada called for a UN force to supervise an end to hostilities; their resolution was supported by fifty-seven countries and opposed by none. Britain, France and Israel agreed to a ceasefire from midnight. The Suez operation was over almost as soon as it had begun. 'By stopping when they did,' Eden's biographer wrote, 'the British had incurred the maximum of odium and the minimum of advantage.' 'I would never have conceived of a government of the United Kingdom functioning as this one has done,' Jawaharlal Nehru, first Prime Minister of India, wrote despairingly on 4 November. 'Whatever the future may bring I fear that respect for the UK has vanished utterly from Asia and Africa.'[8] The 'old' Commonwealth countries, Canada in particular, were dismayed.

One question has been asked over and over again since 1956. Did the Queen know of Eden's secret collusion with the French and the Israelis over Suez, concealed from the world, lied about in Parliament? According to D. R. Thorpe, biographer of Eden, and more recently of Harold Macmillan, she did.[9] She had signed the document approving the calling up of the Army reserves in late summer, and she saw all the Foreign Office and other telegrams that would have revealed what was happening. Did she approve of the operation? The truth is that attitudes at the Palace had reflected the confusion and dismay felt by the nation at large. In the Queen's Private Office Sir Michael Adeane was in favour of armed intervention, while the Deputy and Assistant Private Secretaries, Martin Charteris and Edward Ford, were against it. Both Charteris and Ford were familiar with the Middle East and the Arab world, Charteris having been head of military intelligence in Palestine in 1946, while Ford had acted as tutor to King Farouk and fought in the North African campaign. Neither of them could view with equanimity the prospect of alienating the entire Arab world, the inevitable result of attacking Egypt, symbol of resurgent nationalism, and particularly in conjunction with Israel, less than a decade after the Arab–Israeli war in Palestine in 1948. Britain's oil interests lay in Iraq, where the instability following Suez soon led to the overthrow of the pro-Western royal government. Mountbatten, as First Sea Lord, knew about the invasion plans from the start and in private opposed them. According to a royal aide he 'was always about' at the Palace, and would not have hesitated to let his nephew and the Queen know his informed insider opinion of the operation. According to one of her close advisers, the Queen thought it was 'idiotic'. Prince Philip's reaction has not been recorded; he had been invited to open the forthcoming Commonwealth Games in Sydney, Australia. Incredibly the progression of the Suez crisis had not caused the Palace to cancel or postpone his departure; he had left on board *Britannia* (which had been designated as a hospital ship in the event of war) in October and was off Ceylon when the invasion took place. Perhaps, given the Prince's explosive temperament and the likelihood that on this question he would have shared his uncle Mountbatten's opinions, it was just as well that he was off the stage.

The British Cabinet's reaction was to blame not themselves, the French, the Israelis or the military but the Americans. At the Paris Embassy Harold Macmillan, then Chancellor of the Exchequer in Eden's Government and soon to replace him as Prime Minister, held forth after dinner. 'He is at one time full of optimism about the success of the famous attack,' the Ambassadress, Lady Gladwyn, recorded in her journal on 11 December 1956, 'and then at another moment will talk endlessly in a sort of intellectual pessimism – the end of the white man, the end of Europe, the end of the Commonwealth and Empire, and the fault of the Americans, who don't care.' 'Over port and brandy', as she put it, the next night Macmillan again held forth. This time, 'The great thing was to be rich as we were in the nineteenth century . . . why should we not give up Singapore, sell the Colonies, sell the West Indies too, to America, and just sit back and be rich?'[10] Ironically, the British Embassy was so cold – owing to fuel rationing in the wake of Suez – that Selwyn Lloyd, who had played a principal part in the signing of the Sèvres Protocol, complained and retired to bed ill.

The Suez failure represented a huge dent in the national image and to the British pride nurtured by the Second World War. It brought home that the support of America had won us the war, that American opposition to Suez had crushed it. A survey revealed the feelings of a working-class family, husband, wife and brother-in-law, all aged under thirty: 'They were very concerned about the state of England – what had happened to all her power? England had in the past done so much for backward countries & now they wanted nothing to do with her . . .' Eden himself, in a memorandum 'on the lessons of Suez' written on his return from convalescence in Jamaica, recognized this – too late: 'We had by our action reduced ourselves from a first-class to a third-class power. We revealed our weakness by stopping; and we threw away the moral position on which our world status depended.'

9.   Young Queen

Early in October 1957, the Queen and Prince Philip were in the United States to celebrate the 350th anniversary celebrations of the State of Virginia, the underlying political objective of the visit being to rekindle Anglo-American relations damaged by Suez. Unexpectedly the Soviet Union fuelled the rapprochement. The 4th of October 1957 was America's 'Sputnik Moment', when the Russians perturbed the Western world and astounded the non-aligned nations by launching the first artificial earth satellite into space. The satellite, named *Sputnik*, circled the earth in the astonishingly short time of ninety-five minutes, causing the American scientific and military establishments acute embarrassment. 'I do hope our visit will be of value between the two countries,' the Queen had written to Eden before she left, ' – there does seem to be a much closer feeling between the US and ourselves, especially since the Russian satellite has come to shake everyone about their views on Russian scientific progress!'[1]

She was having a huge personal success, with American opinion openly praising her youth, energy and glamour, contrasting her position as Head of State with that of the ageing President Eisenhower. Just at this triumphant moment, however, waves of criticism from Britain, which had been building since the beginning of the year, reached American shores. The New York *Saturday Evening Post* reprinted an article by the well-known BBC broadcaster and editor of *Punch*, Malcolm Muggeridge, attacking the monarchy as out of touch and socially divisive. 'Does England Really Need a Queen?' the headline ran. He also criticized the Queen as 'dowdy, frumpish and banal'.

The article had originally been published in 1955 but at the time few people had taken any notice; Britain had been in confident mood and there was little anxiety about the national decline that became so evident after Suez. The cause of the disaster seemed to lie in outdated Establishment attitudes orchestrated by men living in a past which was no longer relevant. Newsreel pictures of the time looked and sounded as if they might have been recorded in the 1930s; plummy-voiced commentators talked about 'our men' and 'giving Nasser a lesson'. The Queen, whose image at the Coronation had been linked to the traditional splendours of Britain's historic past, was bound to suffer when Suez revealed that the emperor had no clothes. The monarchy had become the symbol of the nation; in traumatized post-Suez Britain the question was bound to be raised whether that symbol was the right one. The manner of Macmillan's appointment and the outcome of the Margaret/Townsend affair, when the Queen's sister had been seen as a victim of outdated attitudes, reinforced the impression of a nation ruled by a traditional class in its own interests, for which the monarchy was a gilded front.

The Queen, Muggeridge wrote, was at the apex of a social pyramid of snobbishness which was not only out of date in the contemporary world but actively harmful. 'If . . . as I consider . . . such a social set-up is obsolete and disadvantageous in the contemporary world, then the Monarchy is to that extent undesirable,' he had written. Earlier that year, similar criticism of the Queen as representative of outdated snobbery by the young John Grigg, 2nd Baron Altrincham, had caused a storm in Britain, and the thirty-three-year-old peer had been slapped in the face on the steps of the BBC by an enraged British Empire Loyalist. Altrincham called the Queen's Court 'tweedy' and her Household an unimaginative 'second-rate lot', but the public took exception to what was interpreted as personal attacks on the Queen, particularly in her public speeches, when he criticized her high girlish voice, cut-glass accent, and absolute lack of interesting content. Britain, he said, seemed to be compensating for loss of power in the world by lapsing into a state of collective make-believe and British attitudes to the monarchy into unhealthy adulation akin to Japanese emperor-worship. The playwright John Osborne, famous after the success of his play *Look Back in Anger* as the first of the Angry Young Men, weighed in with a denunciation of the monarchy – 'the Royal symbol' as 'a gold filling in a mouth full of decay'.

Muggeridge, Altrincham and Osborne represented the revolt of the intellectuals against the status quo; they were the harbingers of the future but in no way the representatives of the present. Britain was still a deeply and simply patriotic country. Neither the mainstream Conservative nor Labour politicians were interested in attacking the Queen or the monarchy. Among the letters of support that the Queen received was one from twelve 'Teddy Boys', the epitome of young working-class revolt, in Edwardian suits, thick crêpe-soled shoes, and 'mullet' haircuts with Elvis Presley quiffs, notorious for fighting with flick knives and for rocking in the aisles of cinemas to Bill Haley and the Comets in *Rock Around the Clock*.

A world away from the 'Teds', the 'debs' represented everything that Altrincham and Muggeridge despised. Since the days of Queen Victoria, the daughters of aristocratic families had been 'presented' at Court as 'debutantes' once they reached the age of seventeen, their formal curtsey to the Queen signifying that they were ready to 'come out', i.e. to take part in the social season and, if successful, receive offers of marriage from socially and financially desirable men. In those still relatively unliberated days, the majority of upper-class girls of seventeen were still virgins; it was, as Jessica Mitford put it, 'the specific, upper-class version of the puberty rite'. Presentation ceremonies had been suspended during the war years and revived in 1947. The Queen at her Coronation had been attended only by the *crème de la crème* of the aristocracy, six titled daughters of the United Kingdom's senior peers, but things were changing, not necessarily, in the Court's view, for the better. With or without Lord Altrincham, the debutante presentation was devalued in the view of society experts like Betty Kenward, the formidable columnist of *Tatler* magazine, the debs' bible. 'More and more people were trying to buy their way in,' she wrote in 1957. Princess Margaret typically put it more crudely: 'every tart in London was getting in'. 'Presentation acquired an important role in the regulation of society in Britain,' Fiona MacCarthy, herself a former debutante, wrote in her definitive book on the subject. 'It became a kind of bulwark. Defending the inner circle and securing the channels to power, influence and wealth . . . the curtseyers were in, the non-curtseyers excluded from the royal enclosures, members' tents and other well-defended spaces in which the well-bred were separated from the riff-raff.'[2]

1958 was the last year of the debs. 'We had wanted to end it in 1957,' a royal friend told the author, 'but we put it off because we didn't want to be seen to be falling in with Lord Altrincham.' Prince Philip, the modernizer, had longed to end the parade but he was there in March 1958, seated on a throne beside the Queen, over three days when 1,400 girls in batches of between 400 and 500 curtseyed to them, dressed alike in three-quarter-length silk dresses, petal-feathered hats and above-elbow gloves. 'The curtsey itself was part of the mystique. It was a question of leg-lock: left knee locked behind the right knee, allowing a graceful slow descent with head erect, hands by your side. Avoidance of the wobble, definitely frowned upon, relied on exact placing of the knees and feet. The technique had been passed down through generations of debutantes who learned it at Madame Vacani's School of Dancing at 159 Brompton Road in Knightsbridge, a few blocks down from Harrods.' Madame Vacani, 'a squeaky-voiced, effusive, highly-powered tiny lady' who was given to telling her prospective debutante pupils, 'Now, darlings, throw out your little chests and burst your little dresses,' had taught the Queen, Princess Margaret and most of their contemporaries to dance.[3]

Socially and sexually Britain had not changed a great deal for decades. In June 1955 Ruth Ellis, a twenty-eight-year-old 'peroxide' blonde, a club hostess, sometime prostitute and single mother of two, had been sentenced to death for the shooting of her abusive, two-timing lover outside the Magdala pub in Hampstead on Easter Sunday, after he had previously hit her so hard in the stomach that she had a miscarriage. She was hanged in Holloway prison on 23 July, an echo of the public execution of Thomas Hardy's heroine in *Tess of the Durbervilles*. This time it was within the prison walls but nonetheless a large crowd, thousands strong, surged behind a massive police cordon outside Holloway as she died. 'I have been tormented for a week,' the celebrated visiting crime novelist Raymond Chandler wrote on the last day of June, 'at the idea that a highly civilized people should put a rope round the neck of Ruth Ellis and drop her through a trap and break her neck. This was a crime of passion under considerable provocation. No other country in the world would hang this woman.' Things had not much changed since Hardy's day, as a contemporary diarist noted: 'I feel sure that if executions were in public there would be as great crowds today as ever there were.'[4]

The debutante presentation parties vanished into history, a victory for Prince Philip's modernizing initiatives. In May 1956 he had won a victory with another of his more successful innovative ideas: the inauguration of a new tradition of Buckingham Palace lunches for distinguished guests from all professions, trades and vocations. The Palace seemed to be opening up to the people: at Christmas 1957 the Queen made her first televised Christmas broadcast. Prince Philip wrote the final draft of her speech, which the monarch delivered with more directness than usual. Harold Nicolson wrote that the Queen came across 'with a vigour unknown in pre-Altrincham days'. She faced down her critics as 'unthinking people . . . [who] carelessly throw away ageless ideals as if they were old and outworn machinery'. She went on: 'We need the kind of courage that can withstand the corruption of the cynics so that we can show the world that we're not afraid of the future . . . In the old days the monarch led his soldiers on to the battlefield. I cannot lead you into battle, I do not give you laws or administer justice, but I can do something else – I can give you my heart and my devotion to these old islands and to all the peoples of our brotherhood of nations.' The novelty of seeing the Queen performing the annual electronic ritual, instead of just hearing her, united the nation on Christmas afternoon: the 3 p.m. broadcast was seen by 16.5 million people, producing the largest amount of press cuttings since the Coronation. In private she suffered almost as much from nerves as her father had, writing to a friend that the broadcast had ruined the family Christmas.

The next year she starred again in the first live televising of the State Opening of Parliament, on 28 October. The *Manchester Guardian* sneered that the ceremony had little relevance to democracy: 'The Imperial State Crown, the Cap of Maintenance, the Sword of State, the Heralds, the Lord Great Chamberlain and the Earl Marshal make up a beautiful charade, but if all were swept away tomorrow it would make not the slightest difference to the government of the country. They are harmless relics – harmless . . . so long as nobody mistakes them for anything significant . . . Abroad, Britain's reputation as an old curiosity shop will be enhanced and our tourist earnings may benefit.' Twelve million British subjects watched and nine other European countries were treated to the spectacle.

Prince Philip, dressed in the uniform of an Admiral of the Fleet, was seen seated on his 'throne' on the Queen's left but, symbolically, a step down. His six-month tour away from her had created a storm of gossip about a rift in the royal marriage: 'No household in the world is more subject to the hot breath of gossip than Britain's House of Windsor,' *Time* magazine reported on 18 February 1957, as the Queen prepared to fly to Lisbon to meet her husband on his way home in *Britannia*. 'Last week the mongering winds were howling louder around Buckingham Palace than they had since the day of Wallis Warfield Simpson and Edward VIII.' The immediate source of the rumours was the news that Lieutenant Commander Michael 'Mike' Parker, Prince Philip's 'wartime shipmate, good friend and

Private Secretary', had left the Prince and his job at Gibraltar. Parker, as the Palace had known for six months, was being divorced by his wife Eileen, and his departure appeared as if he was being sacrificed to protect the Prince from rumours about his private life. 'Why,' the *Daily Express* demanded, with echoes of the Townsend affair, 'should a broken marriage be a disqualification for royal service? Until a few weeks ago the First Minister of the Queen [Anthony Eden] . . . had been through the divorce courts.' 'Too much Thursdaying,' *Time* captioned a photograph of a bearded Prince and Parker in West Africa, a reference to an all-male dinner club which the press used as a cover word for all sorts of stag and not-so-stag behaviour.

That same month it was announced that the Queen was to create Prince Philip a Prince of the United Kingdom, as Macmillan put it in Cabinet 'in recognition of the great services which HRH has provided to the country and of his unique contribution to the life of the Commonwealth, culminating in the tour which has just concluded'. What the Prime Minister did not say but was almost certainly his intention was that this should knock on the head all the rumours about rifts in the royal marriage by making the Queen be seen publicly rewarding her husband for his services. As if to underline her private feelings, the Queen flew out to Lisbon to greet her husband under the eyes of the world's press. 'After 124 days and twenty-four hours they are TOGETHER AGAIN.' They were 'together again' on a hugely successful visit to Paris in April, the crowds outside the Opéra pressing so close that the mounted guards had to use drawn swords to push them back, while at the Louvre many of the 2,000 distinguished guests resorted to clambering on to the pedestals of statues to get a better view of the couple.

The Queen, it seemed, had trumped Altrincham. When six years later he renounced his peerage and tried to find a Tory seat, honourable and intelligent though he was, he failed to do so. Attacking the Queen was not on the agenda for either of the major parties and books were published extolling the family image that George VI and Queen Elizabeth had worked so hard to establish. Arundel Herald Extraordinary, the journalist Dermot Morrah, a favourite writer with the Palace, published *The Queen at Work* (1958), arguing that the importance of the monarch should lie 'not at all in what she does, but entirely in what she is'. Rejecting Altrincham's idea that the Queen should actively take moral leadership, Morrah argued that her passive role as national icon and mother of an exemplary family was the important one, 'not at all what she does but . . . what she is'. Queen Victoria would not have recognized this royal job description, indeed would have actively rejected it, but her great-great-granddaughter, while privately fascinated by politics and aware through her conscientious and interested reading of State papers and weekly briefings by her Prime Ministers, was, politically, the first passive sovereign. Political historians have criticized her for not using her prerogative and perhaps failing to 'advise counsel and warn' her Ministers, but the Queen saw herself as the repository for confidences from Prime Ministers of Britain and the Commonwealth, a sympathetic informed ear rather than an active ingredient. Dorothy Laird, another favoured author, also played on the family theme but with a note of warning: 'so much has a happy family life become identified with the British Royal Family that it is doubtful whether a sovereign could maintain his sovereignty were this shattered . . .'

'CROWN AND COMMONWEALTH: Canada's Queen on tour' was the headline in June 1959 on the cover of *Time*, featuring the thirty-three-year-old Queen in regal mode, standing on the staircase at Buckingham Palace, in strapless satin with the Order of the Garter, drop pearl and diamond tiara, diamond and pearl necklace and bracelet, her jewels and commanding air once more reminiscent of a young Victoria. The cover story stressed the importance of the Commonwealth in replacing Empire: 'Thus it is not the death groans of Empire but the birth cries of Commonwealth that are heard round the world,' the magazine wrote. 'They were heard a few weeks ago when Singapore, once proud bastion of Empire, became an autonomous state. They will be heard again in a year or two when Nigeria and Rhodesia, Britain's largest African possessions, assume full freedom. The process is continuous; the Commonwealth has many potential members. And if the 19th century sun never set on the Empire, the 20th century satellites have a Commonwealth country always in view.' The magazine followed up with a six-page essay on the Commonwealth, pointing out the ties created by trade and education: Ceylon's [now Sri Lanka] Prime Minister, Solomon Bandaranaike, was at Oxford with Anthony Eden; India's Prime Minister, Jawaharlal Nehru, and the King of Buganda went to Cambridge; the leader of Pakistan, General Mohammed Ayub Khan, trained at Sandhurst, Britain's military academy, as did the Indian Army Chief of Staff. Other political leaders, such as Kwame Nkrumah (London School of Economics) and Singapore's Lee Kuan Yew (Cambridge), completed their higher education in Britain. At the time of writing (June 1959), British universities had some 18,000 Commonwealth students and London was still the mecca for Commonwealth leaders.

The Queen's Canada tour of 1959 – in her constitutional role as Queen of Canada – was intended not only to cement that role in an increasingly nationalistic Canada (for the first time she appointed a French Canadian to be her Governor-General), but as a symbol of the Commonwealth. The global Cold War against Communism was, as ever, the unspoken backdrop. When President Eisenhower joined the Queen and the Prime Minister of Canada, John Diefenbaker, on board *Britannia* for the dedication of the St Lawrence Seaway, linking the US–Canadian Great Lakes with the Atlantic, there were strong echoes of their most important military and political alliance, NATO (North Atlantic Treaty Organization). Still on *Britannia*, she and Prince Philip made an official visit to Chicago, 'only 14 hours but the most lavish 14 hours of pageantry in the city's history'. More than a million Chicagoans lined the Lake

Michigan shore to watch the royal yacht arrive, escorted by seven warships and saluted by more than 500 smaller craft including two Chinese junks; US Air Force and Navy jets thundered across the sky and 'aerial torpedoes exploded parachutes carrying the Stars and Stripes and the Union Jack'. The day ended with a banquet – with gold tablecloths, gold service, 50,000 roses – given by Mayor Richard Daley. In a six-week tour the Queen and Prince had travelled 15,000 miles and seen and been seen by more Canadians than any other reigning sovereigns before flying home, as they had arrived, in a Comet, Britain's first jet airliner, soon to be as disastrously extinct as the once flourishing British aircraft industry. Not everyone had welcomed her – a CBC (Canadian Broadcasting Corporation) interviewer, described as 'Canada's prettiest TV star', appearing for an interview on NBC in New York, declared that 'like most Canadians, I'm indifferent to the visit of the Queen', but, returning home after furious viewers jammed CBC's telephones with protests, she announced that she was taking indefinite leave of absence because of the 'ferocity' of the criticism.

The Queen continued to represent the ideal family: while in Canada she had been obliged to rest for two days at Whitehorse in the Yukon; she was pregnant, although only her immediate entourage and Heads of State knew of it and it was not announced until she reached home in August. In June Martin Charteris had been despatched on a special mission to Accra to tell Dr Kwame Nkrumah, President and virtual dictator of Ghana, a notoriously tricky personage, that she was expecting a baby and would therefore have to cancel her visit to Ghana later on in the year. At Balmoral in August everyone celebrated; the royal couple seemed exceptionally happy together and there were no more rumours of rifts. According to insider sources, the Queen had been keen to try for another baby since her husband's return, although he, apparently, thought two children were enough. People were taken by surprise – Prince Charles was now eleven years old, Princess Anne nearly ten. President Eisenhower, who had been staying at Balmoral, wrote in his thank-you letter that he and his wife were 'delighted about the coming "event", as is everyone in your kingdom'. 'What a sentimental hold the monarchy has over the middle classes!' Harold Nicolson wrote. 'All the solicitors, actors and publishers at the Garrick Club were beaming, as if they had acquired some personal gift.'

As a further sign of the Queen's desire to please her husband, she put forward once again the idea that Prince Philip should have his name connected with his children, the suggestion that had been so decisively rejected by Queen Mary and Churchill in 1952. The Prime Minister, absent in Africa, was informed by R. A. 'Rab' Butler, the deputy premier, that the Queen had 'absolutely set her heart' on a change. A compromise was reached whereby the name of the royal house would remain 'Windsor' but those descendants of the Queen and Prince Philip who had been de-royalized, i.e. no longer called themselves 'Royal Highness', should use the surname 'Mountbatten-Windsor'. It was noted, however, that when HRH Princess Anne married Captain Phillips in 1973, her name appeared on the marriage register as 'Mountbatten-Windsor'. The latest addition to the House of Windsor, Prince Andrew, born on 19 February 1960, was named after his paternal grandfather, Prince Andrew of Greece, another gesture by the Queen to please her husband.

Nine days after Prince Andrew's birth the engagement was announced of HRH Princess Margaret to Antony Armstrong-Jones. The engagement of a controversial but undeniably royal princess to a photographer presaged the social upheaval of the 1960s; it was the perfect beginning to a decade when talent mixed with aristocracy, and rock stars, fashion designers and photographers outshone earls. Armstrong-Jones, known to his friends as 'Tony', was very far from being an Establishment figure. He, unlike later stars like Bailey, had been to Eton and Cambridge, but he was essentially a bohemian and it was that side of him which, apart from his highly-sexed nature, appealed to Princess Margaret. He had no royal connections whatever; his father, Ronald Armstrong-Jones, was a Welsh barrister, the son of a surgeon, who owned, through his mother, a small Welsh estate, Plas Dinas. His mother, Anne Messel, was the daughter of a family of brilliant stockbrokers of German-Jewish descent, who owned a celebrated garden, Nymans in Sussex. Being a photographer in 1960 was considered quite beyond the pale of royal society. Social doyenne Betty Kenward certainly thought so: when politely addressed by Armstrong-Jones she hissed back, 'Don't ever dare speak to me! I *never* speak to photographers.' Courtiers enjoyed relating the story of how the Countess of Pembroke had sent Tony to eat with the servants when he came to photograph her great house at Wilton. Noël Coward, an outstanding snob, was horrified by the engagement. Indeed some of Tony's more intelligent friends who knew both of them foresaw disaster. The Royal Family, however, far less snobbish in their way than their Households were, welcomed him, and the couple themselves were obviously in love.

The wedding of Princess Margaret and Antony Armstrong-Jones was held at Westminster Abbey on 6 May 1960. It was the first great royal spectacular since the Coronation, and was partly designed by the bridegroom himself. Under his instruction the royal couturier, Norman Hartnell, produced a wedding dress of superb simplicity, and a tulle veil ordered by him in Paris fell in clouds from the magnificent Poltimore tiara, bought for the Princess at auction. She herself looked the part of a fairy-tale princess as she was driven to Westminster Abbey in a glass coach. The press sniped about the behaviour of some of Armstrong-Jones's unconventional friends, but the public indulged in one of its periodic orgies of mass participation in and identification with royal events. The sun shone, the bride was beautiful; only the gender roles of the old fairy tale had been reversed, with the bridegroom in the Cinderella part, symbolically connecting the old traditional Royal Family with the new talented popular generation to come.

10. Evening's Empire

'We stand today at the edge of a New Frontier – the frontier of the 1960s – a frontier of unknown opportunities and perils . . .' John Fitzgerald Kennedy declared in a speech in Los Angeles on his 1960 presidential campaign trail. It was indeed a new world for the Queen, as it was for the Commonwealth and Empire, the final disintegration of the latter impelled by the forces of nationalism and the former by the magnetic pull of the newly created European Common Market, established by the Treaty of Rome in 1957.

Early in the New Year of 1960, Harold Macmillan embarked on a lightning tour of southern Africa; in Cape Town towards the end of his visit, speaking to both houses of the white majority Nationalist Parliament, he warned that 'the wind of change is blowing through this continent . . . whether we like it or not, this growth of national consciousness is a political fact'. In return, Prime Minister Verwoerd riposted that South Africa, after a referendum, would certainly become a republic and that there would no longer be a place for the British Queen. The following year South Africa did indeed become a republic and left the Commonwealth. Ghana had gained its independence in 1957; Nigeria would do so in 1960. In Kenya the British Government accepted the principle of black majority rule. Sierra Leone and British Somaliland gained independence that year. On his return from Africa, Macmillan had had an audience with the Queen on 16 February, three days before the birth of Prince Andrew; as always, his biographer wrote, 'he found the monarch well briefed on all the issues'.

The process of transforming Empire into Commonwealth increased the attraction for Britain of joining the European Common Market, but this would prove to be far harder to achieve. The principal obstacle to Britain joining was Churchill's old enemy/ ally General Charles de Gaulle, now President and architect of France's Fifth Republic. De Gaulle feared that Britain's close links with the United States and the Commonwealth would make her a half-hearted member of any European association and he had the power to veto her membership.

The Queen was deployed to soften up de Gaulle's suspicion of the British, and in April he arrived in London for a three-day State visit of 'maximum splendour', in the hope of winning him over. De Gaulle had agreeable wartime memories of her father and mother: at the Buckingham Palace banquet he spoke of the 'most precious encouragements' he had received from the Royal Family. 'Where else, Madame, better than in your presence could I bear witness to my gratitude?' he asked rhetorically, as great Crosses of Lorraine blazed in fireworks outside. The General, not an easy man to win over, was favourably impressed with the Queen. She was, he wrote, 'well-informed about everything [and] that her judgements, on people and events, were as clear-cut as they were thoughtful, that no one was more preoccupied by the cares and problems of our storm-tossed age'. Not even the Queen's knowledge and charm, nor the State dinner at Buckingham Palace, nor a gala night at the Royal Opera House decorated with 25,000 carnations to a design by Cecil Beaton, however, persuaded the French President of British suitability to join the European alliance. As far as he was concerned, the three Great Powers were France, Russia and the United States; as if to underline his independence from NATO, earlier that year France had exploded its own bomb in the Sahara.

The Queen was never anti-European but she was determined to fulfil the vow of dedication to the Commonwealth that she had sworn on her eighteenth birthday in South Africa. The Macmillan Government was eager to see her play her unique part in foreign relations: in the background there was always the Cold War looming; the continuing crisis over Berlin, 1948–61; the failed summit in Paris in May 1960, when Khrushchev had walked out in well-orchestrated protest after the American U-2 spy plane had been shot down over the Urals and its pilot, Gary Powers, captured; Khrushchev's uninhibited bad behaviour at the United Nations, when he had banged his shoe on the desk and Macmillan had emphatically asked for a translation. Neutral countries had to be kept on side by the West, and who better to do it than the non-political figure of the Queen? Moreover, the new Commonwealth countries were eager to have the endorsement of a world celebrity like the Queen paying them a State visit, and invitations rained in on London.

Less than a year after the birth of Prince Andrew, at the end of January 1961, the Queen and Prince Philip embarked on a five-week tour of India and Pakistan via Cyprus and Iran. In Cyprus (independent since 1959) they drank orange juice with Archbishop Makarios, now President, whom Her Majesty's Government had exiled to the Seychelles in 1956, and in Iran they visited the Shah at his personal invitation. Seeing India, the former 'Jewel in the Crown' of Empire, which her father had so much wanted to visit, and where her grandfather and grandmother had held their splendid Durbar in 1912, meant a great deal to the Queen. She had been invited as Queen of the United Kingdom, not as Head of the Commonwealth, as the latter title would have implied that she still had authority over the country. Fears that the visit of the Queen, daughter of the last King-Emperor, and Prince Philip, nephew of the last Viceroy, might lead to anti-imperialist/colonialist demonstrations proved unfounded; 'the mood was to revel, forgive and forget'. In New Delhi more than a million Indians turned out to welcome the Queen 'respectfully and affectionately'. At the Republic Day parade, Lancers of the 61st Cavalry 'pranced past on spirited horses', the 13th Grenadiers Corps 'galumphed' past, and troops of elephants raised their trunks in salute. The Queen laid a wreath of 500 white roses at the shrine of Mohandas Gandhi; the incumbent President, Rajendra Prasad, tactfully recalled that India's relationship with the United Kingdom 'is a part of our history of the past

200 years. The British impact on India has in many ways been an abiding one.'

Otherwise the Queen saw the usual tourist sights: a moonlight visit to the Taj Mahal, lunch at the Lake Palace of Udaipur, a visit to the burning ghats of Benares. One other royal treat involved a far more controversial (in London if not in India) pastime – a tiger shoot organized by the Maharajah of Jaipur with, as was customary, live goats as lures. On the second day Prince Philip despatched a magnificent nine foot eight inch tiger with a single shot. In London the *Daily Mirror* (scornfully described as 'professionally plebeian' by *Time* magazine) parodied the poet William Blake's famous lines:

> Tiger, Tiger, burning bright
> In the forests of the night,
> Tell me, was it just a fluke
> You got potted by the Duke?

Indian reaction, unmoved by the tiger's fate, was mainly one of irritation at Anglo-Saxon sentimentality.

The Queen's next visit, her first to Ghana, in November 1961, was far more controversial – and dangerous. Africa was rapidly becoming the cockpit of the Cold War, with the West and the Soviet Union competing for influence over the newly independent African states. Kwame Nkrumah, now dictator of Ghana, President of a one-party state, had recently visited Moscow and had returned in an anti-Western mood, sacking Western advisers and throwing opponents into jail. There were fears for the Queen's safety: Special Branch was sent out and the Commonwealth Secretary of State, Duncan Sandys, made a preliminary visit to test the atmosphere. British liberal opinion was against the Queen's going to visit an anti-democratic regime, while the Government was genuinely concerned that the Queen might be killed or injured by an assassination attempt when she was with Nkrumah. If the Queen was advised by the Government to cancel plans because of the deteriorating political situation in Africa, Macmillan feared that Ghana would leave the Commonwealth, offering another vacuum for the Russians to fill. While Macmillan dithered, the Queen, however, held out: she had given her promise to go and go she would. As Macmillan wrote in his diary: 'The Queen has been absolutely determined all through. She is grateful for MPs' and Press concerns about her safety, but she is impatient of the attitude towards her to treat her as a *woman* . . . She has great faith in the work she can do in the Commonwealth especially . . .'[1]

In the event, this first-ever visit to Ghana by a British sovereign was a great success. The Government-directed local press called it 'Our Greatest Hour' and a 'fascinating change in the current relations between Britain, the Commonwealth and Ghana', 'a bridge over which the traffic of the future will pass towards the building of a new and prosperous world'. The neo-Marxist *Evening News* wrote that all Ghana had been moved by this 'most modest, lovable of sovereigns', calling her 'the world's greatest Socialist Monarch in history'. The British press, however, according to the Acting High Commissioner there, did their best to stir up trouble 'in their customary surly manner', abusing Nkrumah and reporting scare stories of bomb plots and plans to attach a limpet mine to *Britannia*, enraging the Ghanaian Government to the extent that the correspondents of the *Daily Mail* and the *Daily Express* were prevented from leaving the country and had to be unwillingly bailed out by the High Commissioner. He singled out the *Daily Telegraph* and, as usual, the Beaverbrook-owned *Express* for their racist tone: '. . . no doubt out to prove that when black men govern themselves they make a mess of things, [they] remained incorrigible to the end'. 'We pay a high price for a free Press,' he added, 'and it is an appalling thought that, because a small group of British journalists are determined to abuse the host Government, the good effects of a Royal Tour which has turned out to be an undisputed popular success, may be . . . undermined.'[2] The Queen had endeavoured to neutralize the situation in a speech: 'Let us always recognize that the views of other members of the family, even if they are not the same as our own, nevertheless are genuinely and sincerely held,' she said. Such was certainly not the case in apartheid South Africa, declared a republic in an all-white election in May, where Nationalist opinion was outraged by photographs of the Queen dancing with Nkrumah: the newspaper *Die Oosterlig* complained of the 'honoured head of the once mighty British Empire dancing with black natives of pagan Africa'.

Macmillan, however, did not share the Queen's passion for the Commonwealth. In the summer of 1961 the Government had decided to apply for membership of the EEC and, as the Queen was still abroad, in November de Gaulle and his wife arrived at Macmillan's country home, Birch Grove, for a sticky visit, in the course of which a *Daily Mail* journalist was bitten by a police alsatian. Macmillan saw Britain as the link between Europe and the United States, and was in the process of an assiduous courtship of the new President John F. Kennedy (he was to cross the Atlantic to meet JFK no fewer than seven times during Kennedy's three-year Presidency). When the Commonwealth Prime Ministers arrived for their conference in London in September 1962, Macmillan was left in no doubt of their bitterness at Britain's betrayal of old friendships, and neither undoubtedly was the Queen, who met with them all singly. Sir Robert Menzies, the Australian Prime Minister and an old friend, would have told her exactly what the Commonwealth feeling was. Even before the conference, the Queen had expressed herself as 'worried about Commonwealth feeling' to Macmillan in his weekly audience.

In the end, in January 1963, de Gaulle issued his famous 'Non' to British entry, leaving Macmillan devastated. The Queen's reaction is unrecorded, but when she and Prince Philip toured Australia and New Zealand later that month, they discovered for themselves the difference Britain's European approaches had made to feeling in the 'old' Commonwealth. The crowds were noticeably less overpowering in numbers and enthusiasm than they had been on the

post-Coronation tour just under ten years before. Some of this
could be attributed to familiarity, as television spread the royal
image round the world, but there was also an undercurrent of
doubt as to what Britain – and the Queen – now represented.

And that summer of 1961 a new star had emerged on the world
horizon – Jacqueline Kennedy. Since his inauguration in January, John F. Kennedy had endured a brutal introduction to the
Presidency: the Bay of Pigs disaster in Cuba, when a mismanaged
invasion by Cuban exiles backed by American agencies had ended
in failure, then a difficult summit with de Gaulle in Paris and a
bruising encounter with Khrushchev in Vienna. Jackie, on the other
hand, had conquered Paris with her glamour, chic and fluent French,
to the degree that Jack Kennedy publicly described himself as 'the
man who accompanied Jacqueline Kennedy to Paris'. The Kennedys'
visit to London on 4 June was billed as a private occasion for the
christening of Jackie's sister's new baby, in order to avoid putting
de Gaulle's nose further out of joint – suspicious as he was of Britain's closeness to the US, a relationship which Macmillan had done
everything in his power to foster.

The Queen gave a dinner at Buckingham Palace in the Kennedys'
honour. True to family custom and her innate horror of divorce,
she hesitated about inviting Prince and Princess Radziwill, Jackie's
sister and brother-in-law, with whom the Kennedys were staying.
As Macmillan put it:

> After much hesitation the Queen waived her rule about divorce.
> Prince and Princess Radzinski [as Macmillan persisted in calling
> the Radziwills] were invited, although they had two or three part-
> ners apiece to date. She was very unwilling to do this, or to put
> their names in the Court Circular. I think had the Kennedys been
> staying at the American Embassy, I could have advised the Queen
> to omit the Radzinskis. But since the President and Mrs K. were
> actually staying with the Prince and Princess, it seemed impossible
> to do so.[3]

According to Gore Vidal, Jackie's stepbrother by marriage, Jackie was aware of the proposed Palace veto. The Kennedys had been asked beforehand by the Palace whom they would like to be invited. Jackie proposed the Radziwills, Princess Margaret (whom she wanted to meet) and Princess Marina of Kent, whom Jack remembered from his father Joe's days at the London Embassy. The Palace had apparently intimated that the Radziwills, as divorcees, could not be invited, then backed down. 'Anyway,' Jackie joked, 'the Queen had her revenge. No Margaret, no Marina, no one except every Commonwealth minister of agriculture they could find.'[4] (This was unfair, since Macmillan had seen to it that Kennedy friends like the Ormsby Gores and Jack's sister Eunice were present.)

The Queen and Jackie had nothing in common except horses. Again according to Vidal's version of what Jackie told him, she found the Queen 'pretty heavy-going' and said that 'the Queen was human only once'. Jackie had been telling the Queen about the Kennedy State visit to Canada and the rigours of being on view at all hours: 'The Queen looked rather conspiratorial and said, "One gets crafty after a while and learns how to save oneself." Then she said, "You like pictures?" And she marched Jackie down a long gallery, stopping at a Van Dyck to say, "That's a good horse." '[5] There was more horse conversation between the two women in March 1962, when the Queen invited Jackie, en route home from Pakistan and India, to lunch at Buckingham Palace. 'It was a great pleasure to meet Mrs Kennedy again . . .' the Queen wrote to the President in May. 'I hope her Pakistan horse will be a success – please tell her that mine became very excited by jumping with the children's ponies in the holidays, so I hope hers will be calmer!'

The letter, informal but nonetheless Head of State to Head of State, was written as a result of Macmillan's prompting on his return from yet another visit to Kennedy in pursuit of warm personal as well as political relationships with JFK. He had deliberately made use of his own aristocratic connections in his relationship with Kennedy. Macmillan's wife, Lady Dorothy, was the aunt of the Duke of Devonshire; JFK's favourite sister, Kathleen 'Kick' Kennedy, had married the Duke's elder brother, Hartington, and would have been Duchess herself had Hartington not been killed in Normandy in 1944. The Kennedys were close to the Devonshires and had attended Kick's funeral at Chatsworth after she died in a plane crash in France in 1948. David Ormsby-Gore (later Lord Harlech) had been a friend of Jack's in England before the war; at Kennedy's request Macmillan had appointed Ormsby-Gore Ambassador to Washington, where he and his wife Cissie were very much part of the White House circle. They had all been at the Queen's dinner for the Kennedys at Buckingham Palace in 1961, and the Queen, writing in what her biographer described as 'characteristic Windsor style – a blend of the hostess, the headmistress, the woman of affairs and the well-brought-up schoolgirl who knew how to write letters to order', emphasized the personal connection in a letter to the President after Macmillan's return from yet another visit to Kennedy in May 1962.

> It is a great comfort to know that you and he [Macmillan] are so close, and that you have confidence in each other's judgement and advice; I am sure that these meetings and this personal trust and understanding are of the greatest importance to both our peoples. I was also glad to hear from Mr Macmillan that my Ambassadors are getting on so well and that you are finding them useful. David [Ormsby-Gore] is, as you know, very highly thought of here, and so it is excellent news that he and Cissie are making their mark in Washington.[6]

Five months later Ormsby-Gore was constantly in the White House in an official as well as a private capacity, as the United States and the Soviet Union edged closer to a nuclear confrontation over Cuba. A spy plane out of Texas had detected eight missile sites being constructed in Cuba, and later, on 14 October, another spy plane photographed medium-range ballistic missiles there, capable of being armed with nuclear warheads and of reaching the United States. Two days later Kennedy told friends that the odds 'were somewhere near even' that a nuclear war would break out within the next ten years.

On 5 October 1962, just as the Cuba crisis was developing, the new James Bond film *Dr No* opened in London; the first produced by Saltzman and Broccoli and starring Sean Connery as Bond, its theme, described by a recent historian as 'serendipitously timely', featured as Bond's enemy a Soviet-controlled mastermind aiming to wreck the American test rocket programme from his Caribbean base. Shortly afterwards, John le Carré's spy novel *The Spy Who Came in from the Cold*, a far bleaker view of intelligence and betrayal against the background of the Cold War, was published. Interest in spies and particularly upper-class Cambridge-educated spies had been gaining ground since Guy Burgess and Donald Maclean had defected to Moscow in 1951, only officially admitted in 1955. From 1951 onwards there had been a hunt for the 'Third Man', who had tipped off Burgess and Maclean that the net was closing on them and had made arrangements for their defection. A partially intercepted Soviet transmission had alluded to a 'ring of five'. The Intelligence Services had been increasingly suspicious of Kim Philby, who as head of the Soviet Section of MI6 had been at the heart of Cold War intelligence. Stalin himself read the photographed documents and other information passed to him by the British agents, of whom Philby was the most important of the so-called 'Magnificent Five' (Philby, Anthony Blunt, Burgess, Maclean and John Cairncross). 'The problem for the professionally suspicious minds in the [Moscow] Centre was that it all seemed too good to be true. Taking their cue from the master conspiracy theorist in the Kremlin [Stalin], they eventually concluded that what appeared to be the best intelligence ever obtained from Britain by any intelligence service was at root a British plot. The Five, later acknowledged as the ablest group of agents in KGB history, were discredited in the eyes of the Centre leadership by their failure to produce evidence of a massive, non-existent British conspiracy against the Soviet Union . . .'[7] Philby was a prototype James Bond, 'cool, charming and calculating, a practised seducer and a very smooth operator indeed. Of the three men, he was the most effortless and effective spy, and the information he provided about British and American strategy during the Second World War and its aftermath was beyond price'. In January 1963, Philby, who had been latterly working as the *Observer*'s Middle Eastern correspondent, after interrogation by a British intelligence agent in Beirut where he was living, defected to Moscow, a fact only admitted on 1 July when Macmillan's Government was in crisis and the American press broke the story.

The Queen became aware of the identity of the 'Fourth Man' less than six months later: he was none other than Sir Anthony Blunt, Director of the Courtauld Institute of Art and Surveyor of the Queen's Pictures. Blunt had been a suspect for years. In January 1964, MI5 had finally got hold of real evidence that Blunt had been a Soviet spy from information from Michael Straight, a candidate for an arts job in the Kennedy Administration. In return for Blunt's confession to an MI5 interrogator in April 1964, it was agreed – apparently with previous consultation with Sir Michael Adeane, the Queen's Principal Private Secretary, that he should be given legal immunity and keep his Palace job to avoid alerting the KGB. The Queen, apparently, was told about Blunt; with her habitual discretion and for other, family, reasons she kept him on and said nothing of what she knew. Blunt, whom the Queen scarcely knew, had a history with the Royal Family which the Queen would regard as something that should be repaid by discretion.

Blunt's relationship with the Royal Family went back to George VI, for whom he had undertaken secret missions in the aftermath of the Second World War. He had been sent by the King early in 1945 as an assistant to Owen Morshead, the Royal Librarian, on a mission to retrieve the Kronberg Papers, correspondence between Queen Victoria and her daughter, the Empress Frederick of Germany, at the Friedrichshof, recently captured by General George Patton's Third Army in April 1945. Blunt and Morshead found the documents and deposited them in the Royal Archives at Windsor in August 1945. (In fact, although they took two crates of documents with them, they missed further correspondence between Victoria and her daughter, stolen by American staff at the castle and later returned after their discovery in Chicago.)

At about the same time a large cache of German Foreign Office documents was discovered buried in the Harz mountains, including a file, later known as the Marburg File, concerning the Duke of Windsor's relations with Nazi Germany. Despite Churchill's attempts to suppress them, these were later published in the volumes of the Captured German Documents in 1957. In December 1945 the King had entrusted Blunt with another German mission, to spirit out of Germany a number of valuable objects which belonged to the Princes of Hanover, including the diamond crown of Queen Charlotte, wife of George III, and an extremely valuable illuminated manuscript, the twelfth-century Gospel of Henry the Lion. (Both were returned to the Hanover family after the war; the MS was sold at Sotheby's in 1983 for £8 million). Two years later, in August 1947, the King had sent Blunt abroad again, this time to Haus Doorn, the Kaiser's former home, where he had died in exile. This third royal mission was probably prompted once again by the King's concern that documents might be found there relating to the Duke of Windsor, but there was nothing; all Blunt found were some family objects and copies of nineteenth-century letters. Not one document brought back from Germany by Blunt related to the Duke of Windsor, although in the later confusion following Blunt's unmasking there were rumours that Blunt had found incriminating material and used it to blackmail the Royal Family into covering up for him. Peter Wright, of 'Spycatcher' fame, raised the suspicion by stating that when he interrogated Blunt in 1967, the Palace put an embargo on any questions about his missions to Germany. There was nothing sinister about this to anyone familiar with Palace sensitivities: they wanted to keep the Royal Family out of a case which was not in fact relevant to them and which, further, might have raised awkward bureaucratic questions about the importation of the collections.

The Queen knew about the immunity deal from the beginning and was characteristically tight-lipped about spy stories, telling the Labour Minister Richard Crossman when he attempted to discuss recent Philby press revelations that 'she didn't read that kind of thing'. 'I was suddenly aware,' Crossman wrote, 'that this was not a subject which we ought to discuss.' The Queen barely saw Blunt, who was careful to keep out of the Palace, before his unmasking in 1979 by the investigative author Andrew Boyle, and Margaret Thatcher's reluctant admission of the truth to Parliament. Nevertheless, it was a piquant situation – she knew that he knew she knew but nothing was said – perfectly conveyed in Alan Bennett's 1988 play, *A Question of Attribution*. Blunt performed one more secret mission for the Royal Family in the summer of 1963; according to his biographer, Miranda Carter, he had, only a few months before his confession, negotiated to buy a series of drawings of Prince Philip from Stephen Ward, a key witness at the heart of the Profumo scandal, which was to contribute to the end of Macmillan's premiership.[8]

Ward himself was a social-climbing osteopath whose fatal non-professional speciality was discovering beautiful working-class girls and 'grooming' them to be high-class prostitutes for his upper-class friends. 'High Society' was his goal and was to be his downfall. Among the girls he 'discovered' was Christine Keeler, and her unwitting role in history was to cause the resignation of Macmillan's Secretary of State for War, John 'Jack' Profumo. Profumo, a rich, affable Anglo-Italian, was married to a well-known British actress, Valerie Hobson, who to her credit stood by her husband in the scandal. Profumo met Keeler at Cliveden, Lord Astor's riverside estate in Buckinghamshire, where Stephen Ward had a nearby cottage and a standing invitation to use the swimming pool. One hot weekend there in July 1961 the party round the swimming pool included Keeler and a couple of Ward's other girls, who had been driven down from London by Eugene Ivanov, an attaché and spy at the London Soviet Embassy, another friend of Ward. Profumo began a brief five-week affair with the nineteen-year-old Keeler, who described it as a 'very, very well-mannered screw of convenience'. Profumo broke off the relationship, such as it was, and the matter might have ended there but for Keeler's involvement with two West Indian drug-dealers and a shooting incident outside Ward's flat, where she and another of Ward's protegées, Mandy Rice-Davies, were staying.

Unfortunately for Profumo, who had written a letter to Keeler addressed 'Darling', ending their affair, Keeler sold her story to a Sunday newspaper in January 1963 and the secret, although as yet unpublished, was out among those in the know. In March, the trial of Johnny Edgcumbe, one of the West Indians involved, opened at the Old Bailey and Keeler fled to Spain with a friend of Ward's to avoid giving evidence. The affair was obliquely raised in the House of Commons by enemies of Profumo, who, approached by party grandees to tell them the truth, denied it and the following morning delivered a statement in the House of Commons in which he admitted knowing Ward, Ivanov and Keeler but denied any 'impropriety' in his relations with Keeler, effectively lying to Parliament. Unfortunately for Profumo – and Macmillan – the mixture of war minister, Soviet spy, lord and prostitute was too rich to be ignored, particularly by the Labour Opposition, led by Harold Wilson. The pressure on Profumo became intolerable, he confessed to his wife, Valerie Hobson, and on 4 June 1963 he resigned from the Government. Stephen Ward was put on trial for living off immoral earnings and committed suicide. Rumours circulated about Ward's orgies, attended by politicians wearing nothing but their socks. Prince Philip's name was – quite erroneously – mentioned because of his Thursday Club acquaintance with Ward (hence the sketches acquired by Blunt). The Denning Report on the Profumo scandal, issued in September, became an instant best-seller: although some of the evidence provided during the judge's investigations was apparently so disgusting that the lady typists were sent out of the room, it also definitively proved that there was no intelligence aspect to the affair.

What the whole episode seemed, however, to confirm was the public perception that Britain was ruled by a decadent and immoral class. In the ten years since the Coronation the social atmosphere in Britain had changed. In 1961 the satirical magazine *Private Eye* was published for the first time, subsequently making hay with the Profumo affair. More seriously, in the following year the *Observer* correspondent Anthony Sampson produced his *Anatomy of Britain*, which analysed the British ruling classes as the 'hereditary Establishment of interlocking families which still has an infectious social and political influence on the Conservative party, banking and many industries, has lost touch with the new worlds of science, industrial management and technology ... cherishes irrelevant aspects of the past and regards the activities of meritocrats and technocrats as a potential menace'. Britain, he said, had become 'astonishingly uncommercial', its people had lost their dynamic, were sunk in complacency, were far too snobbish and had carried on a pattern of relationships that was disappearing elsewhere in the world. 'Britain is stagnating in an old world of family connections and complacent assumptions of superiority, while across the Atlantic the Kennedy administration is inaugurating a new environment of professionalism, dynamism and efficiency.'[9] Sampson illustrated his point with a chart showing how the family connections of the Duke of Devonshire included the Prime Minister, the Attorney General, the Secretary for War, the owners of *The Times* and the *Observer*, the Ambassador to Washington and even President Kennedy. The connections of the Duke of Marlborough included the Foreign and Commonwealth Secretaries, the chairmen of Lazard, Guinness and Courtaulds, the owner of the *Daily Express* and the Deputy Governor of the Bank of England. Court circles abounded in Dukes and Earls; courtiers were descended from courtiers; the Queen's closest friends included Viscount Porchester, son of the Earl of Carnarvon, Hugh Euston, son of the Duke of Grafton, and 'Johnny' Dalkeith, son of the Duke of Buccleuch and Queensberry.

It was inevitable that the Court with its pomposities and cere-monial should become a target for the satirists. In March 1963 Ned Sherrin's ground-breaking TV programme *That Was The Week That Was* (otherwise known as *TW3*) signalled the changing mood at the BBC with a sketch entitled 'The Queen's Departure', which lampooned Richard Dimbleby's commentary when the Queen had set out for Australia a few weeks earlier. In the sketch, the royal barge sank while the band of the Royal Marines played the National Anthem. 'Perhaps the lip readers among you can make out what Prince Philip, Duke of Edinburgh, is saying to the cap-tain of the barge as she sinks,' ran the offending commentary. 'It looks to me like "Oh dear, I think we are sinking." And now the Queen, smiling radiantly, is swimming for dear life. Her Majesty is wearing a silk ensemble in canary yellow.' It was not in itself an attack on the monarchy, but rather on the sycophantic attitudes it inspired. Prince Philip was already becoming well known for his explosive attacks on the press, most recently the bawling out of a Scottish newspaper photographer who pursued him as he manoeu-vred his yacht *Bloodhound* through the locks near Fort William. 'Do you want a bloody picture of my left earhole?' the Duke bel-lowed. The next day the Scottish edition of the *Daily Herald* did indeed publish a long-lens photograph of the princely left ear along with a verbatim account of the royal remarks. As long as the Duke's remarks were addressed to the press – 'bloody awful rags etc . . .' – they were treated like a comedy turn and no one minded, least of all the young. But in the summer of 1963 the scandals which engulfed the Macmillan Government inevitably touched the whole Establishment and with it the monarchy.

In a completely unrelated incident, the Queen for the first time in her life found herself the target of booing. 'For three days,' *Time* magazine reported, 'London's genteel West End looked like a battle-field. Near Buckingham Palace, squads of police grappled with leather-jacketed toughs, while chauffeured Bentleys inched their way through. Wild-eyed girls with straggly black hair and blue-eyed girls with golden tresses were frog-walked [*sic*] into paddy wagons. Some 200 people were jailed. Taking advantage of the chaos, a six-man gang waylaid the Dowager Duchess of Northum-berland, sped off in a white Jaguar with her jewels, worth $200,000. Most shocking of all, for the first time in her eleven-year reign, Queen Elizabeth II was booed by her own people.' In fact the Queen was the inadvertent target of left-wing hostility to the State visit to London at the beginning of July of King Paul and Queen Frederika of the Hellenes. The protesters, vocal and violent, were demonstrat-ing on behalf of the Greek Communists imprisoned after the Greek Civil War almost ten years before, and included British supporters of CND (Campaign for Nuclear Disarmament) and intellectual habitual anti-monarchists. Their target was Frederika, called 'the Nazi Queen' because of her membership of the Hitler Mädchen. She was also, as a Princess of Hanover, a great-great-granddaughter of Queen Victoria and therefore a Princess of Great Britain and third cousin of the Queen (and Prince Philip). King Paul was a nephew of Prince Philip's father, Prince Andrew of Greece.

Ironically, the Profumo scandal, often seen as the immediate cause of Macmillan's resignation in the autumn of 1963, was actu-ally the cause of his hanging on in office for another four months. Despite his gloom over the affair, 'the young voter is bored with me', he said, telling the *Daily Express* in July that at the height of the scandal it had been 'touch and go' for several days on his 'chucking it all in'. However, he had resolved that it was his essential duty to carry on: 'I was determined that no British government should be brought down by a couple of tarts.' Macmillan was not brought down by Profumo, his latest biographer, D. R. Thorpe, wrote, 'he was brought down by his prostate'.[10] In fact he had been greatly encouraged by the signing of the Nuclear Test Ban Treaty in Moscow on 5 August. Shortly before that, however, he had welcomed President Kennedy to Birch Grove on 29–30 June, the last time he was ever to see him. Both leaders were shocked by each other's appearance, Macmillan that Kennedy was in pain from his war wounds, while Kennedy saw a Prime Minister suffering from wounds of an even earlier war, tired, older, and doubted that Macmillan would last the year. During the night of 7–8 October the Prime Minister was struck by prostate trouble and driven to hospital the following evening to undergo an operation.

As early as June, when there had seemed to be a possibility that the Macmillan Government might be defeated, there had been an informal agreement that the party leadership should choose their candidate for the Queen to appoint. The alternative was that the Queen should make the appointment of her own will, thus involving herself in internal party politics. While the Queen has been criticized for giving up her constitutional prerogative of appointing her Prime Minister in favour of the easier alternative of one name being suggested to her, it is difficult to see what else she could have done without miring the Crown in party politics. The Palace line in October was 'You choose, we send for.' After taking soundings Macmillan concluded that of the five possibles – 'Rab' Butler, Reginald Maudling, Iain Macleod, Lord Hailsham and Lord Home – Home was the compromise candidate, 'the most generally acceptable . . . because he was the only one not . . . *un*acceptable'. 'The outcome, the selection of Lord Home, cannot be said to have seriously misrepresented Conservative opinion at the time,' the constitutional expert Vernon Bogdanor has written. 'Macmillan was widely criticized for foisting Lord Home on an unwilling party. Yet it is doubtful if criticism of Macmillan is justified. He lacked both the means and the will to secure the premiership for Home against the wishes of the party as a whole.'[11]

At 11 a.m. on Friday, 18 October the Queen arrived at King Edward VII Hospital in Marylebone for Macmillan's last act as premier. She went alone into the hospital boardroom, where a tense and unhappy Prime Minister waited for her, dressed in a white silk shirt for the occasion, a bottle in his bed and a pail underneath it into which bile dripped through a tube. He handed her his final draft of the memorandum detailing the consultation procedures undergone and recommending the appointment of Home. He also discussed with the Queen the last-minute 'midnight meeting' against the choice of Home which had taken place the previous night, and the lobbying of the Palace against him. According to Macmillan's doctor the Queen had tears in her eyes, and Macmillan described her as 'very upset' as he told her, 'I'm afraid I can't go on.' Later that morning Home arrived at Buckingham Palace to be invited to form an administration. The 14th Earl of Home became Prime Minister of Great Britain, renouncing his earldom to become Sir Alec Douglas-Home under recently passed legislation.

The Queen was happy with the choice of Home. He was the closest to her in background, interests and temperament. He was the first she could talk to with a set of shared values and assumptions. There was a feeling of kinship between the Douglas-Homes and the Bowes-Lyons that went back generations. He was an intelligent, charming and honourable man with a deep knowledge of politics – he had been Chamberlain's Private Secretary at the time of the Munich crisis. He was also an old Etonian, a gifted cricketer and a keen shot with a Scottish estate, and it was these latter characteristics that his opponents seized on, beginning with a failed candidate for the leadership, Iain Macleod, whose article headed 'The Magic Circle' in the *Spectator* in January 1964, identifying a 'magic circle' of old Etonians who fixed the succession for one of their own, set the tone for hostile comment. He blamed Macmillan for bouncing the Queen into accepting Home in order to keep 'Rab' Butler out. There was no criticism of Her Majesty as such, but unfortunately for the Queen, the accusations that Home was 'the grouse-moor candidate' recalled the old Altrincham charges against her 'tweedy' circle, reinforcing the Opposition view that the monarchy was at the apex of a snobbish elite. The elevation of Lord Home seemed simply another episode in the history of the inbred, incestuous, class-ridden elite that had controlled British society and politics after the war. By the end of 1963 Kennedy and Pope John XXIII were dead, the Nuclear Test Ban Treaty marked the end of the over-hanging fear of nuclear war and the fragmentation of CND, the Beatles dominated the pop charts and were looking forward to con-quering America, and Harold Wilson was talking of a Britain propelled by the 'white heat' of technological progress. The British Empire, which in 1945 had ruled over 154 million people, now con-trolled just 15 million. In Britain there was general disillusionment with the world that Macmillan and Home had represented; a year later Wilson was elected as the Queen's first Prime Minister with a working-class background.

11. The Royal Family

Shortly after four o'clock on the afternoon of Friday, 16 October 1964, Harold Wilson arrived at the Palace to accept the Queen's invitation to become her fourth Prime Minister. He had won the recent General Election, as predicted, but in the end by a majority of just five seats. Breaking with tradition, he arrived at the Palace with two carloads of supporters, his wife and two sons and his controversial political secretary, Marcia Williams. The Queen's Assistant Private Secretary, Martin Charteris, described the group's arrival as 'a bit of a culture shock' for the courtiers, and indeed it was for the Wilson party. They were given sherry by the urbane Master of the Household, Patrick Plunket, as they sat on a sofa in the Equerries' Room waiting for Wilson to emerge from his meeting with the Queen. Marcia Williams's recollection of the occasion was scornful: 'A number of anonymous Palace individuals were there. To me they all looked exactly alike. As I recall it, the conversation centred on horses. Perhaps it was assumed that everybody was interested in horses though my knowledge of them was minimal and the Wilson family's less. It struck me at the time as an ironic beginning to the white-hot technical revolution and the Government that was to mastermind it . . .'[1]

Horsey conversation was symbolic of the Palace ethos at the time. The Queen was, and is, passionately interested in the racing and breeding of horses, as were her immediate circle. Wilson knew nothing and cared less about horses; his true working-class relaxation was football, as a supporter of his home town team, Huddersfield Town. Despite being from different planets as far as background and interests were concerned, the Queen and Wilson got on extremely well together over the years. Wilson liked intelligent women and never patronized them; the Queen, interested and well-informed as she was in politics and world affairs, had many areas of common ground, and beyond that he could illustrate for her subjects of which she had no knowledge – working-class industrial Britain, Labour politics and the world of the trade unions. Wilson, unlike several of his colleagues in Government, genuinely believed in the value of the monarchy, and while he undoubtedly made use of his good relationship with the Queen for publicity purposes, he protected and helped her over delicate questions such as the royal finances and the Civil List. 'Harold [Wilson] did get on very well with the Queen and she was very fond of him,' a courtier said. 'His Audiences got longer and longer. Once he stayed for two hours, and was asked to stay for drinks. Usually prime ministers only see her for twenty or thirty minutes and it is not normal for them to be offered drinks by the monarch.'[2] 'I think the Queen talked very freely to Wilson,' one of her former Private Secretaries said. In return Wilson found in the Queen a confidante he could trust. 'Harold was very fond of her and she reciprocated it,' Barbara Castle, Wilson's political ally, recalled. 'He made her feel at ease, kept her well-informed . . . He really enjoyed his visits to her and reporting to her.'[3]

Winston Churchill, the Queen's first Prime Minister, celebrated his ninetieth birthday on 30 November, six weeks after Harold Wilson took office. Just over a month later he suffered his last severe stroke and died on Sunday, 24 January 1965. His coffin lay in state for three days in Westminster Hall, an honour accorded to only one non-royal personage in the past century, William Gladstone in 1898. He was, as Roy Jenkins, Wilson's Chancellor of the Exchequer and Churchill's biographer, put it, 'with all his idiosyncracies, his occasional childishness, but also his genius, his tenacity and his persistent ability, right or wrong, successful or unsuccessful, to be larger than life . . . the greatest human being ever to occupy 10 Downing Street'.[4] More than any human being still alive in the twentieth century, Churchill had symbolized Britain

and the British Empire. From Omdurman as a young officer fighting the Mahdi to the trenches of the First World War and finally as
national leader in the Second, Churchill had played an active part
in the drama of his country and of the world. He was given a magnificent State funeral, the first for a commoner since the Duke of
Wellington in 1852. There were 8,000 people attending the ceremony, including the Queen, the Duke of Edinburgh, the Queen
Mother and all the senior members of the Royal Family. Fifteen
Heads of State were there and 112 countries were represented.
Some 350 million people watched the funeral on television worldwide. As de Gaulle had characteristically remarked when told the
news, 'Now Britain is no longer a Great Power.' No one doubted
that Churchill's death marked the end of an era, just as Harold
Wilson's election was the beginning of a new one.

The Queen's visit to West Germany in May 1965 was symbolically both putting an end to the rancours of two world wars, the
last of which had ended only twenty years before, and looking forward to an era of European co-operation which was soon to come.
It was the first visit by a British sovereign to Germany since George
V had attended the wedding of Princess Victoria of Prussia in 1913,
and turned out to be a remarkably successful one. Buckingham
Palace – and that included the Queen and Prince Philip – had ini-
tially been doubtful about the wisdom of reminding everyone,
particularly the British public, of the royal couple's German roots.
In the still divided city of Berlin, the German welcome was particularly warm. The Berlin Wall, sealing off East Berlin from the
West, had been finally completed on 5 January 1964. Before that
date 1,283,918 East Berliners and East Germans had crossed to the
West. With the wall in place, the East German police showed no
compunction in shooting dead anyone who attempted to scale it.
When the Queen and the Duke, accompanied by Willy Brandt and
the Chancellor, Dr Erhart, drove to the Brandenburg Gate, they
were enthusiastically cheered by half a million West Berliners waving paper Union Jacks. In John F. Kennedy Platz, where the late

President had made his famous 'Ich bin ein Berliner' speech, the Queen pledged 'the full support of the British people in the great tasks that lie ahead'. The Vice-President of the Bundestag suggested that German enthusiasm reflected the people's sense of the end of their country's uncomfortable status as a pariah state.

The Queen and the Duke spent ten days in Germany, travelling around by private train. At the castle of Brühl, near the Federal capital of Bonn, the Queen triumphed, looking, as one observer remarked, 'devastatingly beautiful' as she descended the grand staircase to a fanfare of trumpets, the embroidery on her pale blue dress echoing the plasterwork rococo swirls on the ceiling. 'Oh,' said Cecil Beaton somewhat superfluously to Hardy Amies, designer of the dress, 'she looks like *real* royalty.' Finally, in Hamburg, the great port which had once been part of the democratic Hanseatic league (and had suffered terribly when bombed by the Allies in the war), there was the delicate question of her reception at the Town Hall, which had an impressive staircase. There was a tradition that the Mayor of Hamburg would stand at the top to greet the visitor and would never descend to welcome even the Emperor in the days of Empire; the Mayor decided to waive tradition in honour of the Queen: 'I cannot go down to greet even the Queen of England,' he said, 'but I will go down to greet a lady.'

Wilson's willingness to deploy the Queen to facilitate relations in Europe with a view to joining the EEC was equalled by his concerns over what was then Southern Rhodesia, now Zimbabwe, Britain's remaining unresolved problem of her former possessions in Africa. The British Government was insistent that independence must be accompanied by democracy, while Ian Smith, leader of the white settler government in Salisbury, was determined to maintain white minority rule. The situation was different from any other African ex-colonial issue because the white settlers there had not only run their own affairs without major interference for some forty years but were passionately devoted to the image of the Queen as the focus for their loyalty, regarding themselves as essentially 'British'. They wanted Commonwealth membership on their own terms. The British Government was equally determined that they should not be allowed independence or Commonwealth membership without commitment to eventual majority rule. As both Queen of Southern Rhodesia and Head of the Commonwealth, the Queen was therefore a major factor in discussions between London and Salisbury and for both sides of the debate.

Background feeling on the issue was exacerbated by events in South Africa, where on 12 June 1964 Nelson Mandela and seven other African nationalists had been sentenced to life imprisonment. There had been demonstrations outside South Africa House in London, in which fifty MPs took part. The British Government had appealed directly to the South African Government, an appeal which, with others, was contemptuously rejected, with Dr Verwoerd boasting that he had thrown all socialist protests into the wastepaper basket.

Faced with the probability that an increasingly hostile Ian Smith would go for UDI (Unilateral Declaration of Independence), Wilson flew to Salisbury in October 1965 in a last-minute bid to keep Smith on side, bearing with him a hand-written letter from the Queen appealing to Smith to solve the problem. Wilson's object, with the co-operation of the Palace, was to remind Rhodesians of their allegiance to the Crown and hence their duty to follow Her Majesty's Government's advice. But Smith turned the tables on Wilson by reading it aloud at a banquet in the Prime Minister's honour as if it were a personal tribute to himself from the Queen, describing it as 'a wonderful message from this gracious lady – the sort of thing we live for in Rhodesia – our association with the Queen, with Britain and the Commonwealth'. His official reply stated that he and his colleagues had 'embarked on discussion with Mr Wilson in a spirit of utmost sincerity, frankness and goodwill. The Rhodesian people have a special affection for her Majesty and her Majesty the Queen Mother.'[5] Short of sending troops in to fight the loyal settlers, there was not much Wilson could do to prevent UDI, which duly took place on 11 November with a Proclamation of Independence providing for the Queen to be Head of State and ending with the words 'God Save the Queen'. It was a constitutional nonsense: the Rhodesian white community had identified itself with the code of an Empire which had ceased to exist, and with a monarch who was the Head of the Commonwealth and constitutionally under the control of a British Government whose values were now completely different. Both sides had attempted to place the Queen personally in the dispute and put her in a position which endangered her constitutional neutrality. Both had failed, and the consequences were to be bleak for Zimbabwe into the twenty-first century.

Meanwhile at home in Britain, where the Queen was supposed to be kept well informed about every major issue, foreign and domestic, one terrifying secret had been kept from her until 1965. According to Professor Peter Hennessy in *The Secret State*, that secret was the detailed plans for what would happen in the case of nuclear war. 'We agreed,' wrote Commander J. R. Stephens, Keeper of the Government War Book, to his boss, Denys Laskey, head of the Cabinet's Overseas and Defence Secretariat, on 5 March 1965, 'that there is a requirement for the Queen to be informed, wherever she may be . . . of decisions to implement the various stages and procedures for a transition to war.'[6] As Hennessy put it nearly seventeen years after the Berlin airlift and over two years after the Cuban missile crisis, the Palace was, unusually, very largely in the dark about an important area of State. The Queen did not fully know either the drill to be followed should the stage of a nuclear exchange be reached which would leave her kingdom largely a smoking and irradiated ruin, or the plans for carrying on her Government in its aftermath. Only some two years after the Queen's Coronation, the Joint Intelligence Committee report on the H-bomb Threat to the UK in the event of a General War concluded that about ten 10-megaton H-bombs delivered on the western half of the UK from the waters close in off the western seaboard, with the normal prevailing winds, would effectively disrupt the life of the country and make normal activity completely impossible. There could be 18 million casualties, amounting to one third of the population.

While the US President had a special agency to provide instant communications for the President wherever he was, some of the British recommendations for action as recorded in a memorandum after a meeting of a special ad hoc Cabinet Committee in 1961 on 'Nuclear Retaliation' were more like a *Carry On* film: 'The arrangements for recalling the Prime Minister when he is travelling out of London depend at present on communicating with known points on his route. It has been suggested that these arrangements might be supplemented in this country by installing a radio in the Prime Minister's car which would permit messages to be relayed in plain language through the Automobile Association's radio network.'

Further, in May 1962, just a few months from the Cuba crisis, the system was discussed in what Hennessy described as 'an exchange of letters that even P. G. Wodehouse could not have dreamed up' between Tim Bligh, Macmillan's Principal Private Secretary, and Bryan Saunders, his opposite number in the private office of the Minister of Works. Saunders wrote:

> I understand that these radios are to be maintained by Pye's [an electronics company] and it will presumably be necessary for someone to make a daily or weekly call to the AA Control Station as a check that they are in working order.
>
> I understand that if an emergency arose while the Prime Minister was on the road, the proposal is to use the radio to get him to a telephone. Perhaps we should see that our drivers are provided with four pennies [in the early 1960s it was necessary to insert four old pennies and press 'Button A' before a call from a GPO call-box could be connected] – I should hate to think of you trying to get change for a sixpence from a bus conductor while those four minutes are ticking by!

Only the Brits, Hennessy commented, could have come up with a system whereby the Prime Minister is envisaged making a reverse-charge call from a phone box to authorize nuclear retaliation.[7]

As far as the Queen was concerned, provision was to be made for an Emergency Powers Defence Bill for World War Three by which the Queen would make regulations by Order in Council. Among the provision of forces in the event of the outbreak of war, the Government War Book envisaged 'Special duties towards the Royal Family' of one infantry battalion to guard the Queen. Provisions for her protection seemed to have advanced hardly at all since 1940, when the Coates Mission, a hand-picked body of men from the Brigade of Guards and the Household Cavalry, equipped with armoured cars, had supposedly been on standby to protect the Royal Family. On their only alert, a party of guards-men had appeared at the double and proceeded to thrash the Palace shrubbery 'in the manner of beaters at a shoot rather than of men engaged in pursuit of a dangerous enemy', an observer had com-mented. World War Three was a different proposition, as Professor Hennessy wrote: 'Like all else to do with nuclear war, the degrad-ation of the United Kingdom into eleven shrivelled irradiated little fiefdoms filled with wretched and desperate survivors theo-retically governed by men in bunkers and probably ruled, in reality, by armed soldiers and policemen with ultimate powers over life and death . . . is too ghastly to contemplate.' Yet as one of the Queen's Private Secretaries told Hennessy, speaking about the experience of taking part in the late 1970s and early 1980s in 'tran-sition to war' exercises as an FO official: 'It all seemed horribly possible.'[8]

Unofficial war was already continuing in Indo-China when Harold Wilson took office. In response to Khrushchev's pledge in January 1961 of support for 'wars of national liberation' through-out the world, and especially for Ho Chi Minh's escalation of the armed struggle to unify Vietnam by means of the Vietcong guerril-las, President Kennedy had committed Special Forces – the famous

Green Berets – on the ground in South Vietnam against the en-
croachments of Communist North Vietnam. On Sunday, 2 August
1964 the US destroyer *Maddox* was attacked in the Gulf of Tonkin
by three North Vietnamese torpedo boats, and President Johnson
sent Hanoi warning of 'grave consequences' that would result from
further attacks. As American forces in Vietnam escalated, Harold
Wilson's response to Johnson's request for British forces to help was
negative. Indo-China was not and had never been a British sphere
of influence, and Wilson, who had already announced cuts in
Defence, was never going to commit himself. That did not mean,
however, that Vietnam did not loom large on the international
horizon, or in his briefings to the Queen. The extent of the Queen's
knowledge of the situation has been revealed in a letter she wrote
to Lord Avon (the former Anthony Eden) in August 1966. 'The
Russians are in an interesting cleft stick position in Vietnam as their
influence in Hanoi is negligible unless they can get the Chinese to
do it . . . I believe Harold Wilson discovered some interesting hard
facts about this when he was in Moscow.'[9]

Two months later, on 21 October 1966, tragedy hit a small village
in South Wales when a slag-heap collapsed above the mining village of Aberfan, engulfing a school and killing 146 people, most of
them children. The Prime Minister immediately visited the scene,
as did Lord Snowdon and the Duke of Edinburgh. The Queen visited six days later, a delay that was criticized at the time. 'The reason
given was that she did not want to interrupt the work of rescue
and rehabilitation,' her biographer wrote. 'Nevertheless there was
a feeling that her presence was needed, and an opportunity missed.'
'She is negative,' a courtier reflected. 'She never says things like
"For Christ's sake, let's go to Aberfan." She regrets that now – she
would say it was a mistake, that she should have gone at once.' But
when she did get to Aberfan, she climbed over broken planks, cor-
rugated iron roofing and shattered desks to the top of the heap of
slag entombing the school. As she spoke to local families whose

25. The Queen visiting the mining village of Aberfan, South Wales, after the catastrophic collapse of a colliery spoil tip which killed 116 children and twenty-eight adults on 21 October 1966

26. The Queen crowns Prince Charles at his investiture at Caernarvon Castle, 1 July 1969

27. The Queen and the widowed
Duchess of Windsor at the Duke's
funeral, St George's Chapel, Windsor,
5 June 1972 (PA Archive/Press
Association Images)

28. Prince Charles leaving the
New London Theatre with Camilla
Parker Bowles and her husband
Andrew (*rear left*), 14 February 1975
(PA Archive/Press Association Images)

29. Mutual passion: Princess Anne and
her husband Captain Mark Phillips with
their horses, 1976

30. The Queen riding at Balmoral with
her new daughter-in-law the Duchess
of York (Sarah Ferguson), with Prince
Edward behind, autumn 1986

31. Disenchanted: Charles and Diana with the Queen Mother and the Queen, Braemar Games, 1981

32. Mother love: Diana greets Princes William and Harry on *Britannia* in Toronto, 23 October 1991

33. *It's a Royal Knockout*, Alton Towers, June 1987. The Duchess of York, Prince Edward and the Duke of York with Princess Anne and the presenter Stuart Hall in front

34. The People's Princess: Diana in Angola campaigning against landmines for the Halo Trust, an Anglo-American charity, 15 January 1997

35. London newspapers headline the Queen's decision that Charles and Diana should divorce, 21 December 1995

36. The Queen speaks to the nation
on the eve of Diana's funeral,
Friday 5 September 1997

37. The Queen with Jacqueline and Caroline Kennedy at the dedication
of the memorial to President John F. Kennedy, Runnymede, 14 May 1965

38. The Queen and Prince Philip inspect the Liberty Bell, Philadelphia, 1 July 1976

39. The Queen riding with President Ronald Reagan, Windsor, 8 June 1982

40. Michelle Obama and the Queen at a Buckingham Palace reception before the G20 summit meeting, 1 April 2009

41. President Barack Obama appreciates the Queen's speech at a state banquet in his honour at Buckingham Palace, 24 May 2011

42. Teatime in Glasgow: the Queen visits the McCarron family, 7 July 1999

43. Teatime at the Palace: the Queen meets the Arsenal football team, 15 February 2007

children had been buried beneath the rubble, it was obvious that her feelings were deep and genuine. 'There were tears in her eyes as she talked to us,' one woman said. 'She really feels this very deep. After all she is the mother of four children. We had four too and now we have only two.' The Queen placed a wreath at the cemetery where eighty-one children had been buried, and she and the Duke walked to the house of Councillor Jim Williams, who had lost seven relatives in the disaster. 'She was very upset,' Mrs Williams said later. 'She was the most charming person I have ever met in my entire life. Really down to earth.'[10]

The reaction was characteristic of the Queen: passive, self-controlled, reluctant to confront emotional situations. A Mass Observation poll, taken in 1964 and published in 1966, reflected this dual personality. While the Queen was widely regarded as kindly, motherly, natural, charming, unhypocritical and unselfish, a sizable minority also considered her obstinate, cold and with insufficiently wide interests. Few people disliked or disapproved of the Queen, but their enthusiasm, like her image, was passive rather than enthusiastic. The widespread adulation she had enjoyed in the 50s was no longer there; when she had celebrated the tenth anniversary of the Coronation, the occasion had barely been noticed. 'The English,' Malcolm Muggeridge had announced on the Jack Parr show in 1964, 'are getting bored with their monarchy.'

And by 1964 there were other acts more popular and more interesting than the Royal Family — the Beatles and the Rolling Stones. Pop music was no longer considered to be a frivolous, fleeting interest for the young — by the mid-sixties it had become a symbol of Britain and British style. The Beatles in particular were responsible for this cultural development. As the *NME* reported, when they returned to Liverpool in July 1966 'having conquered America, Australia, Scandinavia and Hong Kong', a cheering crowd of 150,000 lined the streets to the civic reception at the Town Hall. Philip Norman wrote: 'The Beatles were no longer a teenage fad, they had become a national obsession.' In June 1965 the Queen presented them (at Harold Wilson's instance) with an honour each, the MBE. There was uproar. One veteran returned his medal in disgust, while at the other end of the scale, Wilson's republican Minister for Economic Development, Tony Benn, was equally out-raged: 'the Beatles have done more for the royal family by accepting MBEs than the royal family have done for the Beatles by giving them. Nobody goes to see the Beatles because they've got MBEs but the royal family love the idea that the honours list is popular, because it all helps to buttress them and indirectly their influence is used to strengthen all the forces of conservatism in society.' He called Wilson's initative 'the most appalling mistake'.[11] The Beatles, obviously, did not agree: outside the Palace Paul McCart-ney quipped – 'tenderly', according to *Time* – 'She was like a mum to us.'

The birth of Prince Edward in March 1964 had completed the Queen's family. She was thirty-eight, still pretty and trim, but her clothes and hairstyle were unaffected by fashion. Her children, too, as they were growing up, looked curiously old-fashioned, as was, indeed, their upbringing. Princess Anne was thirteen when Edward was born, Prince Charles fifteen. Their early years had been entrusted to nannies, first Helen Lightbody, a dominating character who vanished from the Palace after some unspecified row with Prince Philip, then Mabel Anderson, who remained an important figure in Prince Charles's life long after he had out-grown the nursery. Both Anne and Charles had been educated by a governess, Catherine Peebles (known as 'Mispy'), in a school-room at the Palace converted from a nursery. The children probably saw more of their parents' courtiers than they did of their parents themselves, who were always busy and frequently away; Charles and Anne travelled in a familiar cocoon from Palace to Windsor, Sandringham, Balmoral, their movements as regular as clockwork, their surroundings unchanging.

A week before his eighth birthday, in November 1956, Prince Charles, wearing a traditional upper-class velvet-collared coat over his school uniform, and accompanied by his governess, was driven to his first day at school. In terms of royal education it was a large step; neither the Queen nor any of her ancestors had attended school outside the Palace walls. In ordinary people's terms it was not revolutionary – Hill House was a private pre-preparatory school in Knightsbridge run by an ex-Colonel and his wife, designed as a day school for London children of the upper middle class and foreign diplomats. Prince Charles, a shy, diffident child, was frequently ill and therefore did not distinguish himself. In the words of his authorized biographer, Jonathan Dimbleby, 'he was handicapped . . . by a lack of self-confidence which was so inhibiting that although he was well endowed with both intelligence and imagination, these qualities were not yet easy to discern behind the carapace of diffidence and reserve with which he habitually protected himself'.[12] His education was largely determined by his father, who later sent him to two schools which he himself had attended, Cheam in Surrey and Gordonstoun in Scotland. Charles, brought up with his more assertive younger sister in the shelter of nurseries in their various homes, was lonely and miserable at both. No doubt his father, self-confident, self-reliant, athletic and good at sports, had thought these schools would 'toughen him up'; it was no secret in Court circles that he regarded his son as a wimp and that Charles knew it. Before attending these schools he had curiously been given elementary lessons in wrestling and boxing, presumably so that he could protect himself. According to a Palace source he 'loathed' his time there and the Queen knew that he did. In a telling passage in an essay on 'The Advantages of Boarding Schools', he wrote: 'Preparing you for the outside world. Away from your homes for so long' (note 'homes', not home). If he had disliked Cheam, he found Gordonstoun far, far worse, with an atmosphere of fear and loathing, coarseness of behaviour and language, and outright bullying, of which Charles, a shy outsider with sticking-out ears, was a prime target. Even after two years there the bullying was relentless:

> It's such hell here especially at night. I don't get any sleep practic-ally at all nowadays. The people in my dormitory are foul. They throw slippers all night long or hit me with pillows or rush across the room and hit me as hard as they can, then beetle back again as fast as they can, waking up everyone else in the dormitory at the same time. Last night was hell, literal hell . . .[13]

Hitherto the British press had heeded Palace appeals to leave the Prince in peace, issued by the notoriously press-hating Com-mander Colville. But when he was in his second year at Gordonstoun, the 'cherry brandy incident' caused him pain and humiliation, set-ting him up as a press target for the rest of his life. On a school sailing expedition to Stornoway, he had walked with his private detective into a local inn: asked by the barman what he would like to drink, he panicked and asked for the alcoholic drink he knew was served at foxhunting meets. At that moment a woman jour-nalist walked into the bar and the 'cherry brandy incident' became headlines. The Palace unwisely denied that he had bought or drunk alcohol, but faced with the truth had to retract. The Prince was pursued back to Gordonstoun lying on the floor of a Land Rover to avoid the cameras; his private detective was removed from duty. As his biographer put it, he was 'profoundly shaken' by the experience, which fuelled his suspicion of the press. 'For its part,' Dimbleby added, 'the press had been confirmed in its suspi-cion that the word of the Palace was not necessarily to be trusted, and in any case might be usefully ignored. The slide from defer-ence to cynicism in the attitude of the media towards the monarchy and from suspicion to enmity in the attitude of the Prince towards the media was too gradual to locate precisely, but the cherry brandy incident was symptomatic.'[14] The Gordonstoun experi-ence might have 'toughened him up', as his father put it, physically, but it confirmed him in the view that the outside world was a hostile and threatening place. Far from home and his family, he took refuge when he could with his beloved and loving grandmother, Queen Elizabeth, at her house, Birkhall, on the Balmoral estate. There he found solace in solitary sports like deer-stalking and in communing with nature on the mountains, while nearer to home he developed his love of music and theatre and exploring the Royal Library and its treasures at Windsor.

In 1965, in a plan agreed between his parents and Sir Robert Menzies, the Australian Prime Minister, he was sent to Geelong, described as 'the Australian Eton', but actually the Australian branch of Gordonstoun. The real object behind the move was not so much a relief for Charles from the pressures of Gordonstoun but to use him, as the heir to the throne, as a symbol of Britain's and the Royal Family's links with the Commonwealth, weakened by Macmillan's failed approaches to the EEC, and further demonstrated by Australia's military support of the US in the Vietnam war, in which Britain had refused to take part.

Princess Anne, just under two years Charles's junior, was completely opposite in character. A female clone of her father, the Duke, she was self-confident, unsentimental and athletically gifted. Her father and his uncle, Lord Mountbatten, doted on her, and the Queen was proud of her riding abilities and skill with animals. Horse talk dominated the inner family circle or, as Dimbleby put it, 'Princess Anne, who spent many hours in the Royal Mews, was . . . so absorbed by horses that she rapidly acquired the language by which equestrian enthusiasts communicate with each other and with their animals. Like her parents she did not tire of discussing the most arcane details of conformation, training and horsemanship . . . an inexhaustible source of ideas and argument. When, as often happened, Prince Charles revealed himself to be ignorant of the finer points of equine debate . . . he was mockingly taken to task.'[15] Princess Anne, like her father, was intelligent, quick, articulate and gifted with a mastery of detail which was to equip her superbly well for her future public royal duties. Again, as was traditional in the Royal Family, not much store was set by the education of women. In any case, as Anne's biographer, Brian Hoey, pointed out, Miss Peebles, the governess, was so besotted with Charles that when Anne was sent along for lessons in the Palace schoolroom while he was still there, she was practically ignored.[16] After Charles was sent to preparatory school, Anne shared her lessons with two five-year-old girls, daughters of senior courtiers. The Queen was conscientious in visiting the schoolroom, twice a day, morning and evening, but their limited education together ended in September 1963, when at the age of twelve Anne was sent to Benenden boarding school in Kent, another safe upper-middle-class choice. Princess Anne was able but not academic – she left Benenden after five years with only two A-level passes (history and geography) and decided not to apply for university.

All this was a world away from the 'Swinging London' of the 60s, the famous photographers Bailey, Donovan (and, of course, Snowdon) and their model girlfriends, Jean Shrimpton et al., the designers, the discos and the shabby and overrated Carnaby Street in Soho, a way of life featured in the new magazine colour supplements and *Queen* magazine and regularly and wittily satirized in *Private Eye*. London boasted of being 'the Most Exciting City in the World'. *Time* magazine made 'London: the Swinging City' in April 1966, the cover story illustrated by a Pop collage of guitars, dolly birds, mini-skirts and Minis. Much was made of the working-class origins of stars like Michael Caine, Terence Stamp and David Bailey, mixing with the younger, more glamorous members of the aristocracy. In December 1965 *David Bailey's Box of Pin-ups* featured portraits of the inner circle of swinging London, including Mick Jagger, Lennon and McCartney, and Caine. Malcolm Muggeridge was unimpressed by their 'unabashed arrogance', dubbing them 'the relics of the religion of narcissists, of which photographers such as Mr Bailey are high priests'. Controversially, the photographs also featured the hideously violent East End gangsters Charlie,

Ronnie and Reggie Kray, and, separately, Lord Snowdon: the juxtaposition of the Queen's brother-in-law with a gang of East End thugs did not go down well, and Snowdon withdrew permission to publish his picture.[17]

'Suddenly we were being courted by half the aristocracy,' Keith Richards of the Rolling Stones recalled. 'I've never known if they were slumming or we were snobbing. They were very nice people. I decided it was no skin off my nose . . . It was the first time I know of when that lot actively sought out musicians in such large numbers. They realized there was something blowin' in the wind, to quote Dob [Dylan]. They felt embarrassed up there, the Knights in Blue, and they felt they were being left out of things if they didn't join in. So there was this weird mixture of aristos and gangsters, the fascination that the higher end of society has with the more brutish end.'[18]

Jonathan Aitken wrote that a completely new class had been formed, running parallel to the existing system:

> . . . this class, and it is a very small one, compete in fields where although birth and breeding may accelerate progress, success nevertheless depends on merit and talent alone. The class includes actors and public performers of all kinds, authors and journalists, TV men, dress designers, photographers, pop singers and money makers in open markets . . . all the people who are billed as belonging to the classless society or the new aristocracy belong in fact to this new group which, for want of a better terminology, can be called the 'talent' class.[19]

In short, it was a small metropolitan-based clique to which birth, looks, talent and money were the passports. Other names hogged the media headlines and society columns hitherto occupied by debutantes and society parties. In reality things had never been that different: 'In England,' Benjamin Disraeli wrote in his novel *Vivian Grey*, published in 1826, 'personal distinction is the only passport to the society of the great. Whether this distinction arises from fortune, family or talent is immaterial; but certain it is, to enter high society, a man must have either blood, a million, or a genius.' In the end it was to lead to a culture of celebrity so vacuous that appearing on television and being 'famous' was all that mattered, the rest of the population being condemned by a woman known only for her face, figure and ambition as 'civilians'.

In the meantime, Harold Wilson was considering new approaches to joining Europe, following a nonchalantly dropped suggestion by de Gaulle during the 1965 election campaign that Britain might now be welcome in the EEC. When the new Tory leader, Edward Heath, had challenged Wilson to respond, the latter's characteristic response had been: 'One encouraging gesture from the French Government and the Conservative leader rolls on his back like a spaniel.' Barely a week after his re-election, however, Wilson had revised his Cabinet to give two Ministers, George Brown and George Thomson, special responsibility for paving a road towards Brussels. They were soon dropping hints all over Europe that Britain wanted in: in Stockholm in May 1966, Brown had said plainly, 'We want to join.' The situation had changed since the debacle five years ago, when Commonwealth trade ties had been of major importance. Since then Commonwealth countries had increasingly been trading within their regional areas, while in 1964 Britain's trade with Europe had exceeded that with all the Commonwealth put together.

Once again, Wilson planned to use the Queen as a major player to advance his plans. As *Time* put it in a piece entitled 'Once More to Market?' when the Queen paid a State visit to King Baudouin of the Belgians in Brussels in May 1966:

> Officially it was simply a pomp-and-panoply state visit . . . but Brussels is more than just the capital of Belgium these days. With each fresh agreement of the Common Market Six, it becomes more and more the headquarters and repository of the Continent's hopes for unity. Mindful of this the Queen had some carefully

chosen things to say: 'Like so many things in life, what is desirable is not always immediately attainable, but I join with you in hoping that a way be found before long to enable us to cooperate in the wider European unity.'

In the wake of the Queen's affable remarks, Wilson revealed his thinking to his Cabinet colleagues that October. Once again, de Gaulle looked likely to be the major obstacle. Cecil King, the Mirror Group magnate, had recorded in July that the French had 'made it clear that there is no prospect of admitting Britain to the Common Market at this stage. They are not convinced that the Government means business, and there is no question of us joining while we are so deeply in hock to the Americans.'[20] Wilson suggested to his colleagues that the way to allay these fears was for him and his deputy, George Brown, to make 'a tour round Europe to visit the chief capitals and try to clarify the doubtful issues'. The 'Probe', as it was officially known, began in Rome on 15 January 1967 and continued, on and off, for two months. It was a complete waste of time, dubbed by commentator Hugo Young 'the acme of Wilsonian politics: it put on show his fascination with tactics, his professional vanity, his impressionable mind, the grandeur of his self-confidence, his refusal to acknowledge the realities of international power. It was at times comical, at others almost calamitous.'[21] The most important meeting – with de Gaulle in Paris on 24 January – had elements of both. Brown, a mercurial alcoholic whom Wilson indulged to extreme, was 'on his worst form, affectionately calling the proud French head of State "Charlie", and at a reception at the British Embassy publicly unleashing a string of loud-mouthed insults at the ambassador's wife'. When Wilson returned from Paris, he commissioned an expensive set of patience cards with the Cross of Lorraine printed on the back, which he intended to give de Gaulle as a present at their next meeting. There was to be no next meeting – on 27 November de Gaulle again vetoed Britain's application to join the Common Market.

★

By the mid 1960s football had replaced cricket as England's national sport: cricket had an unfashionable elitist, upper-class, even imperialist air about it, and matches took five days as compared with ninety minutes of fast-moving football. The England cricket team was in the middle of a long losing streak, did not even play entertaining cricket, and despite declining spectator numbers the authorities saw no reason to make an effort to attract them back. The historian Dominic Sandbrook illustrated their seigneurial attitude to the game with a quote by Sir Pelham Warner, president of the MCC: 'Cricket is not a circus, and it would be far better that it should be driven back to the village green . . . than yield a jot to the petulant demands of the spectator.'[22] Football was far better adapted to the popular new medium of television, attracting new supporters, including women, who would never have gone to the muddy, crowded grounds to watch a match. In the early part of the 60s, however, the English international team was very much an also-ran. In 1962 they had made it to the World Cup finals in Chile but appeared dull and workmanlike compared with the glamour of South American sides like Brazil, who beat them easily in the quarter-finals. But that year England went on to appoint the dedicated, fiercely patriotic Alf Ramsey to manage the team for the 1966 World Cup. Still, there was not much excitement about the coming event until in March 1966 the World Cup itself was stolen from an exhibition in Westminster Central Hall. It had been lost for a week when a black and white mongrel dog named Pickles, nosing round a hedge in South London, found a tightly wrapped newspaper package which his master discovered to be the Cup itself. Pickles became a national hero, winning a year's free supply of dog food and a medal from the Canine Defence League. He even appeared in a film with Laurence Harvey, Eric Portman and two bulldogs: the spoof *The Spy with a Cold Nose* (1966). When he died in 1973, a nation mourned.

The Queen maintained the royal connection with football established by her father and grandfather, both keen supporters of national matches. The Queen, although naturally preferring events involving horses, had been trained to attend since her youth. She was at Wembley for the opening ceremony on 11 July when England kicked off against Uruguay, and she was there again on 30 July 1966 to present Pickles' (who had also been invited) Jules Rimet trophy to the England captain, Bobby Moore, after England's controversial extra-time victory over (West) Germany. Moore had wiped his hands on the velvet covering of the balcony before shaking hands with the Queen, in order not to dirty her white gloves; he then lifted the trophy to an explosively cheering crowd of 93,000 people, crammed into the stadium. More than 32 million people had watched the match on television, more even than for the Coronation. In London there were the wildest public celebrations since the end of the Second World War. Cheering crowds blocked the streets and danced in the fountains in Trafalgar Square. 'It's like VE night, election night and New Year's Eve rolled into one,'[23] a spokesman for the AA told the *Express*.

Unfortunately for Britain, Harold Wilson and British sporting pride, the resurgence of Britain ecstatically envisaged by the cheering crowds of July 1966 proved to be yet another illusion. Things were about to get much worse. The March 1966 election had been Wilson's finest hour, but within weeks an economic crisis arose which damaged his reputation permanently. A strike by the National Union of Seamen was widely seen abroad as a threat to British exports and to the value of sterling; a policy of cuts, with rising unemployment, led to the devaluation of the pound eighteen months later. On 29 December *The Times* denounced 1967 as a 'beastly year . . . The Government's economic policy collapsed into shambles.' The worst peacetime freeze and squeeze, imposed in July 1966, proved to be of no avail. In the end it was to be devaluation plus stagnation plus the highest level of unemployment for twenty-seven years.

On the evening of the 14/15 March 1968, Wilson involved the Queen in a last-ditch ruse to save the pound from a second devaluation. That afternoon, the Chancellor, Roy Jenkins, had heard that the Americans were contemplating drastic action to relieve pressure on the dollar: Treasury advisers warned him that any American action could create shock waves that could submerge us within twenty-four hours. Sterling had become so exposed and our reserves so nearly exhausted that we were almost bound to be driven off the $2.40 rate. In other words, he said, 'Britain would be forced into a second, utterly humiliating devaluation with horrendous consequences for the domestic economy.' Just before eleven that night the word came that the Americans wanted Britain to close the London gold market to give them time to organize relief for the pressure on the dollar. Jenkins and his advisers decided to shut down the gold market as the Americans asked, but to use this as an excuse to close the London foreign exchange market and proclaim a four-day Bank Holiday to buy time for the beleaguered pound. The Queen was asked to hold a last-minute Privy Council meeting at Buckingham Palace after midnight to declare the Bank Holiday and stave off disaster. She did so, and was 'in extremely chatty form' despite the late hour when Wilson, Jenkins and another Minister arrived to form a quorum with the Queen's Private Secretary; the Bank Holiday was agreed. Jenkins later admitted that had it not been for the Bank Holiday they could have had a 'catastrophic' run on the pound, leading to a second devaluation.[24] But, thanks to a 4-billion-dollar rescue package from Washington, the pound just survived the opening of the markets on Monday morning.

The fun was definitively over: in Asia the bombing of North Vietnam escalated with Johnson's Operation Rolling Thunder, and Chairman Mao initiated his deadly Cultural Revolution. In the Middle East in June 1967 the Israelis rolled over the Egyptians in the Sinai, capturing the West Bank and Arab East Jerusalem and taking over control of thousands of Palestinians. The next year, 1968, was a terrible year for the United States, with the assassinations of Martin Luther King in April and Robert Kennedy in June;

in Europe the Russians crushed the liberalizing Dubček and there were serious protests against the Vietnam War. Lyndon Johnson announced that he would not run again for the Presidency, and that November the Republican Richard M. Nixon defeated the Democrat Hubert Humphrey to become the next President. In 1969 the Troubles began in Northern Ireland, setting a trail of bombing and terrorism whose results are still to be seen today. In June 1970 England crashed out of the World Cup in Mexico, losing to West Germany, and Wilson lost the General Election to the Tory leader, Edward Heath. Symbolically, John Lennon had returned his MBE in January 1969, writing to the Queen: 'Your Majesty, I am returning my MBE as a protest against Britain's involvement in the Nigeria–Biafra thing, against our support of America in Vietnam and against "Cold Turkey" slipping down the charts.'

12.   Rebranding the Monarchy

The retirement in 1968 of Commander Colville from the post of Press Secretary, which he had held for more than twenty years, signalled a sea change in the relations between the monarchy and the media. As far as he was concerned his job was to give out as little information as possible to the press, which he regarded, if not as the enemy, then certainly as a hostile and potentially dangerous force. 'I am not what you North Americans call a Public Relations Man,' he famously told a meeting of American journalists. In return he was widely known, after the Yeti of the Himalayan snows, as 'the Abominable No-man'. He was replaced by William Heseltine, his assistant since 1965, an outgoing, bright Australian, as far from the negative attitudes of his predecessor as it was possible to be. The objective now was to sell the Palace to the public.

The more forward-looking of the Palace Establishment, headed by the Duke of Edinburgh, had been aware for some time of a recession in public enthusiasm for the monarchy. The Queen herself no longer enjoyed the adulation she had become accustomed to since her accession and Coronation. The Duke, with the assistance of Mountbatten and Heseltine, took the view that the Queen and her family should be presented as outgoing, hard-working and accessible. It was time for a relaunch.

The first public spectacular was to be the investiture of Prince Charles as Prince of Wales at Caernarvon Castle on 1 July 1969. It was the fulfilment of a public promise made to the Welsh people by the Queen in 1957, which the nine-year-old Prince, horrified and taken by surprise, had watched on television with deep embarrassment in his headmaster's study at his prep school, Cheam. The ceremony was to be televised and the setting within the castle walls designed by the only Welsh member of the Royal Family, Princess Margaret's husband, Tony Armstrong-Jones, now the Earl of Snowdon. Snowdon had a passion for design which he exercised at every opportunity – he had made his name with his design for the Aviary at London Zoo – and he threw himself into the occasion with huge enthusiasm, even designing his own uniform as Constable of the Castle, a title bestowed on him by the Queen. The original title of Prince of Wales had been created in 1301 by Edward I for his son, apparently to impress the Welsh while he was away hammering the Scots. The first historical re-enactment had been undertaken centuries later in 1911, when George V's eldest son, later Edward VIII, dressed in what he described as a 'preposterous rig' of white satin knee-breeches and stockings, had been forced to undergo a mock-medieval ceremony to boost the local popularity of the Welsh Chancellor of the Exchequer, David Lloyd George, while emphasizing the unity of the United Kingdom.

Unfortunately circumstances had changed since 1911 and, more significantly, since 1957, when the Queen had made her announcement which had raised cheers from thousands of loyal Welsh subjects at the opening of the Commonwealth Games in Cardiff. In preparation for his role, the Queen had decided two years previously that after Trinity College Cambridge the Prince should attend the ultra-Welsh college of Aberystwyth for the summer preceding his investiture. The Welsh Nationalist party, Plaid Cymru, had become much more vociferous and on occasion violent. There had been attacks on Welsh public buildings, and the Queen had apparently told Harold Wilson that she feared for her son's safety. Welsh nationalists had prepared for his arrival and so had the Home Office, with a highly visible security operation at Aberystwyth, billeting some seventy police officers in the town and disguising undercover security men as university cleaners and students. In the circumstances Prince Charles had shown real courage in going ahead with his university term: four students went on hunger

strike in protest at his arrival, a bomb destroyed an RAF radio station nearby and an attempt was made to saw the head off a statue
of his great-uncle David, the previous Prince of Wales, on the
town's promenade.

'There should be no part of the United Kingdom where the
Royal Family cannot go,' declared the Labour Secretary of State
for Wales, George Thomas, nevertheless adding, 'It will require
great moral courage from that young man.' There were bombs on
the eve of the investiture and on the day itself. The royal train was
held up by a hoax bomb, but the next day a real device exploded
in a town thirty miles from Caernarvon, killing the men who were
planting it. In London the BBC pre-recorded obituaries of the
Prince to be broadcast in the event of his assassination. A bomb
went off as the Prince travelled with George Thomas in the ceremonial carriage towards the castle.

In the event, the ceremony was moving because of the obvious
deep feeling of the principal participants, the Queen and the Prince,
she in primrose-yellow Norman Hartnell hat and coat, he in uniform, with a purple surcoat trimmed with ermine as a concession
to theatre. The Queen invested her son with the insignia – the
sword designed for his great-uncle, a golden sceptre and ring
engraved with Welsh dragons, and a coronet which, instead of the
simple gold band that Snowdon had hoped for and which had been
vetoed by the Garter King of Arms, Sir Anthony Wagner, con-
sisted of an elaborate, ugly and modernistic crown studded with
jewels and ornamented with fleur-de-lys and crosses, later described
by the Queen as looking like a candle-snuffer when she put it on
Charles's head. After she had invested him with the insignia, he
knelt in homage, placing his hands between hers to swear the traditional oath as 'liege man of life and limb . . . of earthly worship
and faith and truth I will bear unto you to live and die against all
manner of folks'. It worked; as George Thomas told the Queen,
'. . . it was a far greater triumph than we had a right to expect . . .
Wales has been in a state of euphoria, and at least half a million

dollars came to Caernarvon itself.' The celebrated Barbara Walters of NBC wrote of the 'joy' with which the broadcast had been received in the US, John Betjeman called it 'one of *the* great days of my life . . . It was local and intimate and yet international. It was a family event and yet for everyone.'

There could have been no greater contrast between the mock medievalism at Caernarvon and the scene just under three weeks later, on 20 July 1969, when the American astronaut Neil Armstrong, watched by some 600 million television viewers worldwide, stepped from the lunar module of Apollo 16 on to the surface of the moon: 'That's one small step for man, one giant leap for mankind,' he said as he did so.

The Queen had carried the Caernarvon ceremony off with all the dignity and aplomb that only she could muster in the most extraordinary and potentially risible circumstances. Her deeper instinct was for privacy and for the preservation of her family life as far as possible from the public gaze. She had, like her father, been trained in the principles of Walter Bagehot, who had warned of the fragility of the monarchy's mystique: 'We must not let in the daylight upon magic.' On the advice of her husband and his uncle Mountbatten, whose son-in-law, Lord Brabourne, was a successful film producer, she went even further with a film, *Royal Family*, released that summer. While at Caernarvon the public had been allowed to gaze respectfully on the ceremonial magic of monarchy; with this full-length film they were invited to be with her in the same room, at work with her Private Secretary, at family breakfasts and barbecues, on the royal train, on duty and hard at work.

From its first showing in July 1969 and no fewer than five repeats over the next eighteen months, *Royal Family* attracted 40 million viewers in the United Kingdom alone. The Queen, usually seen stiff and formal in her television broadcasts, appeared absolutely natural, just as she was seen in her own circle: relaxed, radiating happiness and enjoyment, making jokes, always smiling. There were also formal shots of her in uniform, taking the salute on her charger, Burmese, at her official birthday parade. The atmosphere of grand informality throughout the film was epitomized by a clip showing a footman holding out a salver of carefully prepared carrots for her to feed to the horses. She was seen at work with her Private Secretary, Sir Michael Adeane, her manner very crisp and excutive as she opened personal mail and ran over a speech prepared for her next State visit. The forward planning that went into her official year was impressive. She was shown seated, with Bobo standing by her side, both with similar hairstyles and the regulation three strings of pearls, putting together outfits for future tours using coloured sketches for the dresses. At one point she delved into a leather box to bring out a magnificent necklace of gold set with cabochon rubies the size of pigeon's eggs, which had belonged to the Moghul Emperors of India ('the Persians', she called them). 'Rather fascinating,' she says, using the qualified, understated 'Windsorspeak' characteristic of her family. She had never worn the necklace: 'One ought to get a dress designed to wear it with,' she mused. Morning audiences with ambassadors were filmed: on this occasion the introduction of the American Ambassador, the millionaire anglophile Walter Annenberg, seen outside the audience chamber being instructed in procedure by the Marshal of the Diplomatic Corps, a handsome being in a uniform which would not have seemed out of place at the Congress of Vienna in 1815. 'When the doors of the Queen's audience room open,' he said, 'you take one pace forward with your left foot, then stop and bow. Then you walk up to the Queen who is standing about six or seven paces away. As she holds out her hand, you bow again, another little bow as you shake hands . . .' The etiquette was as formal and precise as if it had been the Court of the Emperor of China.

Today 'work of the Queen' scenes like these often feature in television films and the public, while still interested, has become used to them; what was unusual in *Royal Family* were the shots of private family life: the camera behind the Queen's shoulder in a Land Rover as she drove the five-year-old Prince Edward through the snow-covered landscape at Sandringham; picnicking among pine trees and barking corgis beside Loch Muick on the Balmoral estate. In one family picnic scene Prince Philip and Princess Anne are shown in charge of the large iron barbecue which the Prince had made to his own design, the Queen and Princess Anne lighting it with traditional methods – carefully rolled-up newspapers and kindling, carefully set alight with matches – then cooking large fillet steaks. The final scenes of the film were overtly 'family' ones: the Queen and Prince Philip with their two elder children sitting round a family lunch table telling not very funny stories. There are scenes on the royal yacht *Britannia* on State visits, everything planned in advance, not only the menu but also the plate, the dinner services, the cutlery, candelabra, table decorations, flower holders, cruets, all of which had to be carefully packed as the items are so valuable – a dessert plate could be worth £500. This would be done for places as diverse as Nepal and Lusaka, a huge feat of organization and statistics. But the overwhelming impression of the film was of the Queen herself, happy and busy in her public and private life, enjoying her job as much as she did the company of her husband and children. The image was one of a contented, united family, rather charmingly old-fashioned in their kilts, pullovers and shortish haircuts, surrounded by horses and dogs in their traditional British upper-class way of life.

This emphasis on the ideal family was to return to haunt the Queen and her advisers twenty years later when her children's marital disasters revealed the cracks in the fabric. The film innocently whetted the public's appetite for what Muggeridge had called 'the royal soap opera', which was to reach epidemic proportions when things began to go wrong. Having been invited into the drawing room, they were soon going to want to peer into the bedroom.

Milton Shulman, television critic for the *Evening Standard*, warned at the time:

> Richard Cawston's film, *Royal Family*, could not have had a better reception if it had been the combined work of Eisenstein, Hitchcock and Fellini. But the making and showing of such a film with the monarch's co-operation may have constitutional and historical consequences which go well beyond its current interest as a piece of TV entertainment . . .
>
> An old image has been replaced by a fresh one. The emphasis on authority and remoteness which was the essence of the previous image has, ever since George VI, been giving way to a friendlier image of homeliness, industry and relaxation . . .
>
> Judging from Cawston's film, it is fortunate at this moment in time we have a royal family that fits in so splendidly with a public relation man's dream.
>
> Yet is it, in the long run, wise for the Queen's advisers to set as a precedent this right of the television camera to act as an image-making apparatus for the monarchy? Every institution that has so far attempted to use TV to popularize or aggrandize itself has been trivialized by it.[1]

David Attenborough, anthropologist and supremely successful maker of wildlife films, was similarly concerned, telling Richard Cawston, producer-director of *Royal Family*: 'You're killing the monarchy you know, with this film you're making. The whole institution depends on mystique and the tribal chief in his hut. If any member of the tribe ever sees inside the hut, then the whole system of the tribal chiefdom is damaged and the tribe eventually disintegrates.'[2]

In the twenty-first century the intimacy of the *Royal Family* scenes was not to be repeated. The 'work of the Queen' productions became the norm, and Rebecca West's dictum that 'the royal family is ourselves behaving better', which had been the traditional view, was rigidly adhered to. Prince Philip, the Palace modernizer, had been a principal advocate of a no-nonsense, brushing-away-the-cobwebs approach. On a North American tour in Canada at the end of the year he spoke of the monarchy as if it were a non-mysterious, workaday, democratic institution, and its principal figure somebody who was just doing a job. 'If you don't want us, then let us end it on amicable terms and not have a row about it,' he told a press conference in Ottawa. 'The future of the monarchy depends on the national community, and if at any stage the community decides it is unacceptable then it is up to that community to change it. It is up to the people themselves.'[3] He was talking about Canada and the Commonwealth, not Britain. But his remarks seemed to apply, with equal force, at home.

The mock-medieval pantomime of the Investiture at Caernarvon and the intimate domestic picture of *Royal Family* were two prongs of a public relations initiative designed to win over an increasingly uninterested public and at the time they succeeded. The year 1969 was a key one in the history of the monarchy. 'Cynics,' Ben Pimlott wrote, 'detected another motive behind Buckingham Palace's sudden interest in raising the monarchy's public profile: money.' On that same North American tour Prince Philip produced a spectacular example of what he himself called 'dontopedalogy' (putting his foot in his mouth), inadvertently focusing the spotlight on a subject which both the Palace and the Government would have preferred to remain in the dark: the royal finances. In an interview on NBC's *Meet the Press*, Prince Philip announced that the monarchy was broke, or about to be so: 'We go into the red next year, now, inevitably if nothing happens we shall either have to – I don't know, we may have to move into smaller premises . . . for instance we had a small yacht which we had to sell, and I shall have to give up polo fairly soon . . .'[4]

Basically what the Duke was saying was essentially true. The effect of inflation on the Civil List had meant that the sum settled on the Queen on her accession in 1952 – £475,000 a year including an inflation allowance of £70,000 – would no longer cover costs, and the balance would indeed, as he said, go into the red in 1970. On 5 November 1969, five days before the NBC interview, *The Times* had reported that the Queen was overspending her allowance, partly because of the Labour Government's Selective Employment Tax, designed to make businesses and other organizations cut their workforce. (As a result, the Queen's 300 full-time staff had been cut by 15 per cent since her accession.) Prince Philip's remarks, however, ensured bombshell headlines: complaints from a rich man about having to give up luxuries like yachts and polo made the worst possible public impression. A group of dockers in a Bermondsey pub wrote sarcastically to the Prince offering to take up a collection to buy him a polo pony. Barbara Castle recorded a general lack of sympathy for cries of poverty coming from the husband of 'one of the richest women in the world', a phrase which was to have increasing resonance over the years. A worried Harold Wilson raised the issue on 11 November at a meeting of the 'Inner Cabinet' of key Government Ministers, revealing the extent of Government help to the Crown that was already taking place. The Chancellor, he explained, had already arranged to transfer some royal spending to various departments – the Ministry of Works, for instance, now carried the cost of royal castles. The members of the Cabinet were not entirely sympathetic to the Queen's predicament, despite personal admiration for her; the Queen, Richard Crossman noted, paid no estate or death duties, making her 'by far the richest person in the country', an issue which was to break out with increasing insistence over the next twenty years. Skilful and loyal, Wilson kicked the question into touch, his objective being to take the issue out of politics and postpone discussion until after the General Election; he agreed a bipartisan approach with Opposition leader Edward Heath to set up a Select Committee on the Civil List – after the election.

Wilson, to most people's surprise, lost the election held on 18 June 1970 (typically his resignation had to be delayed because the Queen was attending the Royal Ascot race meeting) and was succeeded by Edward Heath. The promised Select Committee on the Civil List began its deliberations just under a year later, in May 1971, this time with a Conservative chairman – the Tory Chancellor, Anthony Barber, and a Tory majority who, to the relief of the Palace, defended the Queen's right to keep details of her personal fortune and the extent of her resources resulting from tax immunities secret. Sir Michael Adeane, the Queen's Principal Private Secretary, continued the 'work of the Queen' theme as seen in *Royal Family*. He stressed how unrelentingly she worked and how she could never look forward to retirement. She received 120 letters a day, and spent three hours reading Foreign Office telegrams, reports of parliamentary procedures, ministerial memoranda and Cabinet minutes. She was in ultimate charge of Buckingham Palace, Windsor Castle, Holyrood House, Sandringham and Balmoral. She travelled more extensively than any of her predecessors. Her volume of work had increased since her accession (the number of centenarians to whom telegrams had to be sent had increased from 225 per annum in 1952 to 1,186 in 1970). Her visits to provincial towns, for instance, were stressful and exhausting: the strain of taking a lively interest in everything, saying a kind word here and asking a question there, always smiling and acknowledging cheers, when driving in her car, sometimes for hours, had to be experienced to be properly appreciated.[5]

In the end it was a generous settlement but passed with a majority of 121 – most Labour MPs abstained, 47 MPs voted against. The Labour Party was far from united on the issue, divided by old-fashioned Labour members like Wilson and Callaghan, and fiery Hampstead socialists like Crossman and Benn. 'The working-class members' (among which he included Wilson and Callaghan) 'love the Queen and she loves them', the diarist Tony Benn wrote crossly. Wilson, according to *The Times*, had gone out of his way 'to be protective towards the Queen and her interests'. 'When it came to re-doing the Civil List Wilson was frightfully helpful,' a courtier recalled. 'He used all his political skills and knowledge to get her what she wanted.' Yet the deal was not as open-handed as it appeared at first sight. The Civil List was to be kept under review by a Board of Trustees, including the Prime Minister and the Chancellor of the Exchequer, who were to report to Parliament every ten years, when the Treasury might make an order increasing the allowance. This altered the relationship between Crown and Parliament in one important respect. Before, the monarch had accepted the Civil List as – in effect – a Coronation gift, unrelated to performance. Now the List was to be continually scrutinized, and future additions to it were likely to depend on the reputation of the Royal Family, the mood of the nation, and the political majority in Parliament. Earlier attempts by monarchs to increase the Civil List in 1904, 1905 and 1920 in mid-reign had remained secret, nipped in the bud by Ministers who pointed out the consequences of the parliamentary debate which would be required. More seriously, the issue of the Queen's private fortune and her tax immunity had been publicly raised, and stonewalled by the Palace. No one doubted how hard the Queen worked, but after the 1971 Committee on the Queen the question of the cost of the monarchy had been brought to public attention. The Civil List Act passed through Parliament on 24 February 1972, a watershed in the relations between the monarchy and the public.[6]

Another – uncomfortable – chapter for the Queen and the Royal Family closed with the death in Paris of the Duke of Windsor. The Duke had haunted his family as the skeleton in the cupboard since his Abdication when the Queen was ten years old, old enough to be aware of the family tensions and particularly of the feelings of her mother and grandmother towards her uncle and, more particularly, towards his wife. The refusal of George VI, backed by Queen Mary and Queen Elizabeth, to acknowledge the former Wallis Simpson as a member of the Royal Family by granting her the title 'HRH' had created a permanent rift which the Duke never forgave. The Windsors had been a taboo subject in the

Queen's circle and she was well aware of what had gone on, including her obligation to continue her father's payment of £10,000 to the Duke as rent for the private estates of Balmoral and Sandringham. The publication of their memoirs by the couple – his entitled *A King's Story*, hers *The Heart Has Its Reasons* – had not helped matters. The Duke had been enraged when the Palace had refused his request to see in typescript passages referring to him in the authorized 1958 biography of the late King by Sir John Wheeler-Bennett. According to the Duke's biographer, Michael Bloch, it was only after the threat of legal action that the Queen allowed him to see relevant portions of the text and then only at proof stage.[7] In the event he could have little about which to complain: there were only the sketchiest of references to Wallis Simpson, and the Windsor marriage at Candé was confined to a one-and-a-half-line footnote. The Queen was naturally concerned that there should be as little washing of dirty linen in public as possible, and she was anxious to be conciliatory. Where her father had refused his brother access to the Royal Archives for his ghostwritten autobiography (published in 1951), the Queen gave him permission to consult them for his 1959 book *A Family Album*, although she disappeared to accompany Prince Philip shooting for the period of the Duke's visit to Windsor.

She had taken a major step towards reconciliation in 1965, visiting the Duke at the London Clinic when he had been there for an eye operation in March, when she met the Duchess, their first sight of each other since 1936, and later walking with him in the gardens at Buckingham Palace during his convalescence. On 7 June 1967, four days after their thirtieth wedding anniversary, the Duke and Duchess of Windsor had attended a Royal Family ceremony together for the first time, at the unveiling of a memorial plaque to Queen Mary. It had been an awkward occasion for all concerned, Queen Mary having been the spearhead of the anti-Wallis faction. The couple had not been invited to the lunch with the royal party afterwards but had been entertained by the Duchess of Kent at

Kensington Palace instead. As Edward VIII's biographer, Philip Ziegler, wrote, 'It was a curious touch of irony that so intimate a family occasion, honouring the woman who had done most to ensure that the Duchess of Windsor should never be accepted as a member of the royal family, should be the occasion at which the Duchess took her place in their midst.'[8] At the Duke's request the Queen later agreed that he and Wallis should be buried side by side in the family burial plot in the grounds of Frogmore at Windsor, and that after his death she would continue to pay his allowance (halved) to the Duchess.

In November 1971 it was revealed that the Duke was dying of an inoperable tumour of the throat. Months later the Queen, while on a State visit to Paris with the Duke of Edinburgh in May 1972, called to see him. The Duke, still lucid although extremely weak and bedridden, on an intravenous drip, insisted on getting up to receive her. She was his sovereign, he told his doctor, and he would receive her properly dressed in the adjoining sitting-room, a drip tube hidden under his shirt attached to flasks behind a curtain. When the Queen entered, he made a supreme effort, standing up and bowing his head in the traditional manner, despite the risk of detaching the drip tube. They sat down and chatted affectionately for about a quarter of an hour. When the Queen left, the doctor noticed that she had tears in her eyes; the old man's gallantry and his resemblance to her father had deeply moved her. He died nine days later, in the early hours of 28 May 1972. His body was flown to Britain in an RAF plane to lie in state in St George's Chapel, where 60,000 mourners filed past over the following two days, not a bad total for an ex-King whose brief reign had ended nearly forty years before. The Duchess was invited to stay at Buckingham Palace for the funeral at St George's Chapel and to lunch at Windsor before the interment of her husband's body at Frogmore. Prince Charles had met her when he had visited his great-uncle in Paris in 1971, when he had described her as 'flitting to and fro like a strange bat', her face rigid from face-lifts, her conversation superficial in the extreme. At Windsor for her husband's lying-in-state, she had seemed to him, and to others, unwell and confused. 'At one point she moved away and stood alone, a frail, tiny black figure, gazing at the coffin and finally bowing briefly . . . she kept saying, "He gave up so much for so little" – pointing at herself with a strange grin,' Prince Charles confided to his diary. The pathos and grandeur of the occasion moved him deeply: 'The whole evening was full of grandeur, simplicity, beauty, and mystery and I shall never forget it. I only wish I had known Uncle David better.'[9]

The Duchess lingered on in the shuttered house in the Bois de Boulogne, increasingly mentally and physically incapacitated, until she died there in a vegetative state on 24 April 1986, aged eighty-nine. Her body was flown to London, escorted by the Lord Chamberlain and met by the young Duke of Gloucester, Prince Richard, who accompanied it to Windsor. The short private service in St George's Chapel was attended by sixteen members of the Royal Family, the American Ambassador and the Duchess's few surviving friends. Her coffin lay in the place previously occupied by her husband, Queen Mary and the preceding Kings of England; on it rested a wreath of yellow and white lilies from the Queen. It was noticeable, however, that the title 'Her Royal Highness' was not on the coffin plaque; nor, even more curiously, was her name mentioned once during the service. Afterwards the Duchess's coffin was followed out of the chapel by principal members of the Royal Family to be taken to its final resting-place in the lawn at Frogmore beside the Duke. In death there was final reconciliation between the family and the woman who had shaken the British throne to its foundations. The Queen was seen to weep.

13.   The Seventies

The Queen's Christmas broadcast for 1973 was censored by her Prime Minister, Edward Heath: a last-minute postscript she had added expressing 'deep concern' at 'the special difficulties Britain is now facing' was vetoed for being too alarmist, any allusion to the crisis being considered bad for morale. Viewers were treated to photographs of Princess Anne's wedding that summer instead.

It was all too reminiscent of 1947/8, when Winston Churchill had described Princess Elizabeth's engagement as 'a flash of colour on the hard road we have to travel'. Edward Heath's one and only premiership (1970–74) had developed in an unending series of crises, which the Queen had rightly described as 'special difficulties'. Between June 1970 and February 1974 Heath declared no fewer than five 'States of Emergency': electricity cuts, miners' and dockers' strikes, collapsing industries (in February 1971 the famous Rolls-Royce company had been declared bankrupt, threatening thousands of jobs and necessitating Government intervention), unemployment, rising commodity prices and inflation, and student riots induced an atmosphere of impending disaster. In Northern Ireland internment, imposed by the Heath Government as a response to the rise in violence of the newly formed Provisional IRA, provoked riots, bombings and reprisals, notably the horrors of 'Bloody Sunday', 30 January 1972, when the British Army shot thirteen people in the Bogside area of Londonderry and an outraged mob burned down the British Embassy in Dublin. The British Government suspended the Stormont Parliament and imposed direct rule from Whitehall. Inevitably there were bombs on the streets of Britain. After the Yom Kippur war of October 1973 and the defeat of Egypt and Syria by Israel, the Arab world united against the West, forcing the price of oil to multiply ten-fold. Heath's response to a threatened miners' demand for a pay rise in the dire economic circumstances was to declare in December 1973 a 'Three Day Week' for British industry in the New Year. Announcing the proposal on television on 13 December, his appearance seemed to predict defeat: 'His face grey with fatigue and his eyes like slits, the Prime Minister had never looked worse on television,' Michael Cockerell commented. 'Ted Heath seemed to match his anagram: the death.'[1] The International Marxist Group announced that 'The objective pre-conditions for a victorious socialist revolution in Britain' were 'ripening fast', and Tariq Ali published a book called *The Coming British Revolution*.[2]

In contrast the Queen, who three years before had been voted the nation's most popular individual, appeared as a symbol of stability. There had been outrage when long-haired students, particular objects of dislike with the British public, had demonstrated against her on a visit to Stirling University in October 1972. Pictures the next day showed a smiling Sovereign walking past students giving clenched-fist salutes and swigging wine from bottles. 'Queen Courageous' declared the tabloids. The next month the Queen and the Duke of Edinburgh celebrated their silver wedding with a thanksgiving service at Westminster Abbey and a dinner at the Guildhall on 20 November. In her speech the Queen emphasized the themes of marriage, family, nation, family of nations. 'We had the good fortune to grow up in happy united families,' she said. 'We have been fortunate in our children, and above all we are fortunate in being able to serve this great country and Commonwealth.'

Within just under a year, on 14 November 1973, she celebrated the wedding of Princess Anne and Captain Mark Phillips. It was a sporting romance: Princess Anne was a superb competitor at equestrian events, so much so that despite her reputation for being rude to reporters, she had been elected the Sports Writers' Association 'Sportswoman of the Year' and the BBC 'Sports Personality of the Year' in 1971. Mark Phillips, a good-looking man of few words, excelled in the area that mattered to her, riding, and was even better at it than she was. The Queen Mother diagnosed the source of the attraction when she reportedly quipped, 'If they have children, they'll have four legs.' As far as the public was concerned, the wedding between the Princess and the handsome Army captain was just what they needed to cheer them up: it helped, too, that the no-nonsense Princess had chosen a middle-class man without a title or a stately home. It made the monarchy seem more democratically accessible. It was the first major royal celebration since the Coronation twenty years before and, like the Coronation, was a genuinely national event. Twenty-eight million tuned in to watch, underlining the huge growth in television ownership over the two decades.

While the Queen's family seemed happy and united, there was another family to which she was devoted which was not faring quite so well under her Prime Minister, Edward Heath – the Commonwealth. Heath, the second of the Queen's Prime Ministers to have a working-class background, was a passionate European. Formal negotiations for Britain's entry had begun in Brussels in July 1970; this time round Georges Pompidou was President of France, but many differences had remained. In May 1971 Heath, taking the initiative, flew to Paris for a two-day conference face to face with Pompidou and managed to convince the French President that British entry was not only possible but desirable. Many people – on both sides – remained sceptical or hostile to the project, as Pompidou had concluded in his statement following the meetings. Heath returned to England to convince his party and the country of the desirability of joining Europe and changed Britain's history. It was a personal triumph. He signed the Accession Treaty marking Britain's entry into the EEC at a formal ceremony at the Egmont Palace in Brussels on 22 January 1972; Britain officially became a member on 1 January 1973. Heath launched 'Fanfare for Europe', intended as a nationwide celebration, but, since four out of ten people opposed EEC membership, it was not and never could have been a success. The Queen and Prince Philip attended a gala night of classical music at Covent Garden to open the festival on 3 January, followed by a dinner at Lancaster House. Heath's heart was 'full of joy at the recognition that Her Majesty the Queen had given to our country's greatest achievement'.[3] He neglected to mention the 300 anti-Europe protesters who had greeted the arrival of the royal couple with shouts of 'Sieg Heil', nor did he apparently notice the 'look of horrified distaste, quickly suppressed ... that crossed the Queen's face when Carl Davis conducted his "modern" adaptation of the National Anthem'.

The Queen, according to some pro-European politicians, was not anti-Europe, but there is little doubt that she did not share Heath's passion for the alliance to the detriment of two other important relationships which she cherished – with the Commonwealth and with the United States. According to Heath's biographer, John Campbell, the Queen was deeply unhappy with Heath's undisguised disrespect for the institution of the Commonwealth in general and most African leaders in particular, and was greatly upset by the rows which had disfigured the 1971 Commonwealth conference in Singapore.[4] The rows had been precipitated by Heath's decision to resume arms sales to South Africa. The Queen would apparently have liked to attend the meeting but Heath would not allow her to go; she did, however, again apparently against Heath's wishes, insist on attending the next Commonwealth Conference in Ottawa in 1973. Britain's entry into the European Community on 1 January 1973 was a turning point for Britain and the Commonwealth. In her Christmas broadcast of 1972, delivered just before the critical date, she tried to reconcile the ideas of Community and Commonwealth: 'The new links with Europe will not replace those with the Commonwealth,' she said optimistically. 'They cannot alter our historical ties and personal attachments with kinsmen and friends overseas. Old friends will not be lost. Britain will take her Commonwealth links into Europe with her.' She concluded, 'We are trying to create a wider family of nations.'

Ben Pimlott called her speech a *cri de coeur*:

> If entry into Europe was a turning point for Britain and the Commonwealth, it was a moment of crisis for the monarchy. The idea of the joining of families . . . was political and economic nonsense, a desperate bid to evade the reality. The truth about signing the Accession Treaty . . . was that it constituted the most decisive step yet in the progressive severance in 'familial' ties between Britain and its former Empire, which had begun with Indian independence. It reduced the remaining links to sentimental and cultural ones . . .
>
> Yet the Queen's own connections with the Commonwealth remained, independent of any decisions taken in London or Brussels. Not only was she Head of the Commonwealth – whatever that now meant – she was also Head of State of a sizeable proportion of its members, and was required to take advice from their governments . . . Britain's entry into the Common Market had made her divided constitutional self more difficult.[5]

Much of the Queen's time from now on would be devoted to overseas tours designed to reassure countries of the 'Old Commonwealth' – Australia, Canada and New Zealand – that Britain's new European commitment would not diminish the links between them. The fact was that they had already been weakened by the strains and shock of Britain's earlier attempts to enter the EEC; as far as the 'Old Commonwealth' was concerned, things would never be the same again. Britain had signalled that her interests lay with Europe and that the 'historical ties and personal attachments' of which the Queen had spoken would inevitably weaken. In Canada the *Toronto Star*, hitherto a supporter of the Crown connection, editorialized as to whether the time had not come for Canada to have its own Head of State instead of one who belonged to a foreign country. On a six-day visit to Australia that year, 1973, the Queen signed what was designed as a first formal step towards cutting the umbilical cord with Britain, the Royal Style and Titles Bill, introduced by the Labour Prime Minister, Gough Whitlam. This stated categorically that when the Queen was in Australia she would be referred to only as 'Queen of Australia', not, as hitherto, as 'Queen of the United Kingdom and of Her Other Realms and Territories'. (In 1975 the dismissal of Gough Whitlam by Sir John Kerr, the Queen's Governor-General and therefore representative in Australia – without consulting the Queen – would give further impetus to anti-British sentiment and a questioning of the validity and desirability of the connection with the British Crown.)

Ever since the Second World War, and indeed since George VI had established friendly relations with President Roosevelt in 1939, the 'special relationship', friendship with the United States had been a tradition at the Palace and particularly with the Queen herself. But Heath, according to Henry Kissinger, President Nixon's Secretary of State, 'was the only British leader I encountered who not only failed to cultivate the special relationship with the United States but actively sought to downgrade it . . .'[6] In October 1970 President Nixon stopped off in Britain for a friendly visit to Heath at Chequers, and the Queen, apparently on her own initiative (and possibly to smooth relations between Nixon and Heath) flew down from Balmoral to join them and meet the President and Mrs Nixon on his first visit to Britain. By the time Heath lost power in 1974 the 'special relationship' had been weakened to such an extent that his biographer felt moved to write: 'From the point of view of Anglo-American relations . . . it is difficult not to feel that Heath's replacement by Wilson in February 1974 gave an opportunity for a fresh start that was badly needed.'

It is hard to credit the claim of his biographer that the Royal Family were 'absolutely potty' about Ted Heath, who rarely exerted himself to charm. Heath's unofficial biographer, John Campbell, has described his relations with the Queen as 'correct but cool'. Heath, physically unappealing, humourless and sexless, was notoriously uncomfortable in the company of most women. 'The Queen found Heath hard going,' a courtier said. 'Ted was tricky – she was never comfortable with him.' They had nothing in common beyond an interest in politics and foreign affairs: Heath's were music and sailing, hers racing and country pursuits. But both were professionals and interested in what the other had to tell them. Heath told an interviewer that he found his weekly audiences rewarding: 'The Queen is very interested,' he said, 'and has a wide correspondence overseas, particularly on overseas stuff she is very useful, and then there is more to it than that. You can speak with complete confidentiality to her. You can say things that you would not say even to your Number Two.'[7]

By the mid-1970s both Nixon and Heath had lost power, destroyed in Nixon's case by the Watergate scandal and in Heath's by economic crisis. At the end of July 1973 the Senate Judiciary Committee voted to impeach President Nixon 'for obstructing justice and violating constitutional rights', as a result of the investigation by the Select Committee on Presidential Campaign Activities, which revealed the presidential involvement in a dirty tricks campaign ('CREEP'), including the Watergate burglary, and the existence of tapes of a paranoid, hate-filled Nixon in the White House ranting against Jews, Italians, Germans, black people and anyone he counted as enemies.[8] Nixon resigned at noon on 9 August 1974, by which time Heath too was out of power, having lost the General Election to Harold Wilson. Heath's decision to go for an election when he did, in the teeth of a long-threatened miners' strike, was unwise, as was his determination to hog the limelight during the campaign, reminding the public that his was a persona for which they did not greatly care. 'Whatever public gesture he made, Heath had a knack of getting it slightly wrong.' Asked to contribute favourite dishes to a cookery book, Heath chose lobster Thermidor with two wine sauces; Wilson's choice was a pasty.[9] 'Lobster Thermidor had a lousy reception in the tabloids and on radio,' a colleague wrote, 'in comparison with Wilson's pasty.' The unspoken question, 'Who governs the country, Heath or the miners?' increasingly seemed to swing towards the latter. The result, against the expectation of a large Tory majority, was a hung parliament, a precursor of the situation in 2010. The Tories had nearly a quarter of a million votes more than Labour, but Labour won 301 seats to the Tories' 297.

At the beginning of 1974, the Queen's constitutionally split personality meant that she had to be in two places at once. Heath's snap General Election, to take place at the end of February, meant that it would fall in the middle of a long-planned South Sea tour. In the past, Prime Ministers had built their election plans round royal itineraries. Heath, facing a national emergency over another miners' strike, and hoping to cash in on it, was not prepared to be sentimental. He expected the Queen to fly back. The royal party set out for the Cook Islands, where the Queen was due to open an airport, at the end of February; from there she travelled on to Christchurch, New Zealand, for the start of the Commonwealth Games. Then she island-hopped through the Pacific: Norfolk Island, the New Hebrides, the British Solomon Islands, Papua New Guinea, and then on to open the Australian Parliament in Canberra as Queen of Australia. Less than thirty hours later, a jet-lagged Queen of the United Kingdom was in Buckingham Palace, ready to receive the Prime Minister of the United Kingdom, or summon a new one.[10] From Friday morning, by which time the final election results were clear, until the afternoon of Monday 4 March when Heath finally resigned, the uncertainty continued as he attempted to negotiate a coalition with the Liberals, led by Jeremy Thorpe. Just as it was to be in 2010, with Gordon Brown clinging on in Downing Street, there were charges of 'squatter' and 'bad loser'. Again, just as it was to be in 2010, the defeated Government's negotiations with the Liberals failed, and by the evening of 4 March Wilson had 'kissed hands' at Buckingham Palace and was once again in 10 Downing Street.

The Harold Wilson of 1974 was a very different man from the

feisty figure who had bounced into Number Ten ten years previously. Eleven years walking the tightrope of party leadership had worn him out, even though he was only fifty-eight, and he was already determined to go when he turned sixty. According to Barbara Castle he had told the Queen of his intention when he became her Prime Minister for the second time, and in March 1976, one week after his sixtieth birthday, he made a surprise announcement of his resignation. His premiership, compared with his previous incumbency and Edward Heath's experience, had been relatively successful: Wilson's objectives had been to keep his party in power and Britain in Europe. In Britain's first-ever referendum, on whether or not Britain should stay in the European Community, held on 5 June 1975, 67 per cent of the electorate voted 'Yes'. As Wilson himself put it, fourteen years of internal argument were over. It was perhaps the greatest triumph of his political career. 'He turned the referendum, which the Left had backed because it saw it as a clever ruse for taking Britain out of the Common Market, into a means of legitimizing, once and for all, the decision to go in; and did so in such a way that it was impossible for anybody except die-hard antis to argue that he had acted unfairly,'[11] his biographer wrote. Even Mrs Thatcher, who had recently replaced Heath as Conservative leader, had put her party's weight behind the Yes campaign and described the result as 'very thrilling'.

The Queen was sorry to see Wilson go; she had liked him and had even formed a certain rapport with his wife, Mary. According to Wilson's own account (differing slightly this time from what he told Barbara Castle), he had informed the Queen of his absolute intention to go in March 1976, while up at Balmoral the previous September. The Queen had dispensed with their detectives and herself driven the Wilsons to a bothy on the estate for a picnic. While Mary laid the table, the Queen filled the kettle; after tea she handed Mary an apron, put one on herself and the two women washed up. Mary Wilson, herself despising pretentiousness, pomp, and certain politicians, wrote a poem about the Queen which described her as a countrywoman (or rather a landowner) yet with an aura. 'Walking free upon her own estate/Still in her solitude, she is the Queen.' On 5 April Wilson gave a dinner party at Downing Street to mark his retirement, which the Queen attended, just as she had for Winston Churchill. That day James 'Jim' Callaghan was elected Leader of the Labour Party, securing the succession as Labour Prime Minister. Since the Conservatives now also elected their leader, the Queen's constitutional prerogative of choosing her Prime Minister in normal circumstances had ceased to exist.

Callaghan, the second of the Queen's Labour Prime Ministers of working-class origins, was as loyal a monarchist as Wilson had been. A tough pragmatist with strong trade-union links, he was open in his admiration for the Queen's abilities but equally honest in his appraisal of his own relationship with the monarch. Unlike Wilson he was under no illusion that he was treated with special favour. 'Each [Prime Minister] thinks he is treated in a more friendly way than the one before,' he told an interviewer. '. . . I'm sure that's not true. The Queen is more even-handed.'

'What one gets is friendliness but not friendship,' Callaghan told Lady Longford.

> Prime Ministers also get a great deal of understanding of their problems – without the Queen sharing them, because she is outside politics. I think she weighs them up – but doesn't offer advice. Of course, she may have hinted at things, but only on the rarest occasions do I remember her ever saying, 'Why don't you do this, that or the other?' She is pretty detached on all that. But she's very interested in the political side – who's going up and who's going down . . .

Callaghan's appraisal of the Queen's understanding of her role was perceptive:

> The Queen has a deep sense of duty and responsibility in this [the political] area, and also sees it as a means of preserving the Royal Family as an institution. If her Prime Minister liked to give the

Queen information and gossip about certain political characters, she would listen very attentively, for she has a real understanding of the value of a constitutional monarchy . . . I think the prestige of the monarchy could deteriorate if she didn't work so hard at it . . . She really knows how to preserve the monarchy and how to conduct herself on public occasions. When to step into the limelight and when to step out. She really is professional in her approach, and I admire her, and I am very, very fond of her.[12]

David Owen, Foreign Secretary in Callaghan's Government, also stressed the Queen's 'friendliness', particularly in circumstances where she felt relaxed, as on board the royal yacht *Britannia*.

On *Britannia* when the last guest goes, the Queen kicks off her shoes and tucks her feet under her skirt on the sofa and talks about the people who've been there that evening in a vivacious way – the face lights up and she becomes really attractive – so you realize how much is kept under control. She gets confidentiality from people because they are treated in such a welcoming and considerate way.[13]

With her husband, Tony Crosland, who was Owen's successor as Foreign Secretary, American writer Susan Crosland travelled to the United States with the Queen and Duke of Edinburgh in July 1976 to celebrate the bicentenary of the Declaration of Independence. She too noted the complete naturalness of the Queen's behaviour in front of her Foreign Secretary and his wife. 'On one occasion when Philip was sounding off about something, the Queen said to him quite sharply, "Oh, Philip, do shut up. You don't know what you're talking about."' When *Britannia* ran into a Force 9 gale two days out of Bermuda, en route to Penn's Landing in Philadelphia, the Queen exhibited great aplomb at dinner when most of the party, including her husband, were ashen-faced.

The Queen rose to say goodnight, resting one hand against the handle of the open sliding door which at that moment began sliding shut, *Britannia* having failed to take a breathing space before

heaving over again. The Queen gripped the handle firmly, pressed
her back to the door and moved with it as it slid slowly shut, her
chiffon scarf flying in the opposite direction. 'Wheeeee,' said the
Queen. *Britannia* shuddered, reeled again. The chiffon scarf flew
the other way. 'Wheeeee,' said the Queen. *Britannia* hesitated before
the next heave. 'Goodnight,' said the Queen, slipping through the
door, Prince Philip half a pace behind her . . . when we foregath-
ered in the drawing room before lunch [the next day] complexions
were better than the evening before. 'I have *never* seen so many grey
and grim faces round a dinner table,' said the Queen. She paused.
'Philip was not at all well.' She paused. 'I'm glad to say.' She gig-
gled. I'd forgotten that her Consort is an Admiral of the Fleet . . .[14]

Time magazine called the Queen's five-day visit to the 'former
colonies of her great-great-great-great-grandfather, George III'
'the most glittering courtesy call of the US Bicentennial'. In blis-
tering heat in Independence Hall in Philadelphia she presented
Britain's Bicentennial gift to the US: a six-ton bell cast by the same
Whitechapel Foundry in London that had made the original Liberty Bell in 1752. In her speech she said that the events of 1776 may
have severed constitutional ties between Britain and the US but
'did not for long break our friendship', and went so far as to thank
the American founding fathers for 'a very valuable lesson'. 'We
learned to respect the rights of others to govern themselves in
their own way,' she said. 'While Elizabeth's forefathers lost a continent two centuries ago,' *Time* noted, 'she won over a nation last
week with her warmth and easy grace.' After a British Embassy
dinner in Washington given for President Gerald Ford, she displayed her sporting knowledge when she met the world-famous
boxer Muhammad Ali, still limping from Japanese wrestler Anto-
nio Inoki's bruising kicks in their recent bout, asking, 'How are
you feeling?' and 'Which leg was hurt the worst?' From New York
she went on with Prince Philip to open the Montreal Olympics,
where Princess Anne was a member of the British equestrian team.

But universally, and at home, Britain's image in the mid to late 70s was one of inescapable, incurable decline: 'a thing in a museum, a dying animal in a zoo', as novelist John Fowles described it in *Daniel Martin* (1977). The strikes and industrial crises of Heath's years had become known as 'the British disease' (there was even a Japanese word for it). In the words of a recent commentator on the 70s, Francis Wheen: 'Once again as during Ted Heath's power cuts and three-day weeks, foreign reporters followed the scent of political and economic putrefaction.'[15] 'Goodbye, Great Britain,' a *Wall Street Journal* editorial concluded. 'It was nice knowing you.' On CBS News of 6 May 1975, the American commentator Eric Sevareid administered the last rites to British democracy:

> It is not merely that her military strength is ebbing and her economic strength weakening but that Britain is drifting slowly toward a condition of ungovernability. It is now a debatable question whether Parliament or the great trade unions are calling the political tune. The country, as one English writer puts it, is sleepwalking into a social revolution, one its majority clearly does not want but does not know how to stop . . .

Comparisons were drawn with Chile, where in 1973 Allende's left-wing government had been overthrown in a military coup. In Portugal in April 1974, the 'Carnation Revolution', a democratic alliance spearheaded by the army, overthrew the dictatorial government. And in Britain itself there was talk of similar coups backed by officers, powerful businessmen, Mountbatten, even the Soviet Union. Tony Benn learned from the commander of the National Defence College, Major-General Bate, 'that there was a movement called PFP [Prince] Philip for President. The Paras were supposed to be involved, and some movement of troops in Northern Ireland was contemplated.'[16] What there certainly was was a general feeling of discontent, expressed by Margaret Drabble in her novel *The Ice Age*, published in 1977: 'All over the country, people blamed other people for all the things that were going wrong – the trades unions, the present government, the miners, the car workers, the seamen, the Arabs, the Irish . . .' Even in football, the area of greatest national pride since the 1966 victory, things were going sour: in October 1973 England was eliminated from the World Cup, and the hitherto relatively unknown phenomenon of football hooliganism was on the rise to the degree that some newspapers ran a weekly 'League of Violence'.

Even the dictator of Uganda, Major General Idi Amin (described by President Nixon as a 'prehistoric monster' and by Lord Home as a 'lunatic'), whose ideas of economic stability had included expelling the Ugandan Asian business community in 1972, had weighed in with sarcastic offers of help to Britain in her troubles. 'In the past few months the people of Uganda have been following with sorrow the alarming economic crisis befalling on Britain,' he wrote to Heath in December 1973: 'I am today appealing to all the people of Uganda who have all along been traditional friends of the British people to come forward and help their former colonial masters . . . who are now victims of measures such as power cuts and inflation.' 'In this spirit,' he teased, 'I have decided to contribute ten thousand Uganda shillings from my savings.' In January 1974 he informed Heath that people of Kigezi district had contributed one lorry-load of vegetables. 'I am now requesting you to send an aircraft urgently to collect this donation before it goes bad.' In January 1975, according to Wheen, he wrote a cheeky letter to the monarch expressing his intention to visit Scotland, Wales and Northern Ireland and offering his services as a peacemaker: 'Your Majesty . . . I should like to use that chance to talk to these people who are struggling for self determination and independence from your political and economic system.' The Queen did not reply.[17]

In the forbidding circumstances, plans for a national celebration of the Queen's Silver Jubilee, her twenty-five years on the throne, in 1977 were regarded with apprehension in Establishment circles and with gruesome delight by the left-wing media. The Jubilee was generally predicted by the British media to be an embarrassing

flop, in contrast to the reactions of foreign newspapers and broad-
casters, who seemed interested and quite unaware of the British
pessimism about the forthcoming event. Twenty-five years after
the Queen's accession, the omens for success were not auspicious:
Britain was wallowing in the worst economic trough since 1945,
with inflation at 16 per cent and 1.5 million unemployed. The
Chancellor had been forced to go to the International Monetary
Fund for a huge loan, which had imposed severe cuts in public
expenditure. 'The Government's line was "We don't want to overdo
this",' Martin Charteris, the Queen's longest-serving Private Secretary, said. They were opposed to a national tour on financial grounds.
'I told them – look, you've never done what I've done – followed
the Queen round in Birmingham and Sheffield and places like that
and seen the glow she spreads around and how people empty out
into the streets to see her.'[18]

The Queen herself could vividly remember her grandfather's
Silver Jubilee in 1935, when aged just nine she had sat with her
grandparents in their carriage driven through wildly cheering
crowds. The success of that Jubilee had taken the King and everyone else by surprise. 'I'm beginning to think they must really like
me for myself,' he had famously remarked after a wildly enthusiastic tour of the East End of London. Her own Jubilee seemed slow
to take off; there were reports of street parties cancelled and lack of
demand for souvenir trinkets. In some areas, the most visible evidence of the coming Jubilee was provided by the efforts of Marxists
and other agitators to discredit it. The Communist Party organized
its own 'People's Jubilee' at Alexandra Palace, and the Trotskyist
Socialist Workers' Party gave out quantities of 'Roll on the Red
Republic' stickers. The *New Statesman* prepared an 'anti-Jubilee'
issue. The Poet Laureate, Sir John Betjeman, wrote an outstand-
ingly dreadful anthem: 'From that look of dedication/In those eyes
profoundly blue/We know her Coronation/As a Sacrament and
true.'[19]

In the end, and contrary to all predictions, the Queen's 1977

Jubilee was a huge popular success. On 6 June she climbed Snow Hill near Windsor to light a bonfire that was the signal for the lighting of one hundred other fires across the country. Next day a million people, as many as for the Coronation, filled the Mall to see the Queen and Prince Philip ride in the State Coach from Buckingham Palace to St Paul's Cathedral for a thanksgiving service; afterwards the royal couple went on a pre-planned walkabout through the City, talking to spectators as they walked, ending at the Guildhall, where she attended a luncheon in her honour at which she gave a speech renewing the vows of service to her people and to the Commonwealth that she had made in Cape Town on her twenty-first birthday. Across the nation there was real community celebration in the cheering crowds who greeted her on her national tour, and in the exuberant street parties in towns and villages across the country – 7,000 in London alone. It was a spectacularly happy moment in a generally miserable decade, and its focus was the Queen herself. 'The Queen had a love affair with the nation,' said Martin Charteris. John Grigg, her former critic as Lord Altrincham, wrote perceptively about her qualities:

> She looks a queen and obviously believes in her right to be one. Her bearing is both simple and majestic – no actress could possibly match it. Wherever she may be in the world, in whatever company or climate, she never seems to lose her poise.
>
> These outward graces reflect the exceptionally steady character which is her most important quality. Through a period of fluctuating fashion and considerable moral disintegration, she has lived up to her own high standards . . . No breath of scandal has ever touched her . . . She behaves decently because she *is* decent.[20]

14.   The Thatcher Years

On 27 August 1979, on a glittering summer morning off the coast of Sligo in the west of Ireland, an IRA bomb detonated by remote control from the shore exploded under the feet of Earl Mountbatten as he piloted his wooden fishing boat to retrieve a lobster pot. He was killed instantly, as were a young local boy, fifteen-year-old Paul Maxwell, and fourteen-year-old Nicholas Knatchbull, one of Mountbatten's twin grandsons. His elder daughter, Patricia, a childhood friend of the Queen, and her husband, Lord Brabourne, were severely injured. Brabourne's mother, who was with them, died of her injuries the next day. On the same day, far to the east at Warrenpoint, County Down, on the border between Northern Ireland and the Irish Republic, another IRA explosion killed eighteen British soldiers. The double strike was, an IRA bulletin claimed, 'a discriminate operation to bring the attention of the English people to the continuing occupation of our country. We will tear out their sentimental, imperialist heart . . . bringing emotionally home to the English ruling class and its working-class slaves . . . that their government's war on us is going to cost them as well.'

The hideous 'execution' – quite apart from the appalling tragedies of the 'working-class' families of the eighteen paratroopers at Warrenpoint – struck at the heart of the British Royal Family. Mountbatten, the last Viceroy of India, Prince Philip's uncle, now seventy-nine years old, was the family's elder statesman. The Queen was at Balmoral when she heard of his death, a devastating blow to the whole of her family. Despite his well-known penchant for meddling and intrigue – he was known, sometimes fondly, sometimes not, as 'Tricky Dicky'– he was much loved, and deservedly so, by the family. He was a valued counsellor for his wide knowledge of public and world affairs, a great supporter of the monarchy and its most distinguished member since Prince Albert. He had been a surrogate father to Prince Philip and uncle to the Queen; Prince Charles called him 'honorary grandfather' and he was perhaps the most devastated of all by his loss. 'I have no idea what we shall do without you if you finally decide to depart,' he had written to Mountbatten earlier that month. Grief-stricken on hearing the news while he was fishing in Iceland, he wrote a heart-felt tribute to his beloved mentor:

> I have lost someone infinitely special in my life; someone who showed enormous affection, who told me things I didn't want to hear, who gave praise where it was due as well as criticism; someone to whom I knew I could confide anything and from whom I would receive the wisest of counsel and advice. In some extraordinary way he combined grand-father, great uncle, father, brother and friend and I shall always be eternally grateful that I was lucky enough to have known him as long as I did. Life will <u>never</u> be the same now that he has gone . . .[1]

Although the increasingly headstrong prince had recently tended to ignore his honorary grandfather's advice, Mountbatten's opinions might have helped him avoid the crucial mistakes he was to make in the coming decade.

Far from becoming, as the Palace had feared in previous years, bored with its monarchy, the public was more and more fascinated by the Queen's family, as the newspapers were discovering to their profit. Princess Margaret had been making the headlines again at the time of her sister's Silver Jubilee, as she had at the time of her Coronation. The Snowdon marriage had been deteriorating since the first happy years; they lived high-profile celebrity lives with friends like Peter Sellers, were always in the news and had both found new loves. Early in 1976 the *News of the World* published a photograph of what appeared to be an intimate shot of the Princess with her 'toyboy', Roderick 'Roddy' Llewellyn, younger brother of the dashing society figure, Welsh baronet Sir Dai Llewellyn. The newspaper had cropped the picture to cut out the Princess's friends, Lord Coke and his wife Valeria, sitting opposite them at a beach bar on the chic private holiday island of Mustique. The photograph precipitated a crisis in the doomed Snowdon marriage; Snowdon moved out of the marital home at Kensington Palace and an official statement was issued:

> Her Royal Highness, The Princess Margaret, Countess of Snowdon, and the Earl of Snowdon have mutually agreed to live apart. The Princess will carry out her public duties and functions unaccompanied by Lord Snowdon.

'There are no plans for divorce proceedings,' the Palace statement ended glibly but mendaciously.

The Snowdon affair dominated the headlines, eclipsing the announcement of Harold Wilson's resignation, proving once again that the public was far more interested in royal personages than it was in politicians. While the political world continued to speculate over sinister motives for Wilson's decision – private scandal, Soviet connections – the majority of readers enjoyed speculation about 'Margaret and Roddy'. Labour politicians seized on the headlines about the affair to attack the Princess and her Civil List allowance. Willie Hamilton, a well-known republican and Labour MP for Fife, pointed out that the Elizabeth Garrett Anderson Hospital for Women was threatened with closure for lack of funds while the Princess's Civil List allowance had risen to £55,000 a year. 'If she thumbs her nose at taxpayers by flying off to Mustique to see this pop-singer chap, she shouldn't expect the workers of this country to pay for it,' he declared, pointing out that she had been on just eight public engagements in the first three months of the year, during which time she had drawn £14,000, 'not bad for eight performances'.[2] The Queen, who as usual had not attempted to interfere, was on good terms with Snowdon and adored the Snowdon children, decided with her advisers that to avoid further damage it was time to draw a line under the scandal. On 10 May 1978 it was announced from Kensington Palace that the Princess was seeking a divorce, stressing that she had no plans to remarry and intended to carry on her duties as the Queen's sister. The Princess celebrated her fiftieth birthday in 1980 with a dinner party attended by the Queen; Roddy Llewellyn discreetly arrived after dinner, escorted by Princess Margaret's close friends the Tennants, who had originally introduced him to her. A year later he married and Princess Margaret was alone again. 'I'm back to where I started with Peter [Townsend],' she told a friend, 'but this time I'm divorced.'

Her role as royal headline star was over: the unwelcome torch had already been handed to the younger generation. The Prince of Wales, as heir to the throne, had been the focus of public and press attention for some time. 'Every working day of my five years at the Palace there was a questioning of who Prince Charles would marry,' Ronald Allison, Press Secretary from 1973 to 1978, recorded. Mountbatten had been a powerful presence even in this aspect of the Prince's life; his objective had been that the Prince should marry his granddaughter, Amanda Knatchbull, daughter of Lady Patricia Brabourne. However, in 1970 Charles had already met the woman who was to be the love of his life, Camilla Shand, great-granddaughter of Edward VII's last (married) mistress, Alice Keppel. Charles and Camilla spent weekends at Mountbatten's house, Broadlands; Mountbatten had encouraged their romance, seeing Camilla as ideal mistress material who could pave the way for Amanda Knatchbull, who was still in her teens, to take over as the virgin bride. 'I believe in a case like yours,' he had written to Charles, 'that a man should sow his wild oats before settling down. But for a wife he should choose a suitable and sweet-charactered girl before she meets anyone else she might fall for.'[3] It was even rumoured that he had used his influence with the Admiralty to get Charles posted overseas to get him away from Camilla, who, while Charles was away serving in the Navy in the Caribbean, married her long-term love, Andrew Parker Bowles, in July 1973.

Mountbatten in his last years had begun to worry about the Prince's selfish bachelor behaviour, as girl succeeded girl after he left the Navy in 1976, warning him that he was 'beginning on the downward slope which wrecked your [great] Uncle David's life and led to his Abdication and useless life ever after . . .' Even before Mountbatten's death, Charles had begun to worry that his uncle might be right. 'I'm told marriage is the only cure for me – and maybe it is!' he had written to a friend on 15 April 1979.[4] The shock just over four months later left him bereft and now entirely dependent on the emotional support and advice of Camilla Parker Bowles. Within eight months the ideal virgin bride appeared, and again Mountbatten's ghost hovered in the background. At a barbecue party in July 1980 he was immediately attracted by the twenty-year-old Lady Diana Spencer, sister of a former girlfriend. The spark that lit the relationship was Diana's empathy over the death of Mountbatten. According to Diana's account to Andrew Morton she told the Prince: 'You looked so sad when you walked up the aisle at Lord Mountbatten's funeral . . . It was the most tragic thing I've ever seen. My heart bled for you when I watched. I thought, "It's wrong you're lonely – you should be with somebody to look after you." '[5]

To Charles and his family, Diana Spencer seemed the ideal choice. Apart from being young, lovely and apparently much in love with Charles, she came from a family with royal connections (her maternal grandmother, Ruth, Lady Fermoy, was a friend and lady-in-waiting to the Queen Mother; her father, Johnnie Spencer, had been equerry to the Queen on her post-Coronation Commonwealth tour; her brother-in-law, Robert Fellowes, husband of her sister Jane, was Assistant Private Secretary to the Queen). Just as importantly for a family as sensitive to the possibility of scandal as the Royal Family, she had no 'previous form' as far as men were concerned. Young and healthy as she was, she would undoubtedly be able to bear the longed-for heir to the Prince of Wales. Friends remarked on the absolute lack of interests between them except for a love of music: Charles was old for his age, Diana young for hers. Camilla, his chief counsellor, actively promoted the marriage; Ruth Fermoy on her deathbed excused Charles on the ground that he was 'driven by his family'. Charles dithered, and his father, rightly concerned that press speculation was making Diana's life impossible, issued an 'either/or' ultimatum. Finally the engagement was publicly announced on 24 February 1981.

The couple were interviewed in the grounds of Buckingham Palace, Charles looking worried and quizzical, Diana very young, her thick fair hair unbecomingly cut, her figure in a mumsy blue suit looking distinctly chubby, but despite her shyness seeming more self-possessed than Charles, who was never at his best in television interviews. Boldly asked by the TV interviewer if they were in love, Diana replied, grimacing, eyes rolling, 'Of course.' Charles famously added his response, 'Whatever in love means.' Around the world, people who watched the interview drew in their breath. It seemed to bode ill for the future. That evening Diana moved to the protection of the Queen Mother at Clarence House to escape the press. Two days later she moved into Buckingham Palace, symbolically cutting herself off for ever from normal life.

Just as the wedding of the Prince of Wales's parents in 1947 had been greeted by Winston Churchill in austerity times as a 'flash of colour on the hard road we have to travel', so the wedding of Charles and Diana in July 1981 lit up the economic gloom after the Labour Government of Jim Callaghan had collapsed following the 1979 'Winter of Discontent', when a series of public sector strikes had left dustbins unemptied, accompanied in the press by graphic photographs of rats feeding on rubbish and bodies unburied in mortuaries. MP Willie Hamilton, who had excoriated Princess Margaret over her Mustique holidays with Roddy Llewellyn, dissented from the general joy, denouncing the whole affair as a deliberate distraction by the Conservative Government, led by Margaret Thatcher, to divert public attention from the latest unemployment figures: 'The winter of discontent is now being replaced by the winter of phony romance with the active connivance of the government.' The *Daily Telegraph*'s reaction was diametrically opposite:

> For a nation more than ever starved of symbols of hope and good-ness in public life, the Royal example, far from fading, becomes more important . . . The best private feelings inspire the greatest public acts. In its monarchy, the British nation has at its pinnacle an institution that commands such feelings and a family that embod-ies them. With so many commoners who hate, it matters more than ever that a Prince who loves should one day sit upon the throne of England.

Within less than two months of the *Telegraph* piece, the 'common-ers who hate' were illustrated by three days of rioting in Brixton, south London, in April, when thousands of West Indian youths fought 3,000 Metropolitan police (followed in July by similar scenes in Toxteth, Liverpool).

Diana became a media star on the day of her wedding, 29 July 1981. In terms of worldwide television, it was the greatest royal event ever staged: three-quarters of a billion people watched as 'Lady Di' became 'Princess Di' and an international icon with the status of Marilyn Monroe and Jackie Kennedy. The beauty she had become was almost unrecognizable from the shy, chubby girl of the engagement interview only five months before. Slim, almost fragile-looking, she was a radiant bride in her over-blown ivory silk dress with its huge train, the magnificent Spencer tiara holding her billowing tulle veil. The moment when the passionate bride kissed her not so passionate bridegroom on the lips on the balcony of Buckingham Palace in full view of the watching millions etched itself on the public consciousness as the remembered image of the 'fairy tale' that the Archbishop of Canterbury, presiding at the ceremony in St Paul's, had pronounced it to be.

From that moment on she (and by connection, the Queen's

family) was never to be out of the limelight and their fortunes were to be linked with her fortunes with disastrous results in the future. Inextricably – and dangerously – the private and public faces of the monarchy were seen as intertwined. Prompted by the romance of the 'princely marriage', polls showed the popularity of the monarchy as higher than it had been even at the time of the Queen's Coronation and her Silver Jubilee. It was the apogee of the twentieth-century monarchy, but dangerously for the institution and for Diana herself, the world became involved in what they saw as 'Our Story' and the fairy-tale princess and her dashing prince became *their* property.

Meanwhile the Queen had been faced with a new phenomenon – her first woman Prime Minister, Margaret Thatcher, who had defeated first Heath for the leadership of the Conservative Party in 1975 and then Callaghan for the premiership in 1979. It marked the acceptance of a sea change in Tory politics and the definitive transition from aristocratic to middle-class dominance of the political system. 'It would have been more difficult for the Tory Party to contemplate electing the daughter of a Grantham grocer to the leadership in 1975 if it had not elected the eldest son of a Broadstairs carpenter [Heath] ten years earlier,' a leading commentator, Hugo Young, wrote, but while Heath had spent a lifetime escaping from his origins – to the rarefied atmosphere of Balliol College, Oxford, and the Albany apartments in Mayfair – Margaret Thatcher gloried in hers. Hard work, thrift and the fight against socialism and the over-mighty welfare state were her mottoes. She was different in her gender and in her outsider status.[6]

'For the Conservative Party, the 1979 election produced an historic victory,' Young wrote.

> But upon its leader the effect was still more elevated, something closer to a transformation. It was the beginning of a period which could later be defined as an era, in which an ordinary politician, labouring under many disadvantages, grew into an international

figure who did some extraordinary things to her country . . . Long before it was complete, the name of Thatcher was taken for granted as one of the givens of British life . . . More than 6 million voters at the 1987 election reached voting age after 1979 and were too young to have known any other government. Analysis of the voting in 1979 showed the largest surge of support came from people usually reckoned to be most unsympathetic to a woman leader: the men and women of the skilled working class. Her victory made her unique not only in the history of Britain but in that of the Western World; her only Eastern equivalent was Indira Gandhi with whom, perhaps surprisingly, she had made friends when they had met in 1976.[7]

It is worth noting that in the nineteenth century the Tory Party, including a strong contingent of reactionary Tory squires, had elected the first and so far only Jewish leader and Prime Minister. There was nonetheless a strong undercurrent of male hostility to Mrs Thatcher in the ranks of her own party, which included Tory grandees who would eventually desert her. And not only Tory grandees: the French Prime Minister, Valéry Giscard d'Estaing, referred to her contemptuously as 'the grocer's daughter', and the official Soviet news agency Tass, worried by her intransigence, had labelled her the 'Iron Lady' as far back as 1976.

Setting Margaret Thatcher up against the Queen (the Queen and 'the Deputy Queen') would be a game that the press would increasingly play in the following decade. It was unfair: Mrs Thatcher was a devoted, even reverent, monarchist. 'No one would curtsey lower than Margaret,' her ex-Ministers affirm. They had no common interests apart from a shared patriotism. Mrs Thatcher was bored by the countryside; when obliged to make the duty visit to Balmoral in August, the ladies-in-waiting struggled to get her out of her habitual high-heeled court shoes into Hush Puppies for picnics, and on the appointed day of departure her suitcase was always early in the hall waiting for the off. Mrs Thatcher's great supporter, in public as in private, her husband Denis, helped lighten the atmosphere by his shared interest in sport and un-PC humour with Prince Philip, particularly when both were playing the role of consort to their wives at Commonwealth conferences.

The widest area of divergence between the Queen and Mrs Thatcher was, as it had been with Edward Heath, the Commonwealth, which in the late 1970s and 1980s meant principally the questions arising from inter-racial conflict in Southern Africa. 'The Queen was sympathetic to the Black cause in Rhodesia and Southern Africa,' the Hon. Lee Kuan Yew, Prime Minister of Singapore, assured the author. Mrs Thatcher was not so committed. For the past fifteen years successive Foreign and Colonial Secretaries and heads of Government had been preoccupied with the settlement in Rhodesia, ever since in 1965 the white minority government under Ian Smith had unilaterally declared independence from Britain. In an effort to placate international hostility and produce a semblance of legality, Smith had held elections in the spring of 1979 which had returned a black Prime Minister, Bishop Abel Muzorewa, but he was generally regarded as a Smith stooge by black nationalist leaders (the Patriotic Front, led by Joshua Nkomo and Robert Mugabe), who had been excluded from the electoral process, and the civil war continued. Lord Carrington, Thatcher's Foreign Secretary, was determined that a proper settlement should be achieved in Rhodesia once and for all, and a Commonwealth conference was fixed to take place in Lusaka, Zambia, in early August. Thatcher at that time knew next to nothing about Commonwealth affairs and her instinct was to regard black nationalists as 'terrorists'. In return the government-owned *Zambia Daily Mail*, comparing Mrs Thatcher unfavourably with the Queen's 'extraordinary loving heart', said the Prime Minister was a racist. Thatcher contemplated not going herself and, it seemed, like Heath, might even have stepped in to prevent the Queen going on grounds of safety after the Rhodesian Government bombed Lusaka. Fortunately, the Secretary-General of the newly formed Commonwealth

Secretariat in London, Sir Sonny Ramphal, persuaded the Rhodesian nationalist leader Joshua Nkomo to declare a ceasefire for the period the Queen would be in Lusaka. In London Thatcher announced that the position was that the Queen would go unless the Government advised her not to: 'the decision we have to make is a very difficult one.'

The Queen was determined to use her unique position and contacts to save the Lusaka Conference, and on 2 July the Palace ended the speculation by saying that previously announced State visits to Tanzania, Malawi, Botswana and Zambia, including four days in Lusaka for the CHOGM (Commonwealth Heads of Government Meeting), would take place as planned.

The Queen did not attend the opening sessions of the conferences and did not play any formal part in their proceedings. Yet she was a familiar and spirit-raising feature of them. She attended a reception and a dinner, and saw each Commonwealth leader for an individual audience. Sir Sonny Ramphal regarded her role as a crucial one:

> First the Queen brought an understanding that it was a post-colonial Commonwealth, something even senior members of the Foreign Office didn't understand. Second, she brought a new quality of caring, a sense that it was an important dimension of her reign, and not just tacked on to being Queen of England. Her success in Commonwealth countries had derived from an awareness that she cared – that they mattered in a sense beyond the British Government. This was a quality that developed very strongly over the years. Third, on her accession she was a young woman growing into international life along with young leaders of the Commonwealth. This was not true with those on the way out at the beginning of her reign, Nehru, Menzies, Diefenbaker. But it was of Kaunda, Nyerere and later Indira Gandhi. She grew up with them, understood them and related to them. They could talk with her and she wasn't talking down. She got to know them very well.

Even at the times when the British Government was at odds with many of these leaders, she was able to understand their point of view without taking sides, and managed to convey to them that she did.[8]

The success of the Lusaka Conference, at which both Mrs Thatcher and the African leaders made concessions, led to the constitutional conference at Lancaster House in London and, after elections, the formal transference of power to an independent Zimbabwe on 17 April 1980.

One event above all enabled Thatcher to play the role of Britannia: the Falklands war. On 19 March 1982 a party of Argentine 'scrap metal dealers' landed – for the second time – on the island of South Georgia, part of the Falklands group of islands, which had been British since 1833 but which Argentina called 'Las Malvinas' and which were now to be the subject of an armed invasion and takeover by the recently empowered military junta, headed by General Leopoldo Galtieri. The invasion was the result of British bungling and inattention almost as much as Argentine ambition. At the Foreign Office there were even plans for a 'lease-back' of the territory to Argentina; when Thatcher found out she apparently went 'thermo-nuclear'. On 2 April Argentine armed forces invaded the islands and Port Stanley surrendered. Mrs Thatcher determined 'with courage and decision', as she herself put it in her memoirs,[9] that the islands were British and must be recovered; a task force was despatched and the two-month war, which cost 255 British lives and more than 650 Argentine dead, began.

On 25 April the capital, Port Stanley, was recaptured: striding 'regally' into Downing Street, Thatcher famously proclaimed 'Rejoice, just rejoice!' On 2 May the Argentine warship *General Belgrano* was torpedoed on her orders by the British submarine *Conqueror* and 368 Argentine sailors drowned, escalating the conflict. Two days after the sinking, the British destroyer HMS *Sheffield* was hit by an Argentine Exocet missile; twenty-one men died and many more were seriously injured, bringing home to the British people that far from being a mere patriotic flourish, serving soldiers and sailors were actually giving their lives. On 21 May troop landings finally took place at San Carlos Bay, but victory was far from certain and the air and naval war, 8,000 miles from home, was a close-run thing. Thatcher had kept her nerve over three strained weeks until the surrender of Port Stanley and final victory. Where defeat would have destroyed her, victory elevated her to a new level, even in Argentina, where the hated junta responsible for the deaths of thousands of *desaparecidos* was destroyed. In Britain, where her reputation had been rock-bottom in 1981, her popularity ratings soared to 51 per cent. It ensured her a second election victory, which until then had been far from certain.

The Queen and Prince Philip had been personally involved in the war: twenty-two-year-old Prince Andrew was serving as a helicopter pilot on the aircraft carrier HMS *Invincible*. Like other families they had watched the progress of the war on television, while the Queen also received bulletins from Downing Street. On 26 May, six days after the first British landings, the Queen spoke about the war for the first time in public as a parent as she prepared to open the Kielder dam in Northumberland. 'Before I begin I would like to say one thing,' she said, 'our thoughts today are with those who are in the South Atlantic and our prayers are for their success and a safe return to their homes and loved ones.' The episode served to remind people of the traditional link between the Royal Family and the Services; the Queen's father, King George VI, had fought at the naval Battle of Jutland in the First World War, her husband, Prince Philip, had an heroic record in the Second, and now their son was serving in the Falklands campaign. For all Mrs Thatcher's understandable triumphalism, the forces' viewpoint was, as the second-in-command of the British land forces, Brigadier Julian Thompson, later put it: 'You don't mind dying for Queen and country, but you certainly don't want to die for politicians.'[10]

Unusually, however, neither the Queen, who after all was head of the armed forces, nor any other member of the Royal Family was invited to the parade and celebration of the victory in the City of London in October at the Guildhall. In the 1945 parade celebrating victory in the Second World War, Churchill and Attlee were positioned at a discreet distance from the saluting base. But now Mrs Thatcher herself, along with the Lord Mayor, took the salute and also supplied the somewhat regal benediction. 'What a wonderful parade it has been,' she said, 'surpassing all our expectations as the crowd, deeply moved and sensing the spirit of the occasion, accompanied the band by singing "Rule Britannia".'

Two Heads of State had visited Britain before the conclusion of the Falklands campaign: one was regally entertained by the Queen at Windsor, the other conspicuously not. Both visits had been planned long ahead, but the war affected them in a significant way. His Holiness Pope John Paul II, one of the most popular popes in history, celebrated for his heroic record as a Polish opponent of Communism, was forced by the circumstances of the war to avoid contact with the Palace or the Government. Argentina was a Catholic country and the Pope could not be seen to be taking sides; it was to be the only foreign tour the Pope made on which he actually avoided meeting the local Head of State or of the Government.

The case of the visit of President Ronald Reagan was very different: with his wife, Nancy, he was invited to stay at Windsor, the first American presidential couple to do so. He was en route to a world summit at Versailles, arranged long ago, but he had more than earned his welcome. During the campaign he had provided crucial military assistance to Britain. The support included everything from Sidewinder missiles to transport aircraft and a vital collaboration on signals and intelligence. The Queen and Mrs Thatcher knew this; the general public did not. Genial, right-wing and fervently anti-Communist, Reagan had bonded with Thatcher at their first meeting in London in 1975, and she had been his first foreign visitor after his inauguration in January 1981. He bonded with Her Majesty on a different, more personal level, a shared passion for horses and riding. He was photographed riding out with the Queen at Windsor and commenting favourably on her handling of her horse. 'It's called the forward seat,' he said of the Queen's riding style (as compared with his more relaxed 'Western' mode), 'the modern riding . . . she was in charge of that animal.' In a speech to both Houses of Parliament on 8 June, the President spoke of the alliance of the two countries against aggression: 'Those young men,' he said, 'fight for a cause, for the belief that armed aggression must not be allowed to succeed.' At a banquet she gave in his honour at Windsor that night, the Queen spoke of drawing comfort 'from the understanding of our position shown by the American people'. She had a personal reason also to be grateful – Prince Andrew, who telephoned her six days later after the war ended, was alive and unharmed.

15.   Family Troubles

On 21 June 1982, less than a year after her marriage, Diana gave birth to a son, Prince William, providing the Queen with, as Her Majesty put it, 'another heir'. On the surface it appeared to be a happy, successful marriage but in private there were difficulties that would lead to a dramatic public implosion within ten years, accompanied by other scandals and shenanigans which increasingly put the Palace at loggerheads with an increasingly ravenous and unscrupulous press.

Public interest in the monarchy had switched from the Queen, who celebrated the thirtieth anniversary of her accession in February 1982, to the younger members of the Royal Family, led, of course, by Diana. The public could not get enough of her: on her first public engagement after the marriage in October 1981, a three-day tour of Wales, the world's press turned up in force. Japanese and American television crews descended on obscure Welsh villages and towns in pursuit of her. Already suffering from bulimia, she was now pregnant, sick and depressed, but managed to show for the first time her extraordinary empathy and skill in dealing with people, in crowds and one on one. 'It was just that ability to talk, to know how to talk to people which was there from day one,' said a member of her staff who accompanied her on the tour. It was also the beginning of her outshining the heir to the throne: 'This was her first walkabout as such,' Dickie Arbiter, one of the royal correspondents there at the time, recalled. 'She did it as if she had done it all her life, trying to please everybody, switching from one side of the road to the other, because all people were doing was, "We want Di, we want Di, we want Di." And that's something he [Charles] had to get used to . . . the trouble was that he was playing the supporting role not the starring role.'[1] 'People wanted to see her not him and he couldn't stomach it,' said an aide. 'I was with Prince Charles and nobody came to us,' a former police protection officer on the tour recalled. 'Everybody wanted her and that was the start of it really. I think she started thinking of herself and people started looking at her as a divine something . . .'

When her pregnancy was announced later that autumn, the Palace took the unusual – and unwise – step of attempting to control the press. Press Secretary Michael Shea invited all the editors of the national Sunday and daily newspapers, television, radio and the Press Association to a special briefing, followed by drinks at Buckingham Palace. Only the editor of the *Sun* decided not to attend. Shea pleaded for the press and photographers to leave Diana alone, and afterwards the Queen circulated among them. It was not an experience she relished, nor did it have the desired effect of inducing the press to toe the line. The editor of the Murdoch-owned Sunday newspaper *News of the World*, referring to recent episodes during the Balmoral holiday, asked the Queen why, if Diana wanted privacy so much, did she go out to buy sweets at shops and not send a servant. The Queen was not amused: 'That was a pompous remark, Mr Askew.' Deference was dead, and inter-tabloid rivalry had developed to such an extent that the newspapers were up for anything that would increase circulation and were not inclined to respect appeals from the Palace. It got worse. In February, when Charles and Diana were on a private holiday on Eleuthera in the Bahamas, she was stalked by tabloid reporters from the *Sun* and the *Star* who took photographs of the pregnant princess in her bikini and published them. 'Carefree Di threw royal caution to the winds to wear her revealing outfit,' ran the *Sun*'s headline. The Queen was outraged, denouncing the tabloids' 'unprecedented breach of privacy'. The two newspapers responded by expressing regret that she should be displeased, but offering no apology and republishing the photographs. It was the beginning of a series of skirmishes between the tabloids and the

Palace, fomented by the behaviour of the younger royals and indeed encouraged by Diana, who let it be known to the offending newspaperman that she had not minded at all.

The Queen herself suffered a major intrusion of her privacy in July 1982 when a thirty-one-year-old schizophrenic, Michael Fagan, broke into the Palace, made his way to the Queen's bedroom at 7.15 a.m. and sat on her bed, holding a broken and bloodied glass ashtray. His intention, he later claimed, was to talk to her about his family problems and slash his wrists in front of her. The Queen behaved with characteristic courage: she pressed the alarm button and attempted twice to call the police, but no one responded. She was on her own. When Fagan asked her for a cigarette, she took the opportunity to manoeuvre him out into the corridor and into a nearby pantry on the excuse of looking for them. Eventually her footman came back with the corgis and she motioned him into the pantry, where he talked to Fagan and offered him a drink before a wandering policeman and a plainclothes man piled in to arrest him. The Queen gave strict instructions that the incident was not to be mentioned but the police report was leaked to the press, revealing the shortcomings in Palace security. It was, as Fagan himself said, 'diabolical'. This was not the first time he had got into the Palace; on the first occasion he had stolen a bottle of wine. This time he had been spotted on the railings near the Ambassador's Entrance on the south front of the Palace, then, climbing through an open office window, he had been seen in the corridor outside the office by a housemaid who assumed he was a workman, and had then been able to go through the corridors halfway round the Palace to the Queen's bedroom on the north front.

Fagan's exploit turned out to be harmless but it underlined the threat of terrorism – and madmen: the Queen had been shot at just over a year earlier as she rode her horse down the Mall for the Trooping the Colour ceremony by a young man who fired six shots at her (they later turned out to be blanks but she was not to know that at the time). She had merely ducked, patted her horse and ridden on. Eight years before there had been a serious attempt, foiled by the courage of the police protection officer, to kidnap Princess Anne from her car on the Mall. Both the Princess and Mark Phillips were unhurt but her bodyguard, the chauffeur, a policeman patrolling the Mall and a passing taxi passenger who tried to tackle the gunman were seriously wounded. The bodyguard, Jim Beaton, was later awarded the George Cross for his bravery. The motive for the attack on Anne had been money – the would-be kidnapper had hoped to gain a million pound ransom. Other violent events in the 1980s were directly related to the ongoing war in Northern Ireland. In 1982 the IRA blew up a squadron of the Household Cavalry in Hyde Park on its way to the daily Changing of the Guard ceremony at Buckingham Palace, and on the same day members of a military band playing in Regent's Park were killed by a bomb under their bandstand. On the night of 11 October 1984, the IRA made its most audacious attempt ever on the British Government at the Tory Party annual conference in Brighton. A bomb planted in Mrs Thatcher's bathroom at the Grand Hotel exploded, killing five and injuring many, including two of the Prime Minister's chief aides, Norman Tebbit and John Wakeham. Mrs Thatcher escaped uninjured, to appear without a hair out of place on television against the backdrop of the ruined hotel and Tebbit on a stretcher being carried, terribly injured, from the rubble. The television pictures shocked the nation, bring-ing to people's minds – if they had not been aware of it before – the continuing dangers of the Northern Ireland situation.

Prince Harry of Wales, the Queen's third grandson and his parents' last child, was born on 15 September 1984. According to Diana herself, her marriage was by then virtually over. After a very pub-lic row between the couple at the British Legion Festival of Remembrance at the Albert Hall in November 1982, when Diana had outraged royal protocol by turning up after the Queen, the press began to pick up on rumours of cracks in the fairy tale. Anne

Robinson, editing the tabloid *Sunday Mirror*, put one of the ablest royal reporters on the story: Diana's family, he reported back, feared that she was anorexic. Robinson ran the story, the Palace complained and she lost her job. On US television the well-connected social columnist Nigel Dempster denounced Diana as a 'monster' and a 'fiend' and alleged that her behaviour was making Prince Charles 'desperately unhappy'. The public did not want to believe it: 'it is important to us that the magic does not die', Robert Lacey wrote. But for the press the fairy-tale marriage in which so many people still invested their faith was turning into a doomed soap opera.

'At the point at which there began to be more hard and fast evidence, her weeping in public . . . cancelling going to places at the last minute, him turning up alone when she had been expected . . . the whispers became more insistent that [the marriage] was indeed going down,'[2] said the well-known media analyst Roy Greenslade. 'And the press loved this because it was a drama . . . in which . . . because of the nature of the Palace's press relations which is "never admit anything, never deny anything" you more or less could get away with anything . . . the royal rat pack began to feed off each other who could outdo the next one with a more outrageous claim.' As *Time* magazine put it in a cover story for the Waleses' visit to the US, their storybook marriage had become a night-time soap opera: 'Palace Dallas' behind the imperturbable Windsor front.

The Queen's second son, Prince Andrew, having returned as a hero aged twenty-two from the Falklands, played his part in Palace Dallas. He was in love with an American actress, Koo Stark. The Queen is said to have liked Koo and welcomed her to Balmoral, but the press, who nicknamed Andrew 'Randy Andy', scuppered the prospect of a marriage by delightedly publishing stills of Koo in a soft porn film, performing in what the papers liked to describe as 'steamy' scenes. The Queen was offended and Prince Philip enraged by Andrew's frolics in Barbados with a woman already well known to the tabloid press. They were delighted, however, when the red-headed Sarah Ferguson came into their son's life. In the comparative isolation in which the Royal Family lived, it was difficult to make friends with new people. Sarah Ferguson came into Andrew's life through polo – and Diana. Polo, essentially a sport for the upper-class and the rich, had been the romantic route for Diana to Charles and, ironically, for Camilla to Charles. Sarah's father, later known to the tabloids as 'Major Ron', was a polo player and womanizer; he was also polo manager to the Prince of Wales. It was at the same barbecue in Sussex, during the Cowdray Park International Polo Festival at which Charles and Diana had shared a romantic moment on a hay bale, that Sarah Ferguson, always known as 'Fergie' to the press, made friends with Diana, an entrée to the royal circle. She was invited to the Waleses' wedding but, significantly, to the church ceremony and not to the wedding breakfast at the Palace. When Diana wanted to make Sarah one of her ladies-in-waiting, she was turned down by the Household (not the Queen) on the grounds that she was 'most unsuitable'. Diana, apparently was 'furious, decided she was going to show them. Diana promoted Fergie's marriage from Day One.'[3]

Fergie's 'unsuitability' for the Palace of those days, in the eyes of the courtiers who worked there, was based, if anything, on her personal life. Her father, although well connected, was regarded as a 'bit of a cad'; there had been a painful divorce, affairs with married women and, perhaps most importantly, no large fortune to support his family. Sarah Ferguson, the second daughter, was born on 15 October 1959. She was just fourteen in 1972 when her mother left home, leaving her and her elder sister Jane in the custody of their father; she later married a polo player, Hector Barrantes, and went to live in the Argentine. The Fergusons' marriage was a victim of the randy, glamorous polo world, and Ronald Ferguson could have walked straight out of Jilly Cooper's best-selling novel *Riders*. Sarah was devoted to her father, whom she called 'Dads', and who, despite the pain of the divorce, had a comfortable Hampshire farmhouse base for the classic 'Sloane' – and sub-Sloane – life:

44. The Silver Jubilee. Crowds in the Mall surround the Queen in the golden State Coach, 1 June 1977

45. Silver Jubilee street party, June 1977. Neighbouring Radcot and Methby Streets in Kennington, London, celebrate the occasion

46. Return from the
Falklands. The Queen
and her family welcome
home Prince Andrew,
Portsmouth harbour,
September 1982

47. The Queen
decorates Corporal
Ricky Furgusson,
The Rifles, with the
Military Cross for his
bravery in Afghanistan,
Buckingham Palace,
7 December 2010

48. Windsor
Castle in flames,
November 1992

49. The destroyed
Brunswick Tower,
Windsor Castle

50. The Queen and
President Mandela
at a state banquet,
Cape Town,
20 March 1996

51. The Queen Mother's birthday, Horse Guards Parade, London, 19 July 2000.
The Queen Mother and Prince Charles enjoy watching Noddy and the Ascent
of Everest pass by, part of a huge pageant to celebrate her 100th birthday

52. A proud
grandmother: Prince
Harry smiles as the
Queen inspects soldiers
at the passing-out
Sovereign's Parade,
Sandhurst Military
Academy, 12 April 2006

53. The Queen escorted
by Prince William during
a visit to RAF Valley,
Anglesey, 1 April 2011

54. The Queen joins Prime Minister Tony Blair and his wife Cherie singing 'Auld Lang Syne' to welcome in the new year at the Millennium Dome, 31 December 1999

55. The Queen and Prince Philip with Prime Minister David Cameron and his wife Samantha outside 10 Downing Street before a lunch to celebrate the Duke's 90th birthday, 21 June 2011

56. The Queen speaking at Dublin Castle on her historic first visit to the Republic of Ireland, watched by President Mary McAleese, 18 May 2011

57. The Queen enjoying a joke with fishmonger Pat O'Connell at the English Market, Cork, 20 May 2011

58. Newly-weds William and Catherine drive from Buckingham Palace to Clarence House in Prince Charles's vintage Aston Martin, 29 April 2011

59. William and Catherine, with village elder François Paulette, paddle across Blatchford Lake, North West Territories, on their visit to Canada, 5 July 2011

pony clubs, gymkhanas, smart secretarial college in London which Camilla Shand had also attended. The college leaving report in 1977 was perceptive: 'Bright, bouncy redhead. She's a bit slapdash. But she has initiative and personality which she will use to her advantage when she gets older.' That advantage would be a ticket for life, marriage into the Royal Family through Diana. A courtier put it unkindly but acutely: 'Fergie's a good girl. She's got no harm in her. She's just vulgar. It's not her fault, that's the way she was born and brought up. That's the milieu. She was a chalet girl having an affair with her boss. She wanted to marry him, she was older than his children, he kicked her out. She cried on Diana's shoulder.'[4]

Diana had been fond of Andrew since her childhood days at Park House, next door to Sandringham, when she had reluctantly attended his birthday parties there and been invited over to play. She was sorry for him after the break-up of his romance with Koo Stark and invited Fergie to dinner to meet him. It was an instant success; they hit it off together. Both were given to boisterous behaviour (Andrew had once turned a fire extinguisher on the press in LA) and 'idiot jokes'. Diana saw to it that Sarah was invited to Windsor for Ascot week in 1985; she sat next to Andrew at lunch in the State Dining Room, where he fed her chocolate profiteroles, and the romance was on. Andrew invited Sarah to a New Year's house party at Sandringham and told her of his love for her: he later proposed, and on 15 March the Queen gave her consent to the marriage. And so there was another fairy-tale wedding, this time at Westminster Abbey, in July 1986, another passionate kiss on the Palace balcony in front of cheering crowds and, as it turned out, another royal marriage to implode.

The Queen liked Sarah Ferguson, 'a breath of fresh air' as the newspapers represented her. She liked her high spirits and the fact that they could go riding together and that Sarah was a country girl who took to the outdoor sporting life at Sandringham and Balmoral like a duck to water. Both she and Prince Philip were grateful that marriage would bring an end to the scandalous headlines – or so they thought and hoped. A leader in *The Times*, in a spectacular misjudgement, greeted her as 'a level-headed and attractive young woman'. Attractive yes, level-headed never. 'Fabulous Fergie', trumpeted one headline. Jean Rook, 'The First Lady of Fleet Street', was less complimentary, calling her 'an unbrushed red setter struggling to get out of a hand-knitted potato sack'. It is impossible to imagine any previous royal bride being described in the press in such terms, and an indication of how far an increasingly disrespectful media was prepared to go.

Mrs Thatcher's major innovation in British politics had been the fearless determination with which she set about attacking the sacred cows and institutions of Britain. Doctors, lawyers, the universities, the trade unions, the nationalized industries, the BBC and the NHS, none of them escaped her reforming zeal and her determination to cut costs, reduce public spending and get value for money for the taxpayer. It was only a matter of time before the same spotlight would be turned on the monarchy again.

One measure above all, the 1984 Trade Union Act, which, among other things, made strike ballots mandatory and outlawed secondary picketing, caused a major shake-up to the newspaper industry, handing vastly increased power to one man, Rupert Murdoch, proprietor of News International, owners of *The Times*, the *Sunday Times*, the *Sun* and the *News of the World*. Power was to pass from the old print workers and journalists to the proprietors. Computers had made the old methods of production obsolete. Murdoch moved his titles from Fleet Street to 'Fortress Wapping', as it was known, surrounded by twelve-foot-high spiked steel railings, razor wire and CCTV cameras to protect the working journalists from the striking print unions. The picketing lasted for almost thirteen months, until the unions accepted severance terms. 'For once,' Roy Greenslade wrote, 'redundancy meant what it said. Most of the men were never to enter a printing works again. Their skills had become obsolete . . . Murdoch [had] transformed the newspaper industry, heralding a new industrial revolution which was to lead directly to the electronic super-highway . . .'[5] Wapping marked the beginning of the end of Fleet Street, as other proprietors moved out following News International's example; 1986, the year of the 'Wapping Revolution', was a revolutionary moment in the history of Britain's national newspaper industry.

Meanwhile the more intellectual section of the media were playing the 'Queen v. the Deputy Queen' game, setting the two leading women, the Queen and the Prime Minister, Mrs Thatcher, up against each other, highlighted by what became known as the *Sunday Times* affair. On 20 July 1986, just before the Commonwealth Games were to be held in Edinburgh (having been boycotted by a number of nations in protest against Britain's – i.e. Mrs Thatcher's – stubbornness over sanctions against South Africa), the *Sunday Times* ran a front-page story that the Queen was deeply unhappy with Mrs Thatcher's policies over a wide number of issues.

'Sources close to the Queen,' the newspaper alleged, 'let it be known to the *Sunday Times* yesterday that she is dismayed by many of Mrs Thatcher's policies. This dismay goes well beyond the current crisis in the Commonwealth over South Africa. In an unprecedented disclosure of the monarch's views, it was said that the Queen considers the Prime Minister's approach to be uncaring, confrontational and divisive.'

Commonwealth unhappiness with Thatcher's policies went beyond her refusal to back sanctions against South Africa. One of the first cost-cutting actions of the new Thatcher Government within six months of taking office in 1979 ordained that differential overseas student fees would be introduced, higher than those for British undergraduates. It was the end of the special connection; as a member of the Commonwealth Secretariat put it: 'It was totally destructive because one of the things about the Commonwealth is that all ruling groups have been educated here. In the early 70s you'd have, say, ten Prime Ministers around the table who knew each other as students in Britain, because they all went to the LSE [London School of Economics] or Cambridge, or Oxford and so on. And she [Thatcher] wiped that out . . .'[6]

The Queen, with unprecedented frankness, had expressed her concern to Commonwealth representatives. In their view, Mrs Thatcher's economizing had hacked at the cultural roots of the connection with the English-speaking Commonwealth. Beyond that, from the Nassau Conference onwards, Mrs Thatcher had handbagged the Commonwealth heads of government at their biennial meetings over the issue of sanctions against South Africa. Her position was that imposing sanctions would harm British exports and throw black South Africans out of work. Commonwealth leaders, both black and white, took the view that sanctions were an important weapon in the battle to end apartheid.

The Queen, the *Sunday Times* said, had authorized her senior officials to make her views known to the world through the newspaper, implying that she had misgivings about Mrs Thatcher's Government which went far beyond the South Africa issue. She disapproved of the lack of compassion for the underprivileged, the handling of the miners' strike in 1984, Thatcher's willingness to accommodate Reagan by granting him permission to use airbases in Britain to launch his bombing of Libya in 1986, and that her policies and attitudes had tended to undermine the liberal consensus which had prevailed in Britain since the war. The *Sunday Times* spoke as if it were the Queen's confidant. 'Far from being a straightforward countrywoman, a late middle-aged grandmother who is most at ease when talking about horses and dogs,' it announced, 'the Queen is an astute political infighter who is quite ready to take on Downing Street when provoked.'

The story showed a complete misunderstanding of the nature of Britain's constitutional monarchy. That the Queen would have authorized a public attack on her Government in a newspaper interview was absurd. If the Queen did feel strongly about certain areas such as the Commonwealth, she might express certain reser-

vations to individual Commonwealth representatives but to claim
that she would intervene directly against a democratically elected
British Government was the opposite of the truth. The warring
queens image was a caricature of both.

The impression persists, however, among politicians and Commonwealth members that the Queen did act as a restraining
influence on Mrs Thatcher in some of her more intransigently
tactless moods. There was speculation that it was advice from the
Palace that widened the celebration of the Downing Street anniversary from a dinner to which Mrs Thatcher and her Cabinet
invited the Queen, to one to which all party leaders and descendants of former Prime Ministers were invited. Another occasion
was the Cenotaph ceremony held on Armistice Sunday in Whitehall, at which the Queen and the leaders of the political parties
lay wreaths. Mrs Thatcher originally refused to allow the newly
formed SDP (Shirley Williams, David Owen, Roy Jenkins and
Bill Rodgers) to take part. A leading member let the feelings of his
party at being thus excluded be known – indirectly – to the Palace.
Mrs Thatcher gave way. Mrs Thatcher, however, could be obdur-
ate on certain issues. The Queen would have liked to visit the
European Parliament in Strasbourg; her Prime Minister resolutely
opposed the idea of giving royal countenance to that despised institution, and the Queen did not go.

Britain seemed to have changed more during the Thatcher era,
the 1980s, than at any time since the Queen's Coronation. The old
mass male employment industries of coal mining and steel making
collapsed after major strikes, ending famously in 1985–6 with the
100,000-strong NUM strike led by the megalomaniac Arthur
Scargill. At the very end of the strike the Queen and Prince Philip
visited *The Times* on the occasion of the newspaper's bicentenary.
While Prince Philip, in his customary forthright way, denounced
the miners' leader as 'a shit', the Queen was introduced to the paper's
labour correspondent, Paul Routledge, as the man covering the
miners' strike. She volunteered that she had been down a coal mine

in Scotland that had closed soon afterwards and, after a pause, added, 'It's all about one man, isn't it?' Routledge replied that perhaps it wasn't about one man and that, having been brought up among them, he didn't think one man could bring out 100,000 men on strike for a whole year. 'There was a pregnant pause,' Routledge recalled, and the party moved on. Eight years later, having written an unauthorized biography of Scargill, he changed his mind: 'With the hindsight that has come from writing this book,' he admitted, 'I now feel that I owe the Queen an apology. By that stage, at any rate, the strike *was* about one man. Scargill may not have started the strike, but one word, one signal from him could have called it off before the struggle plumbed the depths of misery, violence and failure to which it sank . . . The Queen was right.'[7]

No one has discovered what the Queen's feelings were when Mrs Thatcher took the salute of the returned Falklands veterans in the parade through the City of London in October 1982. She may have reflected that the Falklands victory was very much Mrs Thatcher's, but other people had thought it odd to see the Prime Minister standing on the dais instead of the Queen, who is head of the armed forces. Mrs Thatcher did not, however, attend the fortieth anniversary of D-Day in 1984 because she considered it very much the Queen's occasion – perhaps also to avoid the repeated conjecture that she was upstaging the monarch. The press accused Thatcher of ambulance-chasing and elbowing the Royal Family out of the limelight by dashing to be first on the scene of disasters such as the sinking of the ferry *Herald of Free Enterprise* at Zeebrugge, and the destruction of the Pan-Am airliner over Lockerbie.

Another charge related to one of the sillier aspects of Mrs Thatcher's regal behaviour, the use of the royal 'we', to quote the authoritative Hugo Young:

The royal 'we' was a usage heard from the royal lips [in public] only once a year, when the Queen read the Speech from the Throne at the beginning of a parliamentary session. The Prime Minister deployed it much more often. And although there were times when the plural could . . . be said to refer to the government collective[ly], and even to herself and her husband travelling together, there were others when 'we' did not appear on any construction to include anyone but this singular Prime Minister. By 1987 this habit had become almost inextinguishable. 'We are in the fortunate position, in Britain, of being as it were, the senior person in power,' she told a BBC reporter on her way to visit Moscow.[8]

Famously, too, there was her announcement that her son Mark Thatcher and his American wife Diane had had their first child: 'We are a grandmother.' There is no evidence to suggest that the Queen regarded this subconscious self-aggrandizement with anything other than amusement. In general the Royal Family, and the Queen Mother in particular, appreciated Thatcher's courage and patriotism, and her attempts to reverse Britain's decline.

It was, however, far from being all bad news on the economic front. While the old male-dominated unionized workforce had been largely thrown on the scrapheap, commemorated in powerful television drama/documentaries like *Boys from the Blackstuff* and *Gissa Job*, there was expansion in private business and the service industries. The newspaper business had become highly profitable; deregulation in the City – the 'Big Bang' – rocked the cosy 'old boy' network that had been British banking tradition. Hard-working, thrusting south London boys flocked to the trading floors, waving fistfuls of 'readies' as champagne and cocktails flowed in the bars after work. Big American banks set up in the City. The word 'yuppy' – for young upwardly mobile professional – was invented to describe the new businessmen and women, and cries of 'greed' went up to denigrate the 80s.

One million women joined the workforce in the 1980s, mainly in the service industries. In 1976 Steve Jobs had founded Apple and in 1981 IBM developed the Compaq Portable computer. Women's fashion became more assertive, exemplified by the 'big shoulders big hair' look from the US TV series *Dynasty*. Mrs Thatcher gave

up the mumsy dressing of her earlier years for swept-back bouf-
fant hair and mannish suits. The TV satirical series *Spitting Image*
featured her in a man's pin-stripe suit, standing at an urinal;
another scene showed her at the Cabinet table, a waiter by her side
taking an order and asking her, 'And what about the vegetables?'
Thatcher, indicating her Ministers with a sweep of her hand, said,
'Oh, they'll have the same as me . . .'

In the end, however, the 'vegetables' won. In 1987 Thatcher had
won a third term at the General Election, an unprecedented feat,
but the Tories were beginning to lose their nerve. At the beginning of April a wave of protest against the proposed community
charge – 'the Poll Tax' – erupted in violent riots in Central London's Trafalgar Square, reminding the MP Alan Clark of 1981. 'All
the anarchist scum, class-war, random drop-outs and trouble-
seekers . . . infiltrated the march and started beating up the police.'
The Tory Party, he said, was 'lazy, sullen and frightened'. 'In the
corridors and the tea room [of the House of Commons] people are
now talking openly of ditching the Lady [Thatcher] to save their
skins.'[9] Thatcher had alienated some of the leading figures: Nigel
Lawson had resigned as Chancellor of the Exchequer in 1988, and
Geoffrey Howe, deprived by Thatcher in 1989 of the Foreign Sec-
retaryship which he cherished, resigned in November 1990 with an
exceptionally brutal speech to the House of Commons, 'the death
blow' as it was termed. Howe was an apparently mild-mannered
man (the Labour Chancellor Denis Healey described being attacked
by him in Parliament as like being 'savaged by a dead sheep') who
had endured a great deal from 'the Lady' in his successful career at
the top. The key issue for Howe and Lawson was Europe and its
proposed expansion. According to Howe, he had discovered in
October when he flew to Balmoral for a Privy Council meeting
that the Queen had been told – and he had not – that Britain had
agreed to join the ERM (Exchange Rate Mechanism), and when
he had visited Buckingham Palace on the day of his resignation, he
had found the monarch 'full of discreet sympathy'.

At Bruges in September 1988 Mrs Thatcher threw down the gauntlet: 'We have not successfully rolled back the frontiers of the state in Britain, only to see them re-imposed at a European level, with a European super-state exercising a new dominance from Brussels.' She was shown on television banging her fist on her desk and crying defiantly, 'No! No! No!'

Bad by-election results had induced a feeling of doom in the party. At the Lord Mayor's Banquet on 12 November, she hit out at her critics in a characteristically defiant speech, using a metaphor from Denis Thatcher's beloved cricket: 'I am still at the crease, though the bowling has been pretty hostile of late. And in case anyone doubted it, can I assure you there will be no ducking bouncers, no stonewalling, no playing for time. The bowling's going to be hit all round the ground.'

The speech, according to Alan Clark, was greeted with virtually complete silence. Howe's speech the next day in contrast electrified his audience in the Commons: he ended with an open invitation to a leadership contest, ending, 'the time has come for others to consider their own response to the tragic conflict of loyalties with which I myself have wrestled for perhaps too long'. On 14 November Michael Heseltine, a long-time opponent, signified his intention to stand against Thatcher for the leadership of the Tory Party. 'I don't think she realizes what a jam she's in,' Clark had written earlier. 'It's the Bunker syndrome. The saluting sentries have highly polished boots and beautifully creased uniforms. But out there at the Front it's all disintegrating. The soldiers are starving in tatters and makeshift bandages. Whole units are mutinous and in flight.'[10]

On Sunday, 18 November Mrs Thatcher departed for Paris for an important summit, the Conference on Security and Co-operation in Europe (CSCE) with President George Bush and the European leaders. That evening she entertained Chancellor Kohl to dinner at the British Embassy, where she was staying. Kohl, so often her opponent, said what the other leaders had been unable to or dared not say. He referred to the leadership election, telling her supportively that it was 'unimaginable' that she should be deprived of office. On Tuesday night, 20 November, the day of the election, she got the bad news on the first leadership ballot from her Parliamentary Private Secretary, Peter Morrison: 204 votes versus Heseltine's 152 and sixteen abstentions, meaning there would have to be a second ballot. 'Not, I am afraid, as good as we had hoped,' Morrison wrote. Typically, she erupted out of the Embassy en route to a dinner at Versailles to announce to the startled John Sergeant that she was carrying on: 'I fight and I fight to win!' (For his broadcast, so dramatically interrupted, Sergeant won the British Press Guild award for the most memorable broadcast of the year, beating footballer Paul Gascoigne, who had been nominated for bursting into tears during the 1990 World Cup semi-final against West Germany.) 'God alive!' commented Clark. She defiantly repeated this message to the assembled journalists outside Downing Street as she was leaving to make a statement about Paris in the House of Commons next day.

At Downing Street, where she arrived home on 21 November, she found that her husband Denis wanted her to quit. 'Don't go on, love,' he said. Nonetheless she decided to stand for the second ballot, nominated by Douglas Hurd and seconded – with some hesitation – by John Major. She went to the Palace for a meeting with the Queen to inform her of her decision to stand. Later, when she returned to her room in the Commons, a procession of her Cabinet Ministers and loyalists came to see her one by one. Even the most supportive told her she could not win. With her tacit backing, John Major, then Chancellor of the Exchequer, stood against Heseltine and won the premiership. The 28th of November was her last day in office; symbolically, when she went downstairs to her study that morning to check nothing had been left behind – 'it was a shock to find that I could not get in because the key had already been taken off my key-ring'. Just after 9 a.m., with tears in her eyes, Thatcher was driven off to Buckingham Palace to take her leave of the Queen as her eighth Prime Minister. It was the end of an era, and not only for Margaret Thatcher and the Conservative Party.

One historic change had already taken place: on 10 November 1989 the Berlin Wall, major symbol of Communist oppression and the division of Europe, was pulled down. Just a month before, Mikhail Gorbachev had visited the city to celebrate the fortieth anniversary of Communist rule. Forty years before Winston Churchill had warned:

> I do not believe that any people can be held in thrall for ever. The machinery of propaganda may pack their minds with falsehood and deny them truth for many generations of time, but the soul of man thus held entranced or frozen in a long night can be awakened by a spark coming from God knows where, and in a moment the whole structure of lies and oppression is on trial for its life. Peoples in bondage need never despair.[11]

It was announced from Moscow that all the victims of Stalin's purges, from 1930 to 1950, were to be rehabilitated; permission was even given for the serialization of Alexander Solzhenitsyn's prison camp saga, *Gulag Archipelago*, personally approved by Gorbachev. And that year the authorities finally released the death toll from the nuclear disaster at Chernobyl on 26 April 1986. (For three days the Soviet authorities had kept secret the explosion, which had destroyed two out of four nuclear reactors at Chernobyl in the Ukraine. Thousands died as a result of the disaster, but the number of future deaths from cancer from the resulting radioactive cloud, which covered twenty States as far west as Ireland, Spain and Portugal, north to Finland and Norway and as far south as Romania and Turkey, will probably never be known.)

Throughout Eastern Europe, Soviet-sponsored Communist regimes had collapsed like a house of cards. In February the last Russian troops had left Afghanistan, 'a moment of humiliation for the imperial giant', as the historian Martin Gilbert put it, 'but also a moment of truth'.[12]

History has not yet related what the Queen said to Margaret Thatcher at their farewell audience. Among the last things she had done for the Queen was to settle the Civil List for the next decade. Unfortunately for the Queen, the focus on her finances was to be one of the most controversial and dangerous themes of the next few years, aggravated by the behaviour of her closest family and the increasing competitiveness and sense of empowerment of the media.

16.   The Crisis Years

In June 1992, the Queen's own Berlin Wall of privacy around her family life collapsed under the bombshell effect of Andrew Morton's book *Diana, Her True Story*, first serialized in the *Sunday Times* on 7 June. The book told of Diana's psychological problems, the bulimia, self-mutilation and depression, and, worst of all from the Royal Family's point of view, it revealed the failure of the marriage of the heir to the throne and what Diana saw as his responsibility for it, his adultery with Camilla Parker Bowles, and his unkindness to his wife. The British public was shocked and angry. The book affected the Queen both as monarch and mother. For someone who had dignity, duty, self-containment and personal morality at the core of her being, such public revelations were almost unbearable, and were all the worse for being in many respects true, even if one-sided.

The year 1992 marked the fortieth anniversary of the Queen's accession to the throne. In her 1991 Christmas broadcast she had unfortunately chosen to emphasize the family, one of her favourite themes. Reaffirming her determination to serve her people, she had said: 'With your prayers and your help, and the love and support of my family, I shall try and help you in the years to come . . .' Yet within just one month, following the publication in the *Daily Mail* of a photograph showing Sarah on holiday with her Texan lover, the Queen had been informed by the Duke and Duchess of York of their intention to separate. She had asked them to reconsider, but on 18 March an exclusive in the *Daily Mail* trumpeted the story of an imminent announcement of the separation to be made by the Palace, which, indeed, was made the next day.

It was not the first separation in the Queen's immediate family:

in 1989 Princess Anne had announced her split from Captain Mark Phillips, and she was to remarry that year, 1992, Commander Tim Laurence, whose letters to her had been sold by a Palace maid to a newspaper. But the great scandal, the failed marriage of the Prince and Princess of Wales, was still to come. In February the couple had made an official visit to India which had featured the famous 'Princess Alone' photograph of a pensive Diana seated in front of the Taj Mahal, the great romantic monument built by Shah Jehan to the memory of his beloved wife. Charles himself had given a hostage to fortune when, at the same site eight years earlier, he had declared that one day he would like to bring his wife there.

Diana, with her supreme talent for public relations, had created the photo-opportunity for the image of the neglected wife which was to be the theme of the Morton book, following it up with the cruel version of 'the kiss that never was', when at a polo match, as Charles bent towards her for a pre-arranged photo opportunity, she averted her head at the last moment, so that he was pictured pecking ineptly at her neck. Such images caused consternation at the Palace, where the top officials had already picked up rumours of the Morton book and were desperate to shore up the marriage of the heir to the throne. The Queen and Prince Philip were not unsympathetic to Diana: Prince Philip had written her supportive letters before the publication of the book, in one of which he went so far as to say 'what Charles has done is very wrong'. Both still hoped that the marriage would go on, until the serialization broke. Neither believed that Diana had had nothing to do with the book, as she claimed. Prince Philip told her that she had 'destroyed everything'. On 14 June, the day the second instalment of the serialization hit the news-stands, the Royal Family were at Windsor for the Royal Ascot race meeting. As they took part in the traditional drive down the course at the opening ceremony, the Queen had to endure the embarrassing sight of her soon to be ex-daughter-in-law, the Duchess of York, with her two young daughters, Beatrice and Eugenie, waving enthusiastically at her from the rails. Later the Queen and Prince Philip had a meeting with Charles and Diana, at which the subject of divorce was raised but rejected.

The marriage limped on with unbearable strain for all concerned and increasing damage to the image of the monarchy as 'the family on the throne'. The public took sides, most of them with Diana. On a visit to Belfast at the end of June she paid a spectacularly successful visit to the Falls Road, Republican heartland and stronghold of the IRA. An estimated 20,000 people came to 'shout for Diana'. The Morton revelations had made their impact and there was no doubting where popular sympathies lay. As the *Daily Mirror* put it under a banner headline 'WE WANT DI!', front-line Belfast had 'a message for the Royals'. Even the normally anti-monarchist Dublin press reported sympathetically on the Princess. Prince Charles's circle fought back in a way that was equally damaging, claiming that Diana was mentally unstable. The 'War of the Waleses' fought through the press was damaging and painful for the Queen.

It got worse: while the family, ostensibly united, were at Balmoral for the annual summer holiday, suggestive pictures featuring the Duchess of York and her 'financial adviser' John Bryan on holiday in the south of France were published by the *Daily Mirror*. Four days later the *Sun* printed the 'Squidgygate' tapes of New Year's Eve 1989, intimate conversations between Diana at Sandringham and her admirer James Gilbey, which underlined not only the rift between herself and Charles but her difficulties with the Royal Family in general and her relationship with Gilbey. The way in which she had spoken of the family's ingratitude and lack of appreciation of her dutiful public efforts – 'after all I've done for this f . . . ing family' – were difficult for the Palace to come to terms with. The newspaper followed up this scoop with allegations of an affair between Diana and Guards officer James Hewitt. Diana suspected a conspiracy to destroy her, but there was none beyond the destructive effect of the relentless tabloid circulation war that her glamour and defiance had generated.

In the months following the publication of the Morton book,

the Queen and Prince Philip, far from cutting Diana off, had continued to keep in touch. The Prince appealed to her sense of duty, referring to himself as 'Pa' and the Queen as 'Ma', telling her how 'Ma and I' were very worried about the situation and how, when they were first married, they had thought they would have a few years to live their own life; but then when the Queen's father had died, the Queen had had to give up her own family life and he had had to give up his career for the sake of the family. He wanted Charles and Diana to stay together, living separate lives while continuing with their duties. Unfortunately for the Prince's plan, Diana was too modern and too emotional to play the classic role of consort tolerating her husband's mistress.

Matters came to a head in November, when Diana refused to allow their sons to attend a shooting weekend with Charles's particular friends at Sandringham. Charles's patience snapped. On 25 November he and Diana met privately at Kensington Palace and agreed to a legal separation. In the protracted negotiations that followed, the Queen declined to come down on the Prince's side, maintaining her neutrality. On 9 December Mrs Thatcher's successor as Prime Minister, John Major, read out a statement from Buckingham Palace to Parliament, announcing the separation in terms that were more hopeful than realistic. There were no plans for divorce and 'there was no reason why the Princess of Wales should not be crowned Queen Consort in due course'. The Archbishop of Canterbury, when officially consulted before the statement, had wisely said that for the separation to be widely accepted two important provisos should be met: 'Both parents would have to be seen to maintain close bonds with their children; and extramarital love affairs that might be brought to public attention would need to be avoided.' It would soon become obvious that the Archbishop's second proviso was very far from being met.

But for the Queen a very personal tragedy had already occurred. At 11.15 on the morning of Friday, 20 November 1992 (coincidentally the beginning of the Sandringham weekend which was to cause the Waleses' separation and was also the Queen's forty-fifth wedding anniversary), clouds of smoke could be seen rising from the area of Windsor Castle. Fire had broken out in the heart of the castle, which was under restoration, beginning in Queen Victoria's Private Chapel. The fire, started by a restorer's lamp which set a curtain alight, roared almost out of control, running through wall-spaces, tearing through the roof void and devouring the beams in St George's Hall, setting the sky alight with a huge red glow that silhouetted the ancient towers against the night sky. It raged for fifteen hours, devastating 115 rooms.

Before midday the news was round the world, television pictures showing the unbelievable sight of the great castle on the hill in flames. Prince Andrew, who was there, superintending operations, said the Queen, who arrived by three o'clock in the afternoon, was 'absolutely devastated'. Her shock and distress at the destruction of her childhood home were evident to everyone who saw her. She loved Windsor more than anywhere else. For her it was associated with a happy childhood that now seemed like a lost paradise. It was not just memories that had been destroyed but part of the royal heritage that had been entrusted to her; the fire hurt her not only as a person, but as a monarch, enhancing the sense of bewilderment, even of failure, which she felt in the face of the ruin of her children's marriages.

The damage was estimated at £2.3 million an hour as the fire burned through the night, destroying the rooms in the Upper Ward, devastating the part of the castle which had been occupied by the sovereigns of England for at least 800 years.

The total damage at the time was estimated at £60 million, and her subjects' reaction to a pledge on their behalf made by the Secretary of State for National Heritage, Peter Brooke, to pay for the damage was particularly hurtful. The recession was then at its worst, with thousands of homes being repossessed every month. The usually pro-monarchy *Daily Mail* addressed the Queen directly

with a front-page editorial headed, 'Why the Queen must listen':
'Why should the populace, many of whom have had to make huge
sacrifices during the bitter recession, have to pay the total bill for
Windsor Castle, when the Queen, who pays no taxes, contributes
next to nothing?'

The issue of the tax exemption on the Queen's private income
had been gathering strength, fuelled by Britain's severest recession
since the 1930s, since the last settlement of the Civil List in 1990. A
hostile editorial in the Murdoch-owned *Sunday Times,* written on
10 February 1991, at the time of the Gulf War, by the republican
editor Andrew Neil, had attacked the behaviour of the younger
royals for carrying on a privileged lifestyle financed by the public
while the British people were losing their jobs and homes and,
some of them, even their lives at war for their country. A *World in
Action* TV programme in June 1991, based substantially on the
work of Philip Hall, whose book on the subject, *Royal Fortune*, was
to be published a year later in January 1992, had revealed the circumstances of the royal tax exemption. Hall's important argument,
based on ten years' research, was that there was no justifiable historical basis for the exemption and that income tax had been paid
by all the Queen's predecessors except her father, who had been
the first monarch to enjoy such exemption. It had not been until
late 1991 that the Queen, in response to the rising strength of public opinion, and urged on by Prince Charles, had authorized her
advisers to begin discussions on the subject with the Treasury.
According to a courtier close to the Queen, the decision that she
should pay tax on her private income and remove all members of
the Royal Family apart from the Queen Mother and the Duke of
Edinburgh from the Civil List had been reached in April 1992, but
the Palace and the Treasury moved so slowly that they were overtaken by events – the Windsor fire and the hostile public reaction
to the Heritage Secretary's pledge that the loyal public would
pay up.

Four days after the fire, the Queen made a speech at London's

Guildhall at a luncheon given to mark her fortieth (and most inauspicious) year on the throne. She was suffering from a heavy cold and the after-effects of the smoke and fumes at Windsor. She looked and sounded sad as she made a plea for understanding: 'I am quite sure that most people try to do their jobs as best they can, even if the result is not entirely successful . . . There can be no doubt . . . that criticism is good for people and institutions that are part of public life . . . But we are all part of the same fabric of our national society and that scrutiny, by one part or another, can be just as effective if it is made with a touch of gentleness and under-standing . . .' The speech also contained veiled but bitter allusions to the press, which confirmed suspicions that the 'Queen's advis-ers' were still not taking the media seriously as the voice of the public. It would certainly have been better received if an announce-ment of the Queen's decision to pay tax had been made earlier. The *Daily Mail*, still unaware of the decisions that had been taken, was gently reproving: 'We sympathize with the Queen. Of course we do. But these are hard times for most people. Many of them have had a truly horrid year. They have lost their livelihoods . . . Even been driven from their homes. The Queen should pay some tax on her income. And fewer members of her family should be a charge on the Civil List. She should offer to contribute to restor-ing the fabric of Windsor Castle.'

It was not until 26 November, six days after the Windsor fire, that John Major made a surprise announcement in the House of Commons that the Queen and the Prince of Wales had volun-teered to pay tax on their private incomes and that the Queen would reimburse the Civil List annuities to five of the Royal Fam-ily. He informed the House that the National Audit Office would be looking into expenditure on the royal palaces. As a public rela-tions exercise the whole affair could hardly have been handled more ineptly. The timing of the announcement made it seem as if the Queen and the Palace had been panicked by the public reaction into agreeing to pay tax. Three months later the Lord Chamberlain,

Lord Airlie, took the unprecedented step of calling a press conference to clarify the new arrangements – later announcing that the
Windsor restoration, now estimated to cost £30–£40 million
spread over five years, would be paid for without recourse to public funds, while Michael Peat, a top-level accountant for whom the
new title of Finance Director had been created, announced them
on television. Lessons had been learned.

The Queen described 1992, which should have been a year of celebration of the fortieth anniversary of her accession, as her 'annus
horribilis' (cheekily translated by the *Sun* as 'One's Bum Year').
The following year, 1993, the fortieth anniversary of the Coronation, was not going to be better. Within weeks of the December
official announcement of the Waleses' separation, a headline in the
Sun screamed '6 MIN LOVE TAPE COULD COST CHARLES
THE THRONE'. Recorded, curiously, in December 1989, just a
few weeks before Diana's 'Squidgygate' conversation with Gilbey,
it showed that Diana's fears about Camilla being her husband's
mistress were completely justified. Inevitably it was labelled
'Camillagate' by the media. Essentially it was silly, at times 'dirty'
talk between two lovers. 'The tape disclosed an Eeyorish man,
prone to seeing the glass half-empty, in the grip of a long-lived,
intense passion and prone to bad jokes. It left Charles more tarnished than ever and with a most undignified reputation as a man
who dreamed of being re-incarnated as a tampon' and living inside
his lover's trousers.[1] Both 'Camillagate' and 'Squidgygate' were
early examples of the phone-hacking which was later to cost Murdoch's News International and other guilty papers dear.
   For the Queen, the Royal Family and the public in general – both
monarchist and republican – the Morton revelations, the 'Fergie'
photographs, Squidgygate and Camillagate represented a huge
shock, a revolution since the day forty years ago when the Queen –
'the world's sweetheart' – had ridden with her handsome Prince to
her Coronation. As Antony Jay wrote in his book accompanying a

television programme which had been intended as a celebration of the Queen's forty years, the country had changed so much that it seemed more as if 400 years had passed rather than forty.[2] The relations between monarchy and media had undergone the most profound revolution since the days when British newspaper owners had conspired to keep the love affair between King Edward VIII and Wallis Simpson away from the knowledge of the British people. In 1952 only 1,500,000 homes were able to receive the BBC's single-channel black and white television service. There were only three radio networks, all BBC. No newspapers had colour magazines. The press were not expected to take an interest in the private lives of the Royal Family beyond the sickly 'happy family' fare dished out by the Palace press office. Now not only did the press transcribe private conversations of members of the Royal Family and their friends, but the *Sun* went so far as to breach the monarch's copyright by leaking the content of her 1992 Christmas broadcast before she delivered it. The Queen was outraged and consulted lawyers; the newspaper, apparently instructed by its proprietor, Rupert Murdoch, backed down.

The press were not exclusively to blame: beginning with the film *Royal Family*, the 'royals' had been accustomed to seeing themselves on television; Prince Charles had made two television programmes; Princess Anne (now the Princess Royal), Princes Andrew and Edward and the Duchess of York had made fools of themselves in *It's a Royal Knockout*. The show was conceived and organized as a charity event by Prince Edward. The royal party, dressed in Tudor costume, cheered on contestants competing in ridiculous games. Afterwards Prince Edward famously stormed out of an uncomfortable press conference, sarcastically thanking the journalists for their enthusiasm, which did little to endear him to the media and the public. It is hard to imagine Queen Victoria permitting such nonsense, but the Queen consistently and temperamentally has failed to prohibit her children from doing what they wanted and has reaped the consequences. Worst of all, Charles and Diana had used favoured journalists to put their case against each other in the press. As early as May 1991, at a private dinner in Luxembourg, Lord Rothermere, Chairman of Associated Newspapers, publishers of the *Daily Mail,* the *Mail on Sunday* and (at that time) the *Evening Standard*, told Lord McGregor, Chairman of the Press Complaints Commission, that 'the Prince and Princess of Wales had each recruited national newspapers to carry their own accounts of their marital rifts'.

Unfortunately for the heir to the throne, not only did he not have much of a case to put across, but he was an inept media performer and in Diana, 'the wronged wife', he was up against one of the most skilful media manipulators of this or any age, whose deployment of her image as message made the 90s the 'Age of Diana'. The Palace was powerless to control her and, in fact, the Queen and her advisers did not even try, preferring to keep her within the tent rather than outside it. In fact it was Prince Charles who lit the fuse to disaster with his self-justifying television programme, made by the broadcaster Jonathan Dimbleby, accompanied by a sympathetic authorized biography. 'Prince Charles wanted it as a justification after the Morton book,' one of his close circle recalled. Based on interviews with friends and staff and using the Prince's own correspondence and diaries, it was originally officially intended as a television programme to mark the twenty-fifth anniversary of the Prince's investiture at Caernarvon, then expanded to be accompanied by an authorized book. Buckingham Palace was apprehensive, rightly as it turned out. 'He's on a hiding to nothing,' was the general view there, but they were as yet unaware of how personal the programme would be.

The programme, *Charles: The Private Man, the Public Role* went out on 29 June 1994. Its main thrust, the public man, his charities and his views on the causes he believed in, came across as a sympathetic portrait of a good man with serious intentions. It was aimed at the young, the future King's constituency, and showed the Prince, normally an indifferent television performer, at his best as an environmental crusader, speaking articulately, passionately and without notes. With pop star Phil Collins at a holiday camp organized by his successful inner-city youth help foundation, the Prince's Trust, he appeared at his ease and in his element. So far so good, but the programme was always to be remembered when in answer to Dimbleby's 'hook' question as to whether he had been faithful in his marriage, the Prince replied that he had – until it 'had irretrievably broken down'. He went on to describe Camilla Parker Bowles (whom he did not name) as a 'very dear friend' whom he would continue to see. While many applauded him for his honesty, friends, and indeed Camilla herself, were appalled. After all his complaints about 'media intrusion', here was the heir to the throne on television, with his sons, confessing to adultery and not only that but making clear his devotion to his mistress and his intention to carry on exactly as he had been doing in the past. The day after the broadcast, the Prince's Private Secretary, Richard Aylard, admitted in a press conference that the woman in question was Camilla. Charles's admission, coming as it did only a year after the Camillagate revelations, was to have far-reaching long-term consequences: in January 1995 Andrew and Camilla Parker Bowles were divorced.

Diana feigned indifference, but the return match in the blame game was inevitable. Her own relatively transitory affairs had become public knowledge and attacks had been made on her mental stability. Ignoring the advice of her chief media mentors and friends, she decided to take the fatal step of giving a major interview on the BBC's prime TV show, *Panorama*. Several things motivated her: her longing to put her case to the people over the heads of her 'enemies' in the Establishment; her love of publicity on her own terms; her intrinsic belief in the rightness of her own instinct even over all the wise opinions she had been given by people who had only her interests at heart; her determination to counter allegations of borderline personality disorder; and lastly, and least attractively, the desire for vengeance. On Diana's specific instruction the BBC released the press announcement of the forthcoming interview on 14 November, an unwelcome forty-seventh birthday surprise for Charles, pictured in Tokyo cutting a celebratory cake, his face displaying total dismay.

The fifty-five-minute programme went out on 20 November, featuring a dramatic image of Diana. Her face pale, eyes ringed heavily with kohl, wearing minimal jewellery, she was in victim mode but defiant, and seemingly oblivious to the significance of what she said in the context of the monarchy. Apart from references to Charles and Camilla – 'there were three of us in this marriage' – and her desire to reign unofficially as 'Queen of Hearts', the key moment of the programme came when she cast doubt on Charles's fitness to rule. 'It's a very demanding role being Prince of Wales,' she declared, 'but it's an equally [*sic*] more demanding role being King. And because I know the character, I would think that the top job . . . would bring enormous limitations to him, and I don't know whether he could adapt to that.' For her children, and for Prince William in particular, her public admission to her affair with James Hewitt – 'Yes, I loved him, yes I adored him' – was particularly difficult. William, by all accounts, refused to speak to her for days afterwards.

For a Princess of Wales, however aristocratic and beautiful she might be, to question the fitness of the heir to the throne in a hereditary constitutional monarchy was outrageous. It was an obvious bid to bypass Charles in favour of William, with herself as Queen Mother, a role which she told a confidante a few months before her death was one she had envisaged. The Queen decided that the battle of the Waleses had done enough damage to the institution of which she was head and which she held in trust from her ancestors. Just before Christmas 1995 a letter arrived from the Queen, addressed in her own hand to 'Dearest Diana' and ending 'With love from Mama'. Its content, however, was stark: having consulted both the Prime Minister and the Archbishop of Canterbury, the Queen had come to the conclusion that it would be in the best interests of the country to end the uncertainty and for Charles and Diana to take steps to divorce. Charles too wrote a letter to Diana. Their marriage was beyond repair, he said, representing a 'national and personal tragedy', and a quick divorce was the only way to end the 'sad and complicated situation'. The fourteen-year-old 'fairy tale' was over.

On 15 July 1996 Charles and Diana filed their decree nisi, the document declaring that their marriage would be dissolved six weeks later on 28 August. (The Duchess of York had obtained her final decree on 30 May.) The settlement, underwritten by the Queen, was a generous one: Diana received a lump sum of £15 million, plus some £400,000 a year to run her office. Her title was to be 'Diana, Princess of Wales' and she would be 'regarded as a member of the Royal Family' and invited to State and national occasions, when she would be treated as such. Her public role would be 'for her to decide', although working trips abroad would require consultation from the Foreign Office and permission from the Queen (standard practice for members of the Royal Family). She would have access to royal flights and to the State apartments in St James's Palace for entertaining. She would also have use of all the royal jewellery, eventually to be passed on to the wives of her sons. She was, however, to be stripped of the royal title 'HRH'. Some atavistic memory of her father, George VI, refusing the 'HRH' to the divorced Wallis Simpson when she married the Duke of Windsor must have prompted the Queen in this. Rather than have ex-daughters-in-law swanning round the world claiming to be members of the Royal Family, she had stripped Diana and Sarah of the cherished 'HRH'. Once divorced, they no longer had a right to it.

HRH or not, Diana was now a world celebrity of the most glittering order, and her charity activities, such as her spectacular anti-landmines campaign, were making her even more famous and beloved than she had been before. Unfortunately, too, having unwisely dispensed with her official police protection, she was even more hunted by the paparazzi. At 12.23 a.m. on the morning

of 31 August 1997 the Mercedes saloon in which she was travelling with her lover, Dodi Fayed, travelling at speed to escape the
paparazzi, slammed into the thirteenth concrete pillar dividing the
roadway in the tunnel under the Place de l'Alma in Paris. It took
almost an hour to free Diana from the wreckage; she had suffered
life-threatening internal injuries and died in the Hospital of La Pitié-
Salpetrière without regaining consciousness. Her death was officially
announced at 5.45 a.m. Paris time and flashed to an incredulous
world.

If Diana had damaged the monarchy in life, her death shook the
institution as never before. The Queen was at Balmoral with Prince
Philip, Prince Charles and Princes William and Harry when the
British Ambassador in Paris, Sir Michael Jay, telephoned through
the news. Public anger grew exponentially in the days between
her death, the return of her body from Paris and her funeral on 6
September, as the Royal Family remained, apparently uncaring, at
Balmoral. They attended the customary Sunday service at Crathie
church, where Diana's name was not mentioned and had not been
since the royal ruling that, with the loss of her HRH, her name
should be dropped from the prayers for the Royal Family. The
absence of any reference to her apparently prompted Prince Harry
to ask, 'Are you sure Mummy's really dead?'

In conspicuous contrast, the new Prime Minister, Tony Blair, ever
alive to the mood of the moment, told his press officer, Alastair
Campbell, 'This is going to unleash grief like no one has ever seen
anywhere in the world.' In a sure-footed public statement he
dubbed her 'the People's Princess'. 'They liked her, they loved her,
they regarded her as one of the people. She was the People's Princess and that is how she will stay, how she will remain in our hearts
and memories for ever.' The Royal Family's silence about Diana
prompted a mounting wave of criticism which was to reach dangerous levels of hostility by the end of the week. 'DO THEY
CARE?' the *Sun* asked. Isolated on Deeside, they remained unaware
of the gathering hysteria in the capital. In Paris people standing in

the street had clapped as the hearse bearing Diana's coffin passed; on the drive from Northolt airport to London, thousands of people lined the road. Crowds of people – black, white, old and young – queued for up to seven hours to sign the condolence book at St James's Palace; mountains of flowers piled up outside the gates of Kensington Palace, where Diana had lived; sorrowing notes and poems were pinned to the railings. WHERE IS THE QUEEN WHEN THE COUNTRY NEEDS HER? was the banner headline of the *Sun*, stoking up the temperature on 4 September (Thursday) after four days of unofficial grief for Diana. Fury at the paparazzi who had hunted Diana to her death and the press who had paid them was the first reaction, diverted on to the Royal Family by the symbolic issue of the empty flagpole on Buckingham Palace. Traditionally the only flag to fly over the headquarters of the monarchy was the Royal Standard, and that only when the Queen was in residence. Normally when she was away, the flagpole would be empty. After some pressure, the Queen was persuaded to allow the Union Jack to be flown there at half-mast as a traditional symbol of grief until she was in residence.

The Queen and her family flew down to London on Friday 5 September; only then did they get a real sense of what Diana's death meant to the people. Walking out of the Palace gates to mingle with the crowds, they could sense the strange atmosphere, open grief, and, for the first time, an undercurrent of hostility. The atmosphere was so tense that it was reported that the police had been panicked into requesting the presence of the Army in the background. That evening, on the eve of Diana's funeral, the Queen gave a televised broadcast about Diana. Dressed in black, she sat at a window through which the grieving crowds outside the Palace could be seen. Her delivery was firm, solemn and moving; it was perhaps the most personal statement she had ever publicly made. The first paragraph was almost an apology: 'We have all been trying in our different ways to cope,' she said. 'It is not easy to express a sense of loss, since the initial shock is often succeeded by a mixture of other feelings – disbelief, incomprehension, anger and concern for those who remain. We have all felt those emotions in these last few days. So what I say to you now, as your Queen and as a grandmother, I say from my heart.' She paid tribute to Diana as 'an exceptional and gifted human being', concluding that there were 'lessons to be drawn from her life and from the extraordinary and moving reaction to her death . . .' 'The Queen was very grief-stricken by Diana's death,' recorded Dickie Arbiter, the most experienced royal press officer, who had also worked for the Prince and Princess of Wales. 'On the day of the funeral when the Royal Family came out of Buckingham Palace as the gun carriage carrying Diana's coffin passed, the Queen bowed. And the only other time the Queen bows is at the Cenotaph.'[3]

Diana was given a solemn State funeral: her coffin, draped in the Royal Standard, carried three bouquets: a sheaf of white tulips from fifteen-year-old William, white lilies from her brother Charles Spencer and, most movingly, a bunch of Diana's favourite white roses with, clearly visible, a card inscribed 'Mummy' in Harry's twelve-year-old hand. William and Harry walked behind her coffin, with Prince Philip and Prince Charles (reportedly Prince Philip had persuaded a traumatized William to do so by assuring him that he would do the same). As they walked people shouted 'God bless you', wailed and threw flowers on the road. The ceremony took place in Westminster Abbey; 2,000 people were invited, an extraordinary mixture of people representing the range of Diana's life, charities and friendships. Elton John sang the moving 'Goodbye, England's Rose', a rewritten version of 'Candle in the Wind', the requiem he had written for Marilyn Monroe, Diana's heroine, who had died at exactly the same age.

The most dramatic moment was provided by Charles Spencer, whose powerful speech electrified everyone who heard it. Diana, he said, who took her name from the Greek goddess Diana the huntress, had ironically become the 'most hunted woman in the world'. She was 'the very essence of compassion, of duty, of style, of beauty. All over the world she was a symbol of selfless humanity: a standard-bearer for the truly downtrodden, a very British girl whose concerns transcended nationality: someone with a natural nobility who was classless and' – here he could not resist a hit at the Royal Family, who had divested her of her HRH – 'who proved in the last year that she needed no royal title to continue to generate her particular brand of magic'. There was dead silence in the Abbey when Spencer finished his speech. Then, wrote a distinguished journalist who was there:

> A sound like a distant shower of rain penetrated the walls of Westminster Abbey . . . Then it was inside the church. It rolled up the nave like a great wave. It was people clapping, first the crowds outside and then the two thousand inside . . . it was serious applause, and it marked the moment at which the meaning of what was happening on this incredible day was made plain . . . the masses listening outside . . . broke into the abbey. The people wanted to make their feelings felt.[4]

As the coffin began its journey after the service to Diana's family home, Althorp, where she was to be buried, the clapping continued from people crowding the roadside. So many flowers were thrown at the hearse on its way out of London that the driver had to use his windscreen wipers to clear them. It was a feeling of love, appreciation and sympathy that transcended mere celebrity or even royalty. She had indeed been the People's Princess.

For some people the emotion, even hysteria, provoked by Diana's death marked the end of the 'stiff upper lip', of Britishness and 'real men don't cry', which had been a late Victorian public school concept. Journalists, mainly male, mocked the new wave of crying not only in public but ostentatiously so on television, blaming it on the emotional earthquake which had just taken place. Real men disliked the 'Dianafication' of British attitudes. But early September 1997 also marked the cessation of hostilities between the Queen and the press. The Queen had publicly expressed her sorrow, the press were shocked by the role of the paparazzi and the newspaper editors who had paid and encouraged them in literally hounding the Princess to her death. Mohammed al Fayed, father of the Princess's lover Dodi, killed with her in the crash, continued to stir the pot of the conspiracy stew, making wild charges of murder against the British Secret Services prompted, he alleged, by the Duke of Edinburgh's fear that the Princess would have a child by his son, a Muslim. The case was exhaustively investigated and reported in the Stevens Report, which concluded that the driver, Henri Paul, had been over the limit on prescription drugs and alcohol. Propelled to exceed the speed limit – and the limitations of the Alma Tunnel – he had engaged in a reckless race with the motorcycle-riding paparazzi which had ended in the fatal crash into the thirteenth pillar. It was the end of a particularly traumatic period of history for the relations between the British people and the monarchy.

17. Twenty-first-century Queen

The golden wedding of the Queen and Prince Philip in November 1997, which included a service and a walkabout at Westminster Abbey, was treated with respect. Prince Philip, long mocked and caricatured for his gaffes and rudeness (on one famous occasion, visiting Gibraltar, he had gazed up at the Rock, covered with the limestone promontory's celebrated monkeys, and, seeing a posse of newsmen and photographers awaiting his arrival, had asked, 'Which are the monkeys?'), was becoming a national treasure, almost in the tradition of the legendary television figure Alf Garnett. His marriage to the Queen has been an outstanding success. He has carved out a role for himself after the early disappointment of having to give up his own naval career in favour of the second-class role of consort. He sees no State papers, holds no official audiences and officially has no views, nor can he express any for fear of implicating the Queen. As he once complained: 'Because she's the Sovereign everyone turns to her. If you have a King and Queen, there are certain things people automatically go to the Queen about. But if the Queen is also the QUEEN, they go to her about everything.'

'The position of the Queen's consort is, therefore, very much what its holder chooses to make of it; its significance very much lies . . . in the support which the consort is able to give the Queen in carrying out her massive programme of social and ceremonial engagements.'[1] From the beginning of their married life, Prince Philip has seen supporting the Queen as his primary duty. It is impossible now to imagine an important event at which he has not been. They are notably at ease with each other in public and in private. As the Queen's long-serving Private Secretary has said, Prince Philip is the only man in the world who treats the Queen simply as another human being. 'He's the only man who can . . . and she values that. And it's not unknown for the Queen to tell Prince Philip to shut up. Because she's Queen, that's not something she can easily say to anybody else.'[2] Nor is it possible to imagine anybody but the Queen being brave enough to do so.

Prince Philip has overcome initial difficulties by cultivating his own interests, both private and public. He is a talented watercolourist, taught by the Norfolk-based artist Edward Seago; he has given up polo but still takes part in competitive events like carriage-driving. He is involved with hundreds of organizations, particularly connected with young people, notably the Duke of Edinburgh's Award scheme, launched in 1956, the National Playing Fields Association and the Outward Bound Trust. He was the first president of the World Wildlife Fund, of which he has been the international president since 1981. He takes a great interest in scientific and technological research and development; he has been patron of the Industrial Society and president of the British Association for the advancement of science. He is intellectually curious – which the Queen notoriously is not – interested in theology and religion with a small 'r', and has published several books.

On 1 May 1997 Britain had elected its first 'New Labour' Prime Minister, Anthony Charles Lynton 'Tony' Blair, aged not quite fifty-six, the first of the Queen's Prime Ministers who appeared not to have a full understanding of the constitutional significance of the monarch as Head of State as opposed to his own role as the politically elected Leader of Her Majesty's Government. Blair's idea of his position was much more akin to being President of the United States; he was the initiator of what one constitutional expert has called 'prime ministerialism'. Harold Wilson had been accused of running a 'kitchen cabinet' with intimate non-elected advisers like Marcia Falkender, but Blair was the first to deploy a 'sofa government' which simply governed without consulting the regular Cabinet Ministers or the high-level civil servants. 'I am not a great

one for the Establishment,' Blair wrote in his memoir. 'It's probably at heart why I'm in the Labour Party and always will be. I
always felt that they preferred political leaders of two types: either
those who were of them – or at least fully subscribed to their general outlook – or the "authentic" Labour people . . . who spoke
with an accent and who fitted their view of how such people should
be. People like me were a bit nouveau riche, a bit arriviste, a bit
confusing and therefore suspect.'³

Blair's account of his official appointment as the Queen's Prime
Minister is both touching and illustrative. As he drove through the
gates of Buckingham Palace, he was, he said, just longing to get on
with his job, 'straining at the leash of convention, tradition and
ceremony that delayed the doing'. On being shown into the ante-
chamber outside the room where the Queen was, he suddenly
became nervous: 'I knew the basic protocol but only very vaguely.
It is called "kissing hands", the laying on of the Queen's authority
to govern. She was head of state. I was *her* prime minister.' Tempo-
rarily disconcerted by a tall official with a stick who instructed him
on the practical technique of 'kissing hands' – 'You don't actually
kiss the Queen's hands, you brush them gently with your lips' – he
tripped on the carpet as he was ushered in so that 'I practically fell
upon the Queen's hands, not so much brushing as enveloping
them.' The Queen, he found, 'was quite shy, strangely so for someone of her experience and position; and at the same time direct. I
don't mean rude or insensitive, just direct. "You are my tenth prime
minister. The first was Winston. That was before you were born."
We talked for a time, not exactly small talk but general guff about
the government programme, the conversation somewhat stilted.'
The Queen relaxed more when Cherie Blair came in and chatted
about moving the children into Downing Street. 'Contrary to
popular belief,' Blair asserted, 'Cherie always got on well with
her.'⁴ Her refusal to curtsey amused rather than offended the
Queen, who is said to have remarked, 'I can almost feel Mrs Blair's
knees stiffening when I come in.' An indication of the presidential

aura about the Blairs was their apparent acceptance of the title of First Lady bestowed on Cherie by the press, although no such thing existed in British practice.

Tony Blair was as helpful as he could be to the Queen and the Palace over the week following Diana's death, although he could be forgiven for slight exaggeration. He decided to call in Prince Charles as a channel to the Queen: 'Part of my problem with the Queen was that there was no easy point of connection in age, or outlook, or acquaintance. I respected her and was a little [!!] in awe of her but as a new prime minister I didn't know her or how she would take the very direct advice I had to give her.'[5] The Queen had to speak to the nation, the Royal Family had to be visible, he told Charles on the Wednesday before the funeral. At the Queen's request he spoke to her at Balmoral the next day, finding her 'very focused and totally persuaded'. The Palace asked him to read a lesson at the funeral service: 'It was a mark of how pivotal my role had been through the week.' He refused, afraid of the charge of 'muscling in' (which indeed was to be levelled at the time of the Queen Mother's funeral in 2002). The funeral was, in fact, totally organized by the Palace, using a blueprint which had already been drawn up for the Queen Mother. The Queen's broadcast, Blair said, was 'near perfect: it was plain from the language and tone that once she had decided to move, she moved with considerable skill. She managed to be a queen and a grandmother at one and the same time.'[6]

His first traditional visit to Balmoral took place the day after Diana's funeral. 'I was shown up to see the Queen in the drawing room which was exactly as Queen Victoria had left it. I was just about to sit down in a rather inviting-looking chair when a strangled cry from the footman and a set of queenly eyebrows raised in horror made me desist. It was explained that it had been Victoria's chair and that since her day no one had ever sat in it.'[7] Much as Margaret Thatcher had been, or perhaps even more so, he was unused to the culture of country house/stately home weekends of which Balmoral was a royal version, finding it unnerving and totally alien, and the experience 'a vivid combination of the intriguing, the surreal and the utterly freaky'. In private conversation that weekend, Blair was nervous, the Queen, seemingly, also. 'I talked, perhaps less sensitively than I should have, about the need to learn lessons . . . and at points during the conversation she assumed a certain hauteur; but in the end she herself said lessons must be learned and I could see her own wisdom at work, reflecting, considering and adjusting.'[8] A surreal end to a surreal week, he commented, noting with pride that he had a public approval rating of 93 per cent.

For the Queen and, indeed, her family, the end of an era came with the final decommissioning in December 1997 of the royal yacht, *Britannia*, which held so many happy and splendid memories for her. It had been sanctioned by a previous Labour Government under Attlee in June 1951, and had been built at John Brown's shipyard on the Clyde and launched by the Queen herself in April 1953. 'My father felt most strongly, as I do, that a yacht was a necessity and not a luxury for the head of our great British Commonwealth, between whose countries the sea is no barrier, but a natural highway,' she had said in her speech at the time. Professor Sir Peter Hennessy has written that, although no place of safety for the Royal Family in the case of nuclear attack appears designated in public archives, he has always thought the argument that *Britannia* would have served as a hospital ship in time of war 'was a particularly feeble cover story', pointing out that the royal yacht was a fully fledged command and control centre with wash-down facilities to tackle nuclear fall-out.

Tony Blair's Conservative predecessor as Prime Minister, John Major, Britain's youngest premier for 100 years, had done his best for the Queen and *Britannia*. International maritime organization regulations for passenger vessels introduced after the *Herald of Free Enterprise* disaster in March 1987 spelled the end for the ship as she was: updating her to comply would have been more expensive than building a new yacht. Major got on well with the Queen, and his was the decision to go ahead, against Treasury opposition, with spending £60 million of public money on a replacement. By the time Tony Blair decided to cancel the project in 1997, a design had been produced for a 3,280-ton ship only two-thirds the size, which would have been a showcase for British marine technology, the cost of which, at 1997 prices, was a tenth of the money which would be spent on the Millennium Dome, and there were private offers to subsidize running costs.

Symbolically, *Britannia*'s last official voyage in 1997 had been to serve as a base for Prince Charles at one of the final ceremonies of Empire, the transfer of sovereignty over Hong Kong from the United Kingdom to the People's Republic of China, referred to as 'the Return' or 'the Reunification' by the Chinese and 'the Handover' by the British. With Prince Charles to witness the ceremonies were Hong Kong's last Governor, Chris Patten, Tony Blair, Robin Cook, Foreign Secretary, and General Sir Charles Guthrie, Chief of the Defence Staff. The Chinese Government delegation was headed by Jiang Zemin, President of the People's Republic of China, and Li Peng, Premier. Prince Charles, like most liberal-minded people in the West, had been horrified by the massacre of 2,000 demonstrators for greater democratic freedoms for China in Tiananmen Square in Beijing on 3 June 1989, symbolized by the heroic defiance of one young man who had stood in the path of a tank. According to unauthorized leaks of his diary in 2005, Charles referred to the transfer of Hong Kong as the 'Great Chinese Take-away' and the Chinese leaders as 'appalling old waxworks'. With Chris Patten he had sailed away from Hong Kong on *Britannia*, putting the final stop to Britain's imperial story. Blair blithely demonstrated his customary lack of a sense of history when he was completely thrown by the Chinese leader Jiang Zemin's display of his knowledge of Shakespeare, talking and joking about it as if it was the most natural thing in the world, explaining to Blair that this was a new start in UK/China relations and that from now on the past could be 'put behind us'. Characteristically Blair recorded, 'I had at that time only a fairly dim and sketchy under-standing of what that past was.'⁹

When *Britannia* was finally decommissioned on 11 December 1997, the Queen and the Princess Royal were photographed with tears in their eyes. Memories of forty years of family holidays, honeymoons and spectacular State visits were to be obliterated. *Britannia* ended up as a tourist attraction and venue for corporate hospitality in Edinburgh's port of Leith. Poor John Major did not outlast *Britannia*; he was destroyed by Britain's membership of the ERM (Exchange Rate Mechanism) when he, or rather his Chan-cellor, Norman Lamont, was forced by the markets' devaluation of the pound to withdraw on 'Black Wednesday', 16 September 1992. 'With the markets as they were,' he told the Queen, 'we could not have gone on – it would have looked like King Canute.' 'Few political watersheds have been as dramatic as Black Wednesday,' Hennessy wrote. 'The government never recovered, its reputation for economic competence beyond repair.'¹⁰ Sleaze entered the pol-itical vocabulary that autumn too. Major's Government struggled on in increasing disagreement and disarray until the election of May 1997, which the Conservatives lost by the biggest majority since 1832, when Major was replaced by New Labour and Tony Blair.

There were happier family events in the years that followed. On 21 June 1999, Prince Edward, Earl of Wessex, married Sophie Rhys-Jones in St George's Chapel, Windsor, a far less ostentatious spectacle than the ill-fated marriage of Charles and Diana eighteen years before. On 4 August 2000 the Queen Mother celebrated her 100th birthday; the actual celebration had taken place on 19 July with a joyful tribute on the Horse Guards Parade, including a cav-alcade of the century through which she had lived, 'more of a circus than a parade', as her biographer described it.¹¹ There were people representing soldiers of the First World War, ballroom dan-cers from the 1920s, a Second World War fire engine and ambulance, cars of the twentieth century including Enid Blyton's Noddy in his yellow car, the first Mini Minor, James Bond's Aston Martin, and such surprising representatives of twentieth-century Britain as Hell's Angels on their bikes, punk rockers in black and the television characters the Wombles. Then, beginning with the Queen's page leading a pair of corgis, representatives of 170 of more than 300 civil organizations and charities with which the Queen Mother had been associated marched past, with more animals – camels (ridden by members of the Worshipful Company of Grocers, whose emblem is a camel), an Aberdeen Angus bull, Cheviot sheep, chickens and racehorses – with, bringing up the rear, twenty-two holders of the Victoria and George Crosses, the highest awards for gallantry, and a group of Chelsea Pensioners in their bright red uniforms and cocked hats. Second World War planes flew overhead, followed by the Red Devils aerobatic team trailing clouds of red, white and blue. Bands played and 300 children from the Chicken Shed Theatre Company danced. Altogether 2,000 military and more than 5,000 civilians took part in a joyous, sometimes comical spectacle. On her actual birthday the Queen Mother waved from the Buckingham Palace balcony, as she had on VE-Day in May 1945 and again on its fiftieth anniversary in May 1995.

It was to be her last appearance on the balcony: she died, in her 102nd year, at 3.15 on the afternoon of 30 March 2002 at her home, Royal Lodge, in Windsor Great Park. Poor Princess Margaret, who had suffered several strokes, blind and barely able to speak, had died just a few weeks earlier on 9 February. So in her Golden Jubilee Year the Queen lost both her mother and her sister. She was comforted, as she herself said, by the huge turn-out of people in their hundreds of thousands, of all ages and races, who had paid their respects to her mother as her body lay in state in Westminster Hall before her funeral. The scheduled opening hours had to be lengthened to twenty-two hours a day; in freezing weather people waited their turn to pass by the coffin, in queues which wound along the Embankment and across the River Thames. It was an outstanding tribute not only to Queen Elizabeth herself but to what she stood for as part of our history. She had lived through the tragedies of the First and Second World Wars and – just – the terrorist attack on the Twin Towers on 11 September 2001, a defining moment of the twenty-first century which was to lead to conflict in Afghanistan and Iraq and to a new age of terrorism. The Queen's own response to the attack was to order the playing of 'The Star-Spangled Banner' at the Changing of the Guard ceremony at Buckingham Palace.

The Queen had little time for anything but private grieving as she and Prince Philip embarked on twelve months' celebration of her Golden Jubilee: over twelve months the royal couple travelled more than 40,000 miles, to Jamaica, Australia, New Zealand and around the United Kingdom, ending with a visit to Canada. They arrived in New Zealand just after the Prime Minister, Helen Clark, had made a speech in which she condemned the constitutional arrangements with the monarchy as 'absurd' and declared that New Zealand should be a republic. She did not turn up to greet the Queen as she landed from the royal flight. It was certainly a great contrast with the ecstatic welcome the Queen had received on her Coronation tour, but polls that year showed that the majority of New Zealanders still supported the monarchy. They spent five days in Australia, touring Queensland and South Australia and taking in a Commonwealth Heads of Government meeting before returning to the United Kingdom for the Jubilee celebrations between May and July.

Just as at the time of the Silver Jubilee in 1977, there had been dire predictions in the media, notably the *Guardian*, that the event would be a flop. Again, they were wrong. Over the Golden Jubilee weekend, 1 to 4 June, there was the *Prom at the Palace* with the BBC Symphony Orchestra and Chorus, with guest stars Kiri Te Kanawa, Thomas Allen, Angela Gheorghiu and Roberto Alagna; 12,500 people attended, out of 2 million who had applied for tickets. A pop concert, *Party at the Palace*, celebrated fifty years of British achievement with acts including Paul McCartney, Eric Clapton and Cliff Richard. Queen guitarist Brian May played his version of the National Anthem on the floodlit roof of Buckingham Palace, Paul McCartney concluded the evening with numbers such as 'Hey Jude', and the Queen lit the National Beacon at the Victoria Memorial in front of the Palace, the last in a chain of some 2,000 to be lit around the world, echoing Queen Victoria's own Golden Jubilee in 1887. A total of 12,000 guests attended at the Palace, while one million crowded the Mall to watch, listen and sing along to the party, which was displayed on giant television screens. Another 200 million watched the event on television worldwide.

On 4 June there was a National Service of Thanksgiving at St Paul's, to which the Queen rode in the Gold State Coach, then lunch at the Guildhall, where she spoke in terms very different from her miserable fortieth anniversary occasion there in November 1992. 'Gratitude, respect and pride, these words sum up how I feel about the people of this country and the Commonwealth — and what this Golden Jubilee means to me.'

In April 2005, Prince Charles married the woman he should have married the first time round. Camilla Parker Bowles became the Duchess of Cornwall in a civil ceremony at the Guildhall in Windsor, followed by a reception given by the Queen at the castle. It was the first official acknowledgement of their long relationship and a step towards the eventual succession of Prince Charles as King. Everything was kept low-key for fear of hostile reaction from Diana fans, of which there were still many. Cautious statements were made to the effect that when Charles became King she would not be Queen, clearly nonsense, as constitutionally the wife of a King is Queen Consort. Over the following years, loyal journalists promoted Camilla and eventually the Prince was to admit that when he succeeded as King she would be Queen.

In June 1996 the President of the Republic of Ireland, Mary Robinson, paid a visit to the Queen at Buckingham Palace. According to the Irish historian Mary Kenny, the President saw her visits to the Queen as part of a 'modernizing mission' to normalize relations between Britain and Ireland – 'time to drop the baggage, time to move on'. 'The Soldier's Song' was played at Buckingham Palace – with 100 guardsmen in full dress – and the Queen told President Robinson that she would very much like to visit Ireland when the appropriate time came. President Mary Robinson was succeeded in 1997 by another woman, President Mary McAleese, and what Kenny described as a 'very special moment' took place on 11 November 1998 when the Queen and President McAleese stood shoulder to shoulder at Messines Ridge, honouring the dead of the First World War.[12] For Professor Tom Garvin this meeting truly was the end of old hostilities. 'The Empire is gone. The old dependency versus the Empire business is gone as well.' The Queen and President McAleese were to have several more cordial meetings over the years, in Belgium, Britain and Belfast; Mrs McAleese openly stated that the Queen would love to visit Ireland, and that she herself would also love such a visit, but that the event had to wait upon political agreement.

A huge step forward towards political agreement came with the signing of the Good Friday Agreement in Belfast in April 1998, which was little short of an historic breakthrough in the relationships between Britain and Northern Ireland and the United Kingdom and the Republic of Ireland. Following the partition of Ireland in 1922, Churchill had written despairingly of the sectarianism between Catholic and Protestant, Nationalist and Unionist as 'one of the few institutions that has been unaltered in the cataclysm which has swept the world'. A series of twentieth-century Prime Ministers, notably Heath, Thatcher and Major, had attempted a solution, defeated by inborn prejudice and horrific acts of terrorism from the late 1960s on. Tony Blair, for once, in this case felt 'the hand of history' on his shoulder and, indeed, it was partly his history. His mother was a Protestant from Donegal, his wife Cherie a Catholic from Liverpool. By his own account, as Leader of the

Labour Party even before he came to office as Prime Minister he had determined to operate a non-partisan policy with the Conservative Prime Minister in office, John Major, who had begun secret negotiations with the IRA (Irish Republican Army) and brought in Senator George Mitchell from the US to oversee the ceasefire.

One of the key factors in his eventual success was the transformation of the South of Ireland from the despised 'bog-Irish' image to the bounding Celtic Tiger economy after the Republic joined the European Union. Bertie Ahern, the Irish Taoiseach, whose family were Republicans through and through, was equally free of the shackles of history and anxious to move his country forward from its depressing past. With the encouragement of both parties in Ireland, Ulster and Britain, the lines of agreement were laid down. The Republic removed Articles 2 and 3 from the 1937 Irish Constitution, which laid claim to the entire island of Ireland; the British renounced any imperialist claim to the North. Referenda were held in the North of Ireland and the Republic of Ireland, endorsing the agreement by 71 per cent in the North and 94 per cent in the South. Things changed, and changed rapidly. In February 2007 the band at Croke Park stadium in Dublin (scene of the first 'Bloody Sunday' in 1920, when British special troops shot dead fourteen Irish players and spectators in revenge for the murder of fourteen British agents) struck up 'God Save the Queen' before the first rugby international between England and Ireland. Three months later Bertie Ahern was invited to address the joint Houses of Parliament.

There were visits to Ireland by members of the Royal Family – Prince Charles, Prince Philip and Princess Anne; President Mary McAleese met the Queen five times between 1995 and 2008, but the Queen's visit was to be the Big One. As late as 2008 the Irish Ambassador to London said, 'We want this visit to happen, but we want everything to be right.' It was, apparently, 'right' in May 2011, when the Queen and Prince Philip made their four-day State visit to Ireland, 100 years after the Queen's grandfather, George V, had been the last British monarch to visit in 1911. A columnist on the *Daily Telegraph* even raised the possibility of the Republic of Ireland rejoining the Commonwealth, from which it had withdrawn – to the Queen's father's great distress – in 1948. He pointed out that most of the Commonwealth's fifty-four members are republics, including the largest – India – and there is a precedent for a country rejoining as South Africa did in 1994, after leaving when it became a republic in 1961.

On 17 May 2011, wearing emerald green and a radiant smile, the Queen stepped off the aircraft steps and into history as the first monarch to visit the Republic of Ireland. (It had been still part of the United Kingdom when her grandfather, George V, had visited in 1911.) As one commentator pointed out, history was everywhere. 'Ireland's struggle against its imperial overlord' was to be a constant theme during the four-day State visit. Even the military airfield at which she landed, Casement Aerodrome, was named after Sir Roger Casement, hanged by the British for high treason in 1916 after conspiring with the Germans to overthrow British Rule. There was no attempt to disguise the past, no apology, but a sincere theme of regret for many of the terrible things that had happened. With President McAleese, the Queen laid a wreath at the Garden of Remembrance to those killed fighting for Irish independence, and the next day another at the National War Memorial Garden, commemorating Irish soldiers who had fought in the First World War. Above all, for many people, the Queen visited Croke Park, site of the original 'Bloody Sunday'.

The Queen began her speech at the State banquet at Dublin Castle with a phrase in Gaelic; memories of the murder of Mountbatten may have hovered over her but she spoke of 'forbearance and conciliation', of being able to bow to the past but not being bound by it and of the things that might have been done differently or not at all, extending her 'sincere thoughts and deep sympathy to all who had suffered as a consequence of a shared troubled past'. In a piece entitled 'Ireland thanks you, ma'am: we can now let go', a columnist wrote, 'This expression of regret – even if some would quibble that it did not constitute a sufficiently straightforward apology – was more than enough for most Irish people. It seems that deep down in our psyche we really needed to hear the ultimate representative of the British people express regret for the wrongs of the past but only so we could let it go . . .'[13]

Mary Kenny estimated that around 80 per cent had been in favour of the visit, the rest against; there were fears of a terrorist attack, heavy police cordons held back people who had honestly wanted to see the Queen in O'Connell Street, a bus bomb had been discovered the day before and been disposed of, a republican group jeered and whistled in the background at the Garden of Remembrance, but there were no major incidents. Most people agreed with Kevin Myers that there was 'no point in clinging to the wreckage of the past'. 'The ordinary man in the street is favourably disposed towards Britain and the British Royal Family,' he wrote, 'the ordinary man you never hear from, as opposed to the begrudging classes who always raise the banner and conveniently forget that Britain has just loaned us £7 million.'[14] Unmoved by any possible threat to her security, the Queen smiled as she carried out her duties, her courage and dignity appealing, as perhaps no one else in her position could have done, to the majority of the Irish people.

The Commonwealth, so dear to the Queen's heart, seemed barely to register with New Labour as compared with their new allies in the European Union. Significantly, the index to Tony Blair's autobiography, *The Journey*, shows not one single reference to the Commonwealth, although there are numerous pages on Europe. One of the Commonwealth high points for the Queen in recent years had been her visit to South Africa in March 1995, to be greeted with enthusiasm by President Mandela. It was her first visit as Head of State and her first visit to South Africa for forty-eight years, and also a celebration of the return of South Africa to the Commonwealth after an absence of thirty-two years. In November 1999 a referendum was held in Australia on the question of an Australian Republic, producing a 'No' vote of 54.4 per cent against a Republic. Despite the republican argument that it was offensive to expect the many newly immigrated Australians to swear allegiance 'to an elderly Englishwoman, for the most part resident in Berkshire', in fact many Greek, Italian and Vietnamese-born Australians were happy to vote to keep the Queen as their Head of State. In January 2001 the Australian Prime Minister, John Howard, visited Britain at the head of a distinguished delegation including four ex-Prime Ministers, to commemorate the centenary of the creation of the Commonwealth of Australia.

In the summer of 2007 Tony Blair gave way to his Chancellor and chief adversary, Gordon Brown, who seemed to be equally unaware of the constitutional niceties of his position as Prime Minister vis-à-vis the Queen's as Head of State. In June 2009 Brown was invited to join Nicolas Sarkozy and President Barack Obama, with the Prime Minister of Canada, in a celebration of the sixty-fifth anniversary of the Normandy landings on 6 June 1944. Neither the Queen nor any other member of the Royal Family was invited, although the Queen, Prince Philip and Prince Charles had attended commemorative events in France on the sixtieth anniversary in 2004. There was general embarrassment as a result: the White House press secretary Robert Gibbs claimed that they were working to see that the Queen received an invitation, the Palace denied that they were discomfited by the lack of one, and the French Government said it was not up to them to determine the British representation. Gordon Brown is alleged to have said that the event was intended for Prime Ministers and Presidents rather than royals, but the British public as a whole decided to take offence on the Queen's behalf. She was, after all, not only Head of State but head of the armed forces and the only one of those who would attend who had served, however briefly, during the Second World War. In the end Prince Charles went, Gordon Brown was booed by veterans on the beaches, and the Queen went to the Derby.

(A flustered Brown is alleged to have referred to Omaha Beach as Obama Beach.)

In July 2010, the Queen and the Duke visited Canada, always the most problematic from the British monarchist point of view because of its dual Anglo-French heritage. Almost half of Canadians believe the monarchy is 'a relic of our colonial past that has no place in Canada today' and support a referendum on the subject, it was claimed. The author and columnist for the Canadian *Globe and Mail* Leah McLaren reported in the *Daily Telegraph* on 20 July 2010 in a piece headed 'Why cool Queen still melts our hearts'. The royal couple toured nine cities in five days, in soaring temperatures that reached a humid mid-30s. Everyone was drenched in sweat except the Queen, who, despite spending days laying cornerstones and attending State dinners and walkabouts wearing long-sleeved dresses, big hats, ornate jewellery, heavy handbags and long white gloves, never produced so much as a hanky to dab herself. 'How is it possible that someone wearing all that can fail to break a dew? Well, that's the Queen for you,' commented McLaren. She described the visit as a 'roaring success, drawing record-breaking crowds'. Hundreds of thousands of Canadians came out, queueing behind barricades, in airports and car parks, often bursting into tears at the briefest glimpse of Her Majesty, 'now a slightly stooped but smiley 84-year-old grandmother'. 'The truth is,' she went on, 'we keep the Queen around because we love her. And in a time of celebrity narcissism and image-managing politicians, the Queen quietly earns and returns our love.'

However, *the* royal event of 2011 from the world's point of view was undoubtedly the wedding of Prince William to Catherine Middleton at Westminster Abbey on 29 April. An estimated 2 billion people watched worldwide as the glamorous, romantic scenario unfolded. In the United States in particular people got up early in the morning to catch the handsome Prince and his beautiful bride. It was the first truly modern Windsor wedding: there had been 'commoners', as non-royals were known, who had become royal brides, but Lady Elizabeth Bowes-Lyon and Lady Diana Spencer were both earls' daughters. Catherine Middleton's family had genuine working-class credentials. On her mother's side, curiously, Jack Harrison, Catherine's great-great-grandfather, had worked in coal mines in County Durham owned by the Queen Mother's Bowes-Lyon family. Both her parents knew what it was like to work for their living: they had both worked for a British airline, then founded a private company to finance bringing up their family – two girls and a boy – ensuring they could educate them at good schools, moving them up the social scale. Kate went on to earn a place at university, St Andrew's in Scotland, and it was there that she met and eventually fell in love with Prince William. She and William moved in the same circles, shared many of the same friends. Even before they met, their aspirations and interests had seemed to coincide. William went on a Raleigh adventure course in Chile for his gap year; one year later so did Kate, both winning high praise from their leader for their guts, energy and willingness to muck in. Both were sporty, clever enough but not too much so, an advantage in royal circles not known for their intellectual interests. Both had had other loves before they fell for each other, so when they got together they were sure enough what they wanted. There was a brief split, allegedly due to marriage panic on William's side, hardly surprising considering the disaster his parents' marriage had turned out to be. Kate had taken it calmly, being seen out and about with her sister and other friends. Her attitude seemed to be 'Look at me, I can get along without you.' It worked, and within three months they were back together. William, it appeared, could not get along without her.

Nonetheless, an engagement seemed long in coming and had taken everyone by surprise when it had been officially announced in November the previous year. There was a public appearance by the couple, Kate flashing the huge sapphire and diamond engagement ring which Charles had given Diana, a deliberate reminder by William of his dead mother. Part of Kate's appeal for him, you

could conjecture, was, however, that Kate was not at all like troubled, tragic, charismatic Diana. She had a calmness at the centre
which Diana never had, and a stable home life that had been a
haven for William. She was beautiful and stylish, dressed in 'high
street' clothes which girls her age could afford. Most of all the public liked the fact that they were not only in love with each other but
clearly also good friends.

Just like the Queen's own wedding and, indeed, Prince Charles's
to Diana, the marriage of Kate and William echoed Churchill's
words as a 'flash of colour on the hard road we have to travel'. It
took place against a background of world financial crisis, the debt
mountain accumulated after the 2008 banking disasters, and war in
Afghanistan. For everyone it was a chance to have a party and forget their troubles in a shared wave of enjoyment at a romantic
wedding spectacular, executed with the panache customary for
British royal occasions, and royal weddings in particular. A quarter
of a million people lined the Mall leading to Buckingham Palace,
standing twelve deep, waving flags with increasing frenzy as the
State landau with the newly married couple passed on its way to
the Palace, then they flooded after them, avid for the 'balcony
scene' as one twenty-four-year-old history student from Washington DC put it. He had flown over specially, as had two teachers
from Australia, and a Diana fan from Canada. They were there to
watch the kiss, and this time they got not just one brief kiss but a
second lingering one. The royal couple had spent just seven minutes on the balcony but for the watching crowds it was seven
minutes as witnesses to real history. They were there.

Just under a month later President Barack Obama and his wife
Michelle came to London for a State visit from 24 to 26 May, en
route to a G8 summit. It was the first State visit to London by a US
President since that of George W. Bush in 2003. The Queen invited
them to stay at Buckingham Palace. It was not the first time they
had met; on a previous occasion Michelle had been famously photographed with her arm round the Queen in a protective gesture

of spontaneous friendship, and this time no one took offence as they had when Prime Minister Keating of Australia had 'dared' to do the same on the Queen's visit to Australia. The Queen and the Obamas obviously enjoyed each other's company.

For the Duke and Duchess of Cambridge, the title given to William by the Queen on his marriage, the wedding was not just a romantic occasion but the end of their private lives. They were to take part in visits round the country and particularly overseas, as befitted a future King. Earlier that year William had visited New Zealand and Australia, where he had been received with huge enthusiasm. Soon, after a brief honeymoon, they set out together to conquer Canada and America. Everywhere, except in certain parts of French-speaking Quebec, they were greeted with enormous warmth and enthusiasm. They attended Canada Day in Ottawa, visited the burned-out town of Slave Lake, Alberta, played hockey, competed with each other canoeing, ending up with a rodeo, the Calgary Stampede, where, wearing fetching stetsons and jeans, they rode chuck wagons. From Calgary, they flew to Los Angeles.

During their brief visit there William impressed by scoring four goals in a charity polo match for his African charity. He and Kate visited an inner city school, the Inner City Arts Academy, on Skid Row in downtown Los Angeles, where Kate painted a picture of a snail and they both helped the children create a ceramic tortoise. The climax of the visit was a black-tie dinner organized by BAFTA, of which William is president, to promote young British talent in the film industry. Nicole Kidman, Tom Hanks, Barbra Streisand and Jennifer Lopez were there, but there was no doubt who the stars of the evening were: 'William and Kate leave stars star-struck,' blazed the headlines. There was a feeling everywhere they went that they represented the monarchy of the future: two beautiful young people, in love with each other and with life. They were back in Britain for the wedding on 30 July in Edinburgh of Zara, daughter of the Princess Royal, and rugby player Mike Tindall, the man she had loved and lived with for some years. Poignantly, they held their pre-wedding party on the royal yacht *Britannia*, now permanently moored in Leith.

The Queen, like Queen Victoria, is now a matriarch, head of a happy family who, so far, do indeed now represent 'ourselves behaving well'. Her dignity, hard work and sense of duty have ensured her a place in her subjects' hearts. She is a living representative of sixty years of our history and, as politicians become more and more unpopular, tarnished by expenses scandals and media connections, they become less and less representative of the people and the thought of one of their number as President of a Republic becomes less and less attractive. God Save the Queen.

Foreword to Notes, Bibliography and Acknowledgements

This book represents an accumulation of knowledge acquired over the years spent on previous books on royal subjects – George VI, Elizabeth and Diana. I have an extensive archive of interviews with friends, courtiers and employees of the Royal Family, and with politicians, historians and journalists of the time familiar with aspects of the Queen's life and reign. I am deeply grateful to them all for helping me. Most are not named here for reasons of confidentiality.

Similarly, when it comes to colleagues and historians, I have cut the list short and, if anyone feels left out, I would ask them to forgive me. I am principally grateful to the late Ben Pimlott, biographer of the Queen and Harold Wilson, to Philip Ziegler, authorized biographer of Edward VIII, Mountbatten and Edward Heath among other distinguished books, to Hugo Vickers and William Shawcross, biographers of the Queen Mother, and, latterly, to the younger generation of social/political historians, David Kynaston and Dominic Sandbrook.

I would like to express my gratitude to my friend Francis Fulford for giving me the opportunity to study the manuscript volumes, hitherto unknown and unpublished, of the diaries of C. H. Fulford, who acted as unpaid assistant librarian to the Royal Librarian, Sir Owen Morshead, and who lived in the Deanery within the walls of Windsor. I would like to thank Francis for bringing the diaries to my attention and for permission to publish illuminating insights from them into life at the Castle during the years of World War II.

Notes

Chapter 1: *Hyde Park Corner*

1. Author interview with Sir Edward Ford, 22 July 1986.
2. John Colville, *The Fringes of Power: Downing Street Diaries* 1939–1955 (1985), p. 640.
3. Cited in David Kynaston, *Family Britain* 1951 57 (2009), p. 69.
4. Author interview with Sir Edward Ford, 22 July 1986.

Chapter 2: *'Abdication Day'*

1. Massigli to Schumann, Quai d'Orsay, Direction de l'Europe, no. 287, 19 February 1952.
2. The Duchess of York to Princess Elizabeth, 29 December 1935, cited in William Shawcross, *Queen Elizabeth the Queen Mother: The Official Biography* (2009), p.149.
3. Shawcross, *Queen Elizabeth*, p. 368.
4. Author interview with the Hon. Lady Lindsay of Dowhill (Loelia Ponsonby), 28 July 1986.

Chapter 3: *'Us Four'*

1. Lady Elizabeth Bowes-Lyon to Beryl Poignand, n.d., cited in Shaw-cross, *Queen Elizabeth*, p. 100.
2. Lady Strathmore to Arthur Penn, n.d. [18 January 1923], cited in Shawcross, *Queen Elizabeth*, p. 155.
3. Author interview with Lord Charteris of Amisfield, 29 July 1986.

4. See John Julius Norwich (ed.), *The Duff Cooper Diaries, 1915–1951* (2005), 1 November 1923, pp. 181–2.
5. Shawcross, *Queen Elizabeth*, pp.150–51.
6. Cited in Sarah Bradford, *George* VI (1989), p. 116.
7. See John W. Wheeler-Bennett, *King George VI: His Life and Reign* (1958), p. 214.
8. Elizabeth Ring, *The Story of Princess Elizabeth* (1932), p. 124.
9. Marion Crawford, *The Little Princesses,* with an introduction by A. N. Wilson (1993).
10. HRH Princess Elizabeth, in Sarah Bradford, *Elizabeth: A Biography of Her Majesty the Queen* (rev. edn, 1997), p. 65.

Chapter 4: Windsor War

1. Queen Elizabeth to Princess Elizabeth, 13 May 1939, cited in Shawcross, *Queen Elizabeth*, p. 454.
2. Nigel Nicolson (ed.), *Sir Harold Nicolson: Diaries and Letters 1930–1939* (1966), p. 403.
3. Crawford, *The Little Princesses*, cited in Bradford, *Elizabeth*, p. 84.
4. Shawcross, *Queen Elizabeth*, footnote p. 498.
5. Crawford, *The Little Princesses,* p.66.
6. Cited in Bradford, *George* VI, p. 324.
7. Mark Girouard, *Windsor, The Most Romantic Castle* (1993), p. 30.
8. Charles H. Fulford, MS Diary, 12 December 1941.
9. Author interview with Lord Bonham-Carter, 17 January 1989.
10. ibid.
11. Owen Morshead to Queen Mary, 10 June 1940, cited in Shawcross, *Queen Elizabeth*, p. 515.
12. Queen Elizabeth to Queen Mary, 7 January 1941, cited in Shawcross, *Queen Elizabeth*, p. 531.
13. Queen Elizabeth to Queen Mary, 12 May 1941, cited in Shawcross, *Queen Elizabeth*, p. 538.

14. Queen Elizabeth to Princess Elizabeth, 27 June 1944, cited in Shaw-cross, *Queen Elizabeth*, p. 583.
15. Queen Elizabeth to Queen Mary, 4 August 1944, cited in Shawcross, *Queen Elizabeth*, p. 586.
16. Fulford, MS Diary, 21 December 1944.
17. Cited in Bradford, *Elizabeth*, p. 108.
18. Cited in Wheeler-Bennett, *King George* VI, p. 625.
19. Author interview with the Earl of Carnarvon, 25 January 1989.

Chapter 5: Enter the Prince

1. Cited in David Kynaston, *Austerity Britain, 1945–51* (2007), p. 11.
2. Mollie Panter-Downes, cited in Kynaston, *Austerity Britain*, p. 103.
3. Anthony Heap, cited in Kynaston, *Austerity Britain*, p. 104.
4. Fulford, MS Diary, 21 February 1944.
5. Bradford, *Elizabeth*, p. 104.
6. Cited in Philip Ziegler, *Mountbatten: The Official Biography* (1985), 19 January 1947, p. 457.
7. Lady Pamela Hicks, cited in Ben Pimlott, *The Queen* (1996), p. 139.

Chapter 6: Young Couple

1. Cited in Bradford, *Elizabeth*, p. 132.
2. Princess Elizabeth to Queen Elizabeth, 22 November 1947, cited in Shawcross, *Queen Elizabeth*, p. 630.
3. Kynaston, *Austerity Britain*, p. 275.
4. Colville, *The Fringes of Power*, p. 625.
5. Martin Charteris, cited in Bradford, *Elizabeth,* p. 155.
6. Cited in Hugo Vickers, *Elizabeth, the Queen Mother* (2005), p. 283.
7. Pimlott, *The Queen*, p. 165.
8. Frank Prochaska, *Royal Bounty: The Making of a Welfare Monarchy* (1995), pp. 237–8.

9. Roy Strong, *Visions of England* (2011), p. 19.
10. Cited in Pimlott, *The Queen*, p. 170.

Chapter 7: Coronation

1. David Kynaston, *Family Britain* 1951–57 (2009), p. 299.
2. Pimlott, *The Queen*, p. 222.
3. 23 November 1953, in Graham Payn and Sheridan Morley (eds.), *The Noël Coward Diaries* (1982), p. 223.
4. United Kingdom High Commissioner in New Zealand to Secretary of State for Commonwealth Relations, 25 February 1954, PRO 84/3/1.

Chapter 8: A New and Dangerous World

1. CAB 129/74. Governor of Trinidad to Colonial Secretary, No. 29, 7 February 1955.
2. Cited in Bradford, *Elizabeth*, p. 207.
3. *The Times*, 26 October 1955.
4. See Kynaston, *Family Britain*, pp. 524 and 525.
5. Cited ibid., p. 619.
6. Nicolson (ed.), *Sir Harold Nicolson: Diaries*, 25 April 1956.
7. Robert Rhodes James, *Anthony Eden* (1986), p. 581.
8. Cited in Ziegler, *Mountbatten*, p. 541.
9. D. R. Thorpe, *Eden: The Life and Times of Anthony Eden, First Earl of Avon* (2003).
10. Miles Jebb (ed.), *The Diaries of Cynthia Gladwyn* (1995), pp. 194–5.

Chapter 9: Young Queen

1. Pimlott, *The Queen*, p. 285.
2. Fiona MacCarthy, *Last Curtsey: The End of the Debutantes* (2007), pp. 11–12.

3. ibid., p. 9.
4. Cited in Kynaston, *Family Britain*, pp. 489–90.

Chapter 10: Evening's Empire

1. 13 November 1961, see Harold Macmillan, *Pointing the Way, 1959–1961* (1972), p. 472.
2. PRO Prem 11/3509, 29 December 1961.
3. Harold Macmillan, diary entry for 11 June 1961, Mss Macmillan, dep. 42. Bodleian Library, Oxford.
4. See Gore Vidal, *Palimpsest: A Memoir* (1995), pp. 371 2.
5. ibid.
6. The Queen to President John F. Kennedy, 20 May 1962, Kennedy Papers, cited in Pimlott, *The Queen*, pp. 316–17.
7. Christopher Andrew and Vasili Mitrokhin, *The Mitrokhin Archive: The KGB in Europe and the West* (1999), p.156, cited in Peter Hennessy, *The Secret State: Preparing for the Worst 1945–2010* (rev. edn, 2010), p. 19.
8. Miranda Carter, *Anthony Blunt: His Lives* (2001), p. 450.
9. Anthony Sampson, *Anatomy of Britain* (1962), cited in Dominic Sandbrook, *Never Had It So Good: A History of Britain from Suez to the Beatles* (2008), p. 569.
10. D. R. Thorpe, *Supermac: The Life of Harold Macmillan* (2010).
11. Vernon Bogdanor, *The Monarchy and the Constitution* (1995), pp. 96–7.

Chapter 11: The Royal Family

1. Marcia Falkender, *Inside Number Ten* (1972), p. 17.
2. Cited in Ben Pimlott, *Harold Wilson* (1993), p. 524.
3. Author interview with Baroness Castle of Blackburn, 26 January 1994.
4. Roy Jenkins, *Churchill* (2001), p. 912.
5. Cited in Pimlott, *The Queen*, pp. 347–8.

6. Hennessy, *Secret State*, p. xxxv.

7. ibid., pp. 393–4.

8. ibid., p. 208.

9. 26 August 1966, AP30A (Lord Avon Papers).

10. See Pimlott, *The Queen*, p. 371.

11. Tony Benn, *Out of the Wilderness: Diaries 1963–67* (1987), 13 June 1965.

12. Jonathon Dimbleby, *The Prince of Wales* (1994), p. 29.

13. ibid., p. 65.

14. ibid., pp. 69–70.

15. ibid., pp. 54–5.

16. Brian Hoey: *Anne: The Private Princess Revealed* (1997), p. 18.

17. Dominic Sandbrook, *White Heat: a History of Britain in the Swinging Sixties* (reprint edn, 2008), pp. 269–70.

18. Keith Richards, with James Fox, *Life* (2010), p. 202.

19. Jonathan Aitken, *The Young Meteors* (1967), pp. 272–3.

20. Cecil King, Diary, 5 July 1966, cited in Sandbrook, *White Heat*, p. 388.

21. Hugo Young, *This Blessed Plot: Britain and Europe from Churchill to Blair* (1998), pp.191–2.

22. Cited in Sandbrook, *White Heat*, p. 307.

23. See ibid., p. 323.

24. Roy Jenkins, *A Life at the Centre* (1992), pp. 237–8.

Chapter 12: Rebranding the Monarchy

1. Cited in Bradford, *Elizabeth*, pp. 359–60.

2. ibid., p. 353.

3. Pimlott, *The Queen*, p. 392.

4. Bradford, *Elizabeth,* p. 360.

5. Pimlott, *The Queen*, p. 402.

6. ibid., p. 405.

7. Michael Bloch (ed.), *Wallis & Edward: Letters 1931–1937* (1986).

8. Philip Ziegler, *King Edward VIII: The Official Biography* (1990), p. 556.

9. Cited in Dimbleby, *The Prince of Wales*, p. 180.

Chapter 13: The Seventies

1. See Philip Ziegler, *Edward Heath, The Authorised Biography* (2010), p. 416.
2. Francis Wheen, *Strange Days Indeed: The Golden Age of Paranoia* (2009), p. 51.
3. Ziegler, *Edward Heath*, p. 297.
4. John Campbell, *Edward Heath: A Biography* (1994), p. 494.
5. Pimlott, *The Queen*, p. 416.
6. See Ziegler, *Edward Heath*, p. 374.
7. ibid., p. 319.
8. Wheen, *Strange Days*, p. 118.
9. Ziegler, *Edward Heath*, p. 430.
10. Pimlott, *The Queen*, p. 418.
11. Pimlott, *Harold Wilson*, p. 654.
12. Elizabeth Longford, *Elizabeth R* (1983), pp. 278–80.
13. Author interview with Lord Owen, 22 November 1994.
14. Susan Crosland, *Tony Crosland* (1982), p. 345.
15. Wheen, *Strange Days*, p. 251.
16. ibid., p. 256.
17. See ibid., pp. 238–9.
18. Author interview with Lord Charteris of Amisfield, 24 November 1994.
19. *Telegraph* and other sources, cited in Pimlott, *The Queen*, p. 556.
20. *Sunday Times*, 5 May 1977.

Chapter 14: The Thatcher Years

1. Diary, 27 August 1979, cited in Dimbleby, *The Prince of Wales*, p. 267.
2. Cited in Bradford, *Elizabeth*, pp. 407–8.

3. 14 February 1974, see Ziegler, *Mountbatten*, p. 687.

4. Cited in Dimbleby, *The Prince of Wales*, p. 261.

5. Andrew Morton, *Diana, Her True Story — In Her Own Words* (rev. edn, 1997), p. 33.

6. Hugo Young, *One of Us: A Biography of Margaret Thatcher* (1990), p. 52.

7. ibid., p.135.

8. Author interview with Sir Shridath Ramphal, 20 December 1993.

9. See Margaret Thatcher, *The Downing Street Years* (1993).

10. Young, *One of Us*, p. 283.

Chapter 15: Family Troubles

1. Author interview with Dickie Arbiter, 23 February 2004, cited in Sarah Bradford, *Diana* (1997), p.101.

2. Author interview with Professor Roy Greenslade, 10 September 2005.

3. Author interview, 10 April 2006, in Bradford, *Diana*, p. 149.

4. ibid.

5. Roy Greenslade, *Press Gang: How Newspapers Make Profits from Propaganda* (rev. edn, 2004), p. 476.

6. Author interview, 18 November 1993, cited in Bradford, *Elizabeth*, p. 385.

7. Paul Routledge, *Observer*, 5 September 1993, cited in Bradford, *Elizabeth*, p. 389.

8. Young, *One of Us*, p. 491.

9. Alan Clark, *Diaries* (1993), 2 April 1990, p. 290.

10. ibid., 4 November 1990, pp. 342–3.

11. Winston S. Churchill, 1949, see Martin Gilbert, *Challenge to Civilization: A History of the Twentieth Century, Volume Three 1952–1999* (1999), p. 672.

12. ibid., p. 673.

Chapter 16: The Crisis Years

1. Jeremy Paxman, *On Royalty* (2006), pp. 252–3.
2. Antony Jay, *Elizabeth R: The Role of the Monarchy Today* (1992).
3. Author interview with Dickie Arbiter, 23 February 2004, *Diana*, p. 381.
4. See Brian MacArthur (ed.), *Requiem: Diana Princess of Wales 1961–1997, Memories and Tributes* (1997), p. 6.

Chapter 17: Twenty first century Queen

1. See Ronald Allison and Sarah Riddell (eds.), *The Royal Encyclopedia* (1991), p. 451.
2. Confidential interview.
3. Tony Blair, *A Journey* (2010), pp. 143–4.
4. ibid., pp.13–14.
5. ibid., p.147.
6. ibid.
7. ibid., p.150.
8. ibid.
9. ibid., p.126.
10. Peter Hennessy, *The Prime Minister: The Office and Its Holders since 1945* (2000), p. 465.
11. Shawcross, *Queen Elizabeth*, p. 1.
12. Mary Kenny, *Crown and Shamrock: Love and Hate between Ireland and the British Monarchy* (2009, reprint 2010), p. 32.
13. Matt Cooper, *Sunday Times*, 22 May 2011.
14. Cited in *Sunday Telegraph*, 14 May 2011, Neil Tweedie, 'Will the Irish give the Queen a warm welcome?'

Bibliography

Aitken, Jonathan, *The Young Meteors* (1967).

Airlie, Mabell, Countess of, *Thatched with Gold* (1962).

Allison, Ronald, and Riddell, Sarah (eds.), *The Royal Encyclopedia* (1991).

Aronson, Theo, *Princess Margaret: A Biography* (2001).

Bagehot, Walter, *The English Constitution*, new edn with introduction by Richard Crossman, (2003).

Benn, Tony, *Out of the Wilderness: Diaries 1963–67* (1987).

Benn, Tony, *Office without Power: Diaries 1968–72* (1988).

Blair, Tony, *A Journey* (2010).

Blakeway, Denys, *The Last Dance: 1936: The Year of Change* (2010).

Bloch, Michael (ed.), *Wallis & Edward: Letters 1931–1937* (1986).

Bogdanor, Vernon, *The Monarchy and the Constitution* (1995).

Bradford, Sarah, *George VI* (1989).

Bradford, Sarah, *Elizabeth: A Biography of Her Majesty the Queen* (rev. edn, 1997).

Bradford, Sarah, *Diana* (rev. edn, 2007).

Brendon, Piers, and Whitehead, Philip, *The Windsors, A Dynasty Revealed* (1994).

Campbell, John, *Edward Heath: A Biography* (1994).

Carter, Miranda, *Anthony Blunt: His Lives* (2001).

Clark, Alan, *Diaries* (1993).

Colville, John, *The Fringes of Power: Downing Street Diaries 1939–1955* (1985).

Crawford, Marion, *The Little Princesses* (new edn, with an introduction by A. N. Wilson, 1993).

Crosland, Susan, *Tony Crosland* (1982).

De Courcy, Anne, *Snowdon: The Biography* (2009).

Dimbleby, Jonathan, *The Prince of Wales* (1994).

Douglas-Home, Charles, and Kelly, Saul, *Dignified and Efficient: The British Monarchy in the Twentieth Century* (2000).

Eade, Philip, *Young Prince Philip: His Turbulent Early Life* (2011).

Falkender, Marcia, *Inside Number Ten* (1972).

Gilbert, Martin, *Challenge to Civilization: A History of the Twentieth Century, Volume Three 1952–1999* (1999).

Girouard, Mark, *Windsor: The Most Romantic Castle* (1993).

Greenslade, Roy, *Press Gang: How Newspapers Make Profits from Propaganda* (2004).

Hall, Phillip, *Royal Fortune: Tax, Money & the Monarchy* (1992).

Harris, Kenneth, *The Queen* (1994).

Haseler, Stephen, *The End of the House of Windsor: Birth of a British Republic* (1993).

Heald, Tim, *The Duke: A Portrait of Prince Philip* (1992).

Healey, Denis, *The Time of My Life* (1989).

Hennessy, Peter, *The Prime Minister: The Office and Its Holders since 1945* (2000).

Hennessy, Peter, *The Secret State: Preparing for the Worst 1945–2010* (2010).

Hoey, Brian, *Anne: The Private Princess Revealed* (1997).

Horne, Alistair, *Macmillan 1957–1986* (1989).

Howard, Anthony (ed.), *The Crossman Diaries: Selections from the Diaries of a Cabinet Minister 1964–70* (1979).

Hurd, Douglas, *Memoirs* (2004).

Ingham, Bernard, *Kill the Messenger* (1991).

Jay, Antony, *Elizabeth R: The Role of the Monarchy Today* (1992).

Jebb, Miles, *The Diaries of Cynthia Gladwyn* (1955).

Jenkins, Roy, *A Life at the Centre* (1992).

Jenkins, Roy, *Churchill* (2001).

Kenny, Mary, *Crown and Shamrock: Love and Hate between Ireland and the British Monarchy* (2010).

Kynaston, David, *Austerity Britain, 1945–51* (2007).

Kynaston, David, *Family Britain, 1951–57* (2009).

Lacey, Robert, *Majesty: Elizabeth II and the House of Windsor* (1983).

Logue, Mark, and Conradi, Peter, *The King's Speech* (2010).

Longford, Elizabeth, *Elizabeth R* (1983).

MacArthur, Brian (ed.), *Requiem: Diana Princess of Wales 1961–1997, Memories and Tributes* (1997).

MacCarthy, Fiona, *Last Curtsey: The End of the Debutantes* (2007).

Macmillan, Harold, *Riding the Storm, 1956–1959* (1971).

Macmillan, Harold, *Pointing the Way, 1959–1961* (1972).

Macmillan, Harold, *At the End of the Day, 1961–1963* (1973).

Marr, Andrew, *The Making of Modern Britain* (2009).

Morton, Andrew, *Diana: Her True Story – In Her Own Words* (1992).

Nicolson, Nigel (ed.), *Sir Harold Nicolson: Diaries and Letters 1930–1939* (1966).

Norwich, John Julius (ed.), *The Duff Cooper Diaries (1915–1951)*, 2005.

Paxman, Jeremy, *On Royalty* (2006).

Payn, Graham, and Morley, Sheridan (eds.), *The Noël Coward Diaries* (1982).

Pimlott, Ben, *Harold Wilson* (1993).

Pimlott, Ben, *The Queen: A Biography of Elizabeth II* (1996).

Pope-Hennessy, James, *Queen Mary, 1867–1953* (1959).

Prochaska, Frank, *Royal Bounty: The Making of a Welfare Monarchy* (1995).

Rhodes James, Robert (ed.), *Chips: The Diaries of Sir Henry Channon* (1967).

Rhodes, James, Robert *Anthony Eden* (1986).

Richards, Keith, with James Fox, *Life* (2010).

Roberts, Andrew, *A History of the English-Speaking Peoples since 1900* (2007).

Rose, Kenneth, *King George V* (1984).

Rose, Kenneth, *Kings, Queens & Courtiers* (1985).

Sandbrook, Dominic, *Never Had It So Good: A History of Britain from Suez to the Beatles* (2005).

Sandbrook, Dominic, *White Heat: A History of Britain in the Swinging Sixties* (2006).

Sandbrook, Dominic, *State of Emergency: The Way We Were: Britain, 1970–1974* (2010).

Shawcross, William, *Queen Elizabeth the Queen Mother: The Official Biography* (2009).

Strong, Roy, *Visions of England* (2011).

Thatcher, Margaret, *The Downing Street Years* (1993).

Thorpe, D. R., *Eden: The Life and Times of Anthony Eden, First Earl of Avon (1897–1997)* (2003)

Thorpe, D. R., *Supermac: The Life of Harold Macmillan* (2010).

Vickers, Hugo, *Alice: Princess Andrew of Greece* (2000).

Vickers, Hugo, *Elizabeth, the Queen Mother* (2005).

Vidal, Gore, *Palimpsest: A Memoir* (1995).

Warwick, Christopher, *Princess Margaret* (1983).

Wheeler-Bennett, Sir John W., *King George VI* (1958).

Wheen, Francis, *Strange Days Indeed: The Golden Age of Paranoia* (2010).

Whitelaw, William, *The Whitelaw Memoirs* (1989).

Wilson, A.N., *The Rise and Fall of the House of Windsor* (1993).

Windsor, HRH Duke of, *A King's Story: the Memoirs of HRH the Duke of Windsor, K.G.* (1951).

Young, Hugo, *One of Us: A Biography of Margaret Thatcher* (1990).

Young, Hugo, *This Blessed Plot: Britain and Europe from Churchill to Blair* (1998).

Ziegler, Philip, *Crown and People* (1978).

Ziegler, Philip, *Mountbatten: The Official Biography* (1985).

Ziegler, Philip, *Elizabeth's Britain: 1926 to 1986* (1986).

Ziegler, Philip, *King Edward VIII: The Official Biography* (1990).

Ziegler, Philip, *Harold Wilson* (1993).

Ziegler, Philip, *Edward Heath: The Authorised Biography* (2010).

Acknowledgements

I would like to thank specifically the people who have helped and encouraged me with this book. My agent, Gillon Aitken, and his associates Andrew Kidd, Leah Middleton and Imogen Pelham. My editor, Eleo Gordon, who has been a stalwart and inspiring support, with her assistant Ben Brusey. The magisterial technical director at Viking, Keith Taylor, whose expertise has been vital to the success of my books, has once again been key to the publication of this one, and I would like to thank him yet again and also his copy-editor Annie Lee, for her work in producing superb proofs. Claire Hamilton has co-operated with sensitivity and skill in researching the photographs so important to this book on the Queen's Jubilee – her reign and our lives. Douglas Matthews, king of indexers, has produced his usual superb work for me, as he has before over many years.

At home, I have relied upon the expertise of my husband, Will Bangor, for reading the proofs, and Jane Hayes for her invaluable technical assistance and support.

Index